*More True Tales*
*of Old-Time Kansas*

*Let us remember that the times which future generations delight to recall are not those of ease and prosperity, but those of adversity bravely borne.*
—Charles W. Eliot, 1877

DAVID DARY

# *More True Tales of Old-Time Kansas*

UNIVERSITY PRESS OF KANSAS

# To Jacob, Cristian, and Jeremy

Published by the University Press of Kansas (Lawrence, Kansas 66045), which was
organized by the Kansas Board of Regents and is operated and funded by Emporia
State University, Fort Hays State University, Kansas State University, Pittsburg State
University, the University of Kansas, and Wichita State University

Photo credits: p. 77—State Historical Society of Missouri; p. 81—Mrs. Mabel L. Bennett, Pagosa Springs, Colorado; pp. 223, 227, 228, 244, and 245—David Dary; all
others—Kansas State Historical Society

Library of Congress Cataloging-in-Publication Data

Dary, David.
  More true tales of old-time Kansas.
  Bibliography: p.
  Includes index.
  1. Kansas—History.  2. Frontier and pioneer life—
Kansas.  3. Pioneers—Kansas—Biography.  I. Title.
F. 681.5.D36  1987  978.1  87-6152
ISBN 0-7006-0331-X
ISBN 0-7006-0329-8 (pbk.)

Printed in the United States of America
10 9 8 7 6 5 4 3 2 1

# CONTENTS

Preface       vii

PART I    OVER THE TRAILS

William Becknell, Father of the Santa Fe Trail      3
Indian Trails and Isaac McCoy      9
Martias Dias's Escape across Kansas      14
Seth M. Hays and Council Grove      17
When Horace Greeley Followed Kansas Trails      24
Lizzie Johnson Williams, the First Cow Woman to
    Come up the Trail      33

PART II    BURIED TREASURE ON THE PLAINS

Outlaw's Treasure in Cowley County      39
Entangled Legends about Treasure in Ellis County      43
The Treasure Legend That Wasn't      49
The Missing Indianola Treasure      55
Legends of Treasure in Morton County      58
Abram B. Burnett's Treasure      61
Legends about Treasure in Lincoln County      64
The Devil's Den Treasure      66
The Mysterious Iron Box in Sedgwick County      69

v

## PART III THE LAWLESS AND THE LAWMEN

Bloody Bill Anderson 73
Dutch Henry, Horse Thief 80
The Rescue of John Doy 90
The Most Violent Town in Kansas 94
James M. Daugherty's Kansas Journey 100
Gunfights and Gunfighters 104

## PART IV THE FAMOUS AND THE OBSCURE

The Saga of Lew Cassel, Trapper 115
The Jordan Massacre 123
John O'Loughlin, Trader and Town Builder 129
Hugh Cameron, the Kansas Hermit 133
John Baxter and the Town That Was Named
    for Him 142
Eugene Fitch Ware, "Ironquill" 146
Theodore R. Davis's First Journey across Kansas 154

## PART V TORNADOES, FLOODS, GRASSHOPPERS, BLIZZARDS, AND PRAIRIE FIRES

When Tornadoes Were Called Cyclones 165
Before the Dams Were Built 173
When Grasshoppers Ruled the Day 179
Some Kansas Blizzards 185
Prairie Fires 192

## PART VI PEOPLE, PLACES, AND THINGS

The Real Birthday of Kansas 203
The Kansas River in History 207
Theodore Weichselbaum, Trader and Beer Maker 218
The Lost Kansas Cattle Town 225
Tellers and Portrayers of Tall Tales about Kansas 233
Some Kansas Fish Stories 242
"Bear" Facts about Kansas 247
When Every Town Had a Band 251

Notes and Credits 256

Index 270

# PREFACE

This book is a sequel to my *True Tales of Old-Time Kansas,* published in 1984 by the University Press of Kansas. It is a new collection of stories about people, places, things, and events in what today is Kansas.

These stories, many of which are appearing in print for the first time, provide something of the flavor of life in Kansas during the nineteenth and early twentieth centuries. As in my earlier collection, many of these stories touch on the struggles and hardships that pioneers encountered as they attempted to adjust to life in early Kansas. The tales reflect the pioneering spirit, the love of freedom and individualism, but also a healthy respect for nature. Still other stories have been included simply because they are good stories, and I wish to share them with the reader. If some of them seem romantic, so be it. Kansas history is colorful. It is filled with as much romance and adventure as are the histories of most other western states, but many writers of Kansas history have viewed the colorful as perhaps too commonplace and unworthy of repeating. Unfortunately, much that has been written about Kansas is dull and plodding.

As a chronicler of life in the Old West, I find much enjoyment and satisfaction in discovering an old tale or legend, seeking to verify it if possible, uncovering new facts if they exist, sometimes visiting the area where the story was set, and then retelling the story in a fresh yet factual form, to be read by Kansans everywhere, savored, and enjoyed.

I am indebted to many people whose names appear in the text and notes. I also want to express my gratitude to Howard Turtle, the retired editor of *Star*, the Sunday magazine of the *Kansas City Star*, who many years ago encouraged me to search for tales and legends, and to Gene Murray, his successor, who encouraged me to place the stories between two covers in book form. And thanks to the fine staff at the University Press of Kansas for encouraging me to complete this second collection of such stories.

May you enjoy them.

David Dary

Lawrence, Kansas
Along the Kaw
1987

## Part I

# OVER THE TRAILS

*If you would not be forgotten as soon as you are dead, either write things worth reading or do things worth writing.*

—Benjamin Franklin

# William Becknell, Father of the Santa Fe Trail

In 1803, when France sold the Louisiana Purchase, including what is now Kansas, to the United States, it was common knowledge among frontiersmen of Missouri country that white men had already criss-crossed the plains several times between Spanish Santa Fe and what is now Missouri. The earliest white traders to reach Santa Fe from Missouri may have been Pierre and Paul Mallet in 1739, but Spanish officials denied the Mallets' request to open trade between Missouri and Santa Fe because all commerce in New Spain was controlled by the home government in Europe. The Spanish government wanted to maintain its monopoly over the raw goods that were produced in New Spain. This policy continued into the nineteenth century, even though many other white traders made their way across what is now Kansas to Santa Fe during the intervening years. Some of these traders, apparently having bribed Spanish officials to look the other way, successfully traded guns for mules. But other white traders were arrested and jailed.

The barriers still existed in 1821, the year when Missouri became a state and Mexico won her independence from Spain. The news of the start of the Mexican Revolution, which probably reached Missouri by late spring or early summer in 1821, received much attention. On June 25 the *Missouri Intelligencer,* a newspaper published at Franklin, ran an advertisement inserted by William Becknell, an experienced plainsman and veteran of the War of 1812. Becknell sought seventy men who would be willing to join together and invest in an expedition whose purpose was purportedly to trade for horses and mules and to trap fur-bearing animals somewhere west of Missouri.

By early August, only seventeen men, not seventy, had applied. They met, organized a company, and elected Becknell captain of the expedition. Some of the men may have put up gold and silver as their part of the investment, and some may have provided trading goods. By September 1, 1821, the day that the expedition crossed the Missouri River at Arrow Rock and headed west to cross modern Kansas, there were about twenty men in the party.

Most written accounts suggest that the expedition intended to trade with Indians on the southern plains, but Becknell probably had his sights set on Santa Fe from the beginning. He knew, as the explorer Zebulon M. Pike had reported earlier, that Governor Don Facundo Melgares of New Mexico was a fair man who was also friendly toward Americans. Becknell was aware that the people of New Spain were declaring their independence from Spain, so the timing of his journey was no coincidence, even though he apparently was a very cautious man.

From the beginning, Becknell was vague about the destination of the expedition, perhaps fearing that if he were to announce it as Santa Fe, word would reach there before the party had left Missouri. If so and if the Mexican revolution were to fail, Spanish soldiers might be waiting for him. Becknell played it safe from the outset, although most of the men in the party probably had a good idea where they were going. Unfortunately for historians, Becknell's own account, as published later by the *Missouri Intelligencer* at Franklin, Missouri, does not provide much help. His terse account contains little detail.

On Tuesday morning November 13, 1821, about six weeks after leaving Arrow Rock, Missouri, Becknell and his party met a group of Spanish soldiers in what is now eastern New Mexico. The Spaniards were very friendly, though they spoke no English and no one in Becknell's party spoke Spanish. The two groups camped together for the night, and on the following morning the soldiers took the Americans to a village on the Pecos River, whose inhabitants, Becknell recalled, "gave us grateful evidence of civility and welcome." In the village he met a Frenchman who could speak

Spanish. Becknell possessed enough French to communicate with the man, who was then hired as an interpreter. It was probably from him that Becknell learned about the success of the Mexican Revolution, although he may have guessed as much from the warm reception that he and his men had received. Soon after arriving in Santa Fe, Becknell met with Governor Melgares, who expressed his desire that Americans should come to Santa Fe. "If any wished to emigrate, it would give him pleasure to afford them every facility," the governor said to his visitor.

Members of Becknell's party turned a handsome profit with their trading goods. When they gathered to plan their return trip to Missouri, all but one of them announced that they wanted to stay in Santa Fe. The village, the people, and the life in Santa Fe delighted them. Becknell and a man named M'Laughlin were the only two members of the party to leave for Missouri; they were joined on the trip by two other traders who had arrived in Santa Fe later than Becknell and his group. The four men left for Missouri in mid December and arrived in Franklin early in 1822, about forty-eight days later. Tradition has it that when they unloaded their pack animals on the main street of Franklin, rawhide packages containing silver dollars were dumped on the sidewalk. One of the traders, perhaps Becknell himself, cut the thongs on a bag, and its silver coins spilled out, clinking on the stone sidewalk and rolling into the gutter. One Franklin resident who had invested $60 in Becknell's expedition received $900 as her share of the profits. The dream of profit from the new trading route had been realized, and the dream of regular trade between Missouri and Santa Fe would soon become a reality.

Becknell spent much of the winter of 1822 preparing to take a larger trading party back to Santa Fe. He formed a company of twenty-one men, and they purchased $3,000 worth of trade goods. The merchandise was loaded onto three farm wagons, and in mid May, 1822, the party left Franklin, Missouri, bound for Santa Fe. On May 22 they crossed the Missouri River on the ferry at Arrow Rock, and by early June they had entered what is now Kansas. The party traversed the rolling prairie, which soon gave way to the plains as they followed a southwesterly course. These were the very first wagons to cross the plains.

On his first expedition a year earlier, Becknell and his group had followed the Arkansas River to a point just east of where La Junta, Colorado, stands today. There they had forded the river and headed southwest, crossing over the 7,834-foot-high Raton Pass while leading their packhorses, which were laden with trade goods. Remembering the difficulties that he had experienced in getting the packhorses over the pass, Becknell, on his second journey, chose to look for a more level route to Santa Fe so as to reduce the risk of losing the party's three wagons. At a point probably in present-day Rice County, Kansas, Becknell again crossed the Arkansas River. It cost the party no small effort and trouble to bring the wagons safely across. Exhausted, they made camp on the south bank of the river.

At about midnight their horses were frightened by some buffalo, as the country abounded with the shaggies. Twenty horses ran off in different directions, while Becknell and a few others gave chase. Two of the men, searching together, ran into a party of Osage Indians the following morning. The two were stripped of their clothing, whipped, and robbed of their horses, guns, and other belongings before the Indians turned them loose. Naked and embarrassed, they made their way on foot back to their camp on the river. Meantime, another man, searching alone for the horses, was taken prisoner by another group of Osages, who escorted him to their camp. The Indians apparently planned to rob him; but Auguste P. Chouteau, a trader from Missouri, was conducting business in the camp, and he persuaded the Indians to free their prisoner, who then made his way to safety.

Six days later, William Becknell and his party resumed their journey. Although they were more watchful than ever for Indians, they saw none as they followed the Arkansas River west along its south bank, past the river's great bend, to about where Dodge City, Kansas, stands today. There the party turned southwest, crossing the sand hills and entering what was to become known as the Cimarron Desert. This is not a true desert; it is a sixty-mile stretch of arid land that has little vegetation, much alkaline dust, and little water. Becknell and his men, however, no doubt viewed the region as a desert, especially after their water supply was exhausted.

Just as they had begun to think they would not survive, the party came upon a stray buffalo, which had taken a deep drink in the Cimarron River, farther to the southwest. The groggy buffalo was killed and cut open, and the men drank the water in the buffalo's stomach. They were thus able to reach the Cimarron River itself, where they quenched their thirst and filled their water containers. After resting and regaining their strength, the party continued southwest across what is now the Oklahoma and Texas panhandles until they reached the Canadian River in modern northeastern New Mexico. The country was rockier near the Canadian River, but they made good time with their wagons as they neared the site of today's Watrous, New Mexico. There, Becknell was on familiar ground. He had traveled over the same country a year earlier after traveling through Raton Pass to the north, and he had no difficulty in leading his party to San Miguel, where the men divided into small groups to conduct their trading in and around Santa Fe.

The expedition soon turned a reported profit of 2,000 percent on an investment of $3,000 in trading goods, which probably included broadcloth, muslin, drills, prints, some taffeta, calico, linen, velveteen, and other textiles. In addition, Becknell's party may have sold clothing, buttons, buckles, handkerchiefs, razors, razor strops, writing paper, thread, needles, thimbles, knitting needles, scissors, pots, pans, coffee mills, knives, shovels, hoes, axes, and other tools. They may even have taken a few cases of sherry and claret to Santa Fe. It was possible to carry a great quantity of small items in the expedition's three wagons, which were also sold. Becknell's wagon had cost him about $150 in Missouri. He sold it for $750 before leaving Santa Fe. The owners of the other two wagons did likewise.

Later, after returning to Missouri, Becknell reported that the New Mexicans wanted "goods of excellent quality and unfaded colors." He found that the people of Santa Fe suspected the traders of bringing goods that were "the remains of old stock, and sometimes damaged." But he observed that if one brought good trading merchandise, the New Mexicans, with plenty of "money and mules" to spend, would not hesitate to pay the price demanded if the articles "suit their purpose, or their fancy."

The story of Becknell's second journey to Santa Fe contains many of the ingredients emphasized by writers of western novels and those who have produced traditional films about the American West. Such works tend to stress the pioneers' hardships, determination, adventure (romantic by today's standards), and freedom from restraints. While these elements constitute or are important parts of their accomplishments (and make for good entertainment), they often have overshadowed the simple facts that traders were in search of profit and that in their roles as businessmen, they brought capitalism—the investment of capital in businesses—to the West.

To some degree, Becknell has been the victim of this misguided emphasis. He does have a secure place in history books as the man who opened regular trade between Missouri and Santa Fe, who took the first wagons from Missouri westward across what is today Kansas, and who pioneered in the use of the shorter Cimarron, or dry, route to Santa Fe. But these adventuresome firsts have overshadowed another first, one that is perhaps not as exciting but probably had a more lasting effect: Becknell was the man who organized the first stock company of traders to cross the western plains.

In 1824, after having made two trips to Santa Fe and back, Becknell decided to engage in trapping in the mountains of New Mexico, because the prices of trade goods in New Mexico were falling due to an increase in the quantity of goods being brought from Missouri and because an export duty of 3 percent was being imposed on all specie exported from Mexico. Becknell, however, did not find trapping to his liking; he apparently had little success; and he eventually went back to Missouri, never to return to New Mexico. In 1835 he sold his farm in Missouri and moved to what was then the Mexican province of Texas. He and his family settled on Sulphur Fork Prairie, a few miles west of modern Clarksville in northeastern Texas. There Becknell prospered, not as a trader of goods, but as a farmer, cattle broker, and stock raiser. He also served as a Texas Ranger and as a representative in the Congress of the Republic of Texas. Becknell, the father of the Santa Fe trade, spent the rest of his life in northeastern Texas, where he died on April 25, 1856, at the age of sixty-eight.

# Indian Trails and Isaac McCoy

The fall of 1831 was when Rev. Isaac McCoy, two other white men, and several Indian chiefs from the Wyandotte, Delaware, and Shawnee tribes set out from what is now Missouri to find locations for new Indian reservations in present-day Kansas. The summer had been rainy and wet, and the grass on the prairies was so high and thick that it obstructed travel except along heavily used Indian trails. The small party, traveling by horseback, followed the Osage River to a point near where Ottawa, Kansas, now stands. There they turned north. At some point in present-day southern Douglas County one of the men, who happened to look back, expressed alarm; in the distance he saw a prairie fire, which was bearing down on the party from the south. A strong southerly wind was pushing the fire along at a rapid speed.

The party of horsemen stopped and looked toward the oncoming sheet of flames. Moments later, a Delaware chief leapt from his saddle, threw himself into the tall grass, and struck a fire. Soon the flames from his fire were raging. The party soon leaped through the back flames that had been set by the Indian into the area that had already burned. When the approaching prairie fire reached the party, the back fire had burned a large area. There the men lay down flat on the ground and held their hands over their mouths. The hot air from the prairie fire was almost suffocating, and hot cinders and burning grass were flying around the men and their horses, which had been securely tied. When the fire had passed—it

This illustration by George Catlin, titled "Prairie Fires in the West," depicts the terror that Rev. Isaac McCoy, others in his party, and the Indians must have felt as a prairie fire was bearing down on them in the fall of 1831.

did so quickly—the men's faces, hands, and clothing were blackened.

After the sweeping flames had pushed north, well beyond where the party had sought refuge, the men mounted the horses and continued northward. On the following day they reached the Kansas River, where they camped in a thick undergrowth of trees and bushes along a ravine that was located just north of what is now Mount Oread, the site of the University of Kansas in Lawrence. The prairie fire had not burned that far north.

McCoy and the others decided to wait in camp a day or more until the burning ashes and cinders on the prairie to the south, on the other side of Mount Oread, had either blown away or been cooled by the south wind, which was still very strong. In the meantime the party hoped to make contact with some Kansa Indians, who reportedly were hunting in the neighborhood; but by the end of the second day, members of the group had seen no one. As the third day dawned, however, a lone Indian could be seen to the south, standing on the treeless northern edge of what is now Mount Oread. The Reverend Isaac McCoy and another white man in the party started toward the Indian. To their surprise, the Indian did not run; he stood like a statue. When the two white men reached him, they spoke to the Indian in his native tongue, but he did not utter a syllable. He ignored them; he stood like a person in thought or like someone who is remembering other years.

It was then that the white man who was with McCoy took some Indian ornaments from his pocket. They were ornaments like those which the squaws wore. At the sight of one ornament, a tear appeared in one of the Indian's eyes. He then spoke, and the two men conversed quietly for several minutes. During the conversation the man who had accompanied the Reverend Mr. McCoy to the top of the hill asked where the Indian's family and tribe were. The white man explained that the party wished to see the principal chiefs and to "form an amnesty, so that other Indians, by the request of our Great Father at Washington, might come and live upon the lands" near where the men stood.

McCoy's companion related: "Pointing to each side of the river east and west, and after learning from him all we desired, we asked him down to our camp to have some breakfast, an invitation which he cordially accepted." And in camp, this white man held a long conversation with the Indian, who told the following story:

> The time was when our tribe was as numerous as the leaves on these trees, and a long time ago a party of our warriors and young men, myself among them, went on an excursion away to the north. We encountered a band of Pawnees, a battle ensued, and after many hours of hard fighting, we came off conquerors leaving many of the Pawnees, and capturing one young brave, or Pawnee chief. Returning home with many scalps and our prisoner, we reached in safety our village, then lying on a creek over the hills yonder about four miles away. Our old men, squaws, and children came out to meet us, and when we had sung the song of the dead of our band and had recounted our valiant prowess in battle, a council was held and our Pawnee chief, it was decided should be tortured and burnt

at the stake, and the spot where you saw me this morning [on present Mount Oread] was the place selected.

As several days would intervene before the time, to give our tribe time to all come in, my sister became acquainted with the prisoner, as he was placed in my charge and confined or tied in my lodge. At length, the fatal day came, hundreds of our warriors and people had assembled; the stake had been planted, the victim tied to it, and faggots [twigs, sticks, and branches] from this grove had been gathered in abundance and piled around him. The burning brand was about to be placed to them, when my sister rushed through the crowd, scattered the faggots, seized the burning brand and hurled it far down the mound's side, and turning around to us taunted us as cowards and squaws, torturing and burning a lone captive because we had him in our power. I have become acquainted with him, said she. I know he is a brave, he fears not your implements of torture or the burning flame, he rather seeks and invites so glorious a death; he longs to go to the hunting lands of his fathers, and warriors slain in battle, or burnt at the stake; and now, if you torture and burn him, then torture and burn me. I am his friend, and my spirits shall go with his to the happy land of the Indian's long home; we are ready; kindle your flames—turning and throwing her arms around the captive warrior—for when he dies I will also die.

For a while we all stood aghast, but recovering from our stupor several of the chiefs, among them myself, rushed in and seized and placed her in the hands of friends while we rearranged the pile, applied the torch, and soon his voice was heard in the flames accusing us of not knowing how to torture or burn, asking us to call on the spirits of our warriors which he had assisted to torture and burn, and they would answer that you are only children and squaws in the matter. Then he would call on the spirits of his warriors to witness his fortitude and death as became a Pawnee brave, and also to avenge his fate, taunting us until his voice was hushed in death and his blackened and charred corpse fell loosened by the burning cords. Then again it was that my sister broke away from those who had her in charge, rushed forward and fell on his burning body, crying: cowards, heap on your burning brands. I scorn your warriors, and hate my family and tribe. Kill, torture, burn me, for my spirit shall go with my Pawnee brave.

All that I know, love, or hold dear, is him; he is gone, I shall and will go too.

We again rescued her from the still burning pile, took her away, and gathering the charred remains of the captive, dug a grave, and buried him near the spot where you first saw me. It was then that my sister appeared calm and asked of us for one moment, to see and stand over the place where he was buried, promising that if permitted, she would return to our village and try and forget her dead warrior.

Most of our tribe had left, the few that remained granted her request, myself among them, yet my eyes closely watched her, fearing she would do some act that might deprive her of life. Standing for some minutes near and by his grave, her eyes intently looking up toward the blue sky, she suddenly sprang like an antelope down the side of the mound, chanting at intervals as she could catch her breath, the death song of our tribe, and bounding along the opposite bank of this ravine as with the wings of an eagle, gained the bank of the river yonder, and before we who had started in pursuit, could reach her, she had disappeared, and when we came to the spot where we last saw her, with a shout of triumph she sank amid the dark and muddy waters of the river, and its curling waves rolled over her forever.

Every year since that day, on its annual return, I have visited that spot where you saw me this morning, have heard by the winds of night the voice of the Pawnee brave mingle with the spirit voice of my sister, taunting me and my tribe as cowards, as children. But I shall visit it no more; my time has fully come. I shall soon be gathered to the land of my fathers, but how shall I meet the spirits of my sister and her brave?

According to the unidentified white man who repeated the story, the Indian trembled as he finished telling it. His colorless cheeks and pallid lips told the agony of his soul. When he had finished, he stood up, and McCoy and the others watched as the Indian tottered out of their camp and feebly made his way towards the west. They watched him until he was out of sight.

# Martias Dias's Escape across Kansas

The name Martias Dias will not be found in Kansas history books, but long before Kansas Territory was established, he had made history in what is now the Sunflower State. Dias, a Mexican, was a servant who accompanied Texas' Santa Fe expedition to New Mexico in 1841. The expedition was something of a combined diplomatic-military-commercial venture that in June left Austin, in the Republic of Texas, bound for Santa Fe. Mirabeau Buonaparte Lamar, president of Texas, hoped to establish Texas jurisdiction over part of New Mexico and thereby to capture some of the Santa Fe trade that Missouri was enjoying.

The expedition, which consisted of perhaps twenty-four ox-drawn wagons, carrying merchandise and supplies, plus about three hundred men, failed. It was defeated, not by man, but by the terrain. The expedition got lost on the arid plains of what is now western Texas and eastern New Mexico, and the men suffered for want of food and water. When they did reach New Mexico, they surrendered to Governor Manuel Armijo's Mexican soldiers.

The Texans were cruelly treated, being marched on foot to Mexico City, where they were imprisoned (they were released in April, 1842); but Martias Dias and some other Mexican servants, who were working for the Texans, were freed in Santa Fe. One of the servants soon reported, however, that Dias was a regular Texas soldier and that he had served with Col. Jack Hays, a Texas soldier and ranger. This was true; in fact, Dias was one of about three

14

hundred men in the Texas military who had buried the victims of the Alamo in 1836.

Dias, who apparently did not deny his past, was jailed in Santa Fe and was suspected of being a Texas spy. He spent the winter of 1841 and the early spring of 1842 in the jail. In April of 1842, some friends, perhaps other servants with the Texas Santa Fe expedition who had remained, smuggled tools to Dias in the jail, and he began to dig his way to freedom. Late one night he broke out and fled from Santa Fe on foot. Hiding by day and traveling only at night, Dias made his way to Taos, about fifty-five miles north and a little east of Santa Fe.

At Taos, Martias Dias stole a horse and a mule under cover of darkness. First riding one animal and leading the other, he would travel some distance and then stop. After changing animals, Dias would continue on, his goal being to reach Missouri. At one point, about thirty or forty Indians discovered Dias and gave chase on foot, but Dias, who was mounted on his mule, quickly got away from the Indians. He made his way over Raton Pass and reached Bent's Fort, on the Arkansas River in what is now southeastern Colorado. In 1842 the Arkansas River was the international boundary between the United States and Mexico.

Between Taos and Bent's Fort, Dias had been without any food except some roots and herbs; he had no weapons with which to defend himself or to kill wild game. And his worn clothing left him little protection from the cold spring nights or the warm sun during the daytime. Dias must have been a sight when he rode into Bent's Fort, where he was welcomed and was given food and new clothing. After he had rested for a day or two, Dias was given provisions, and he resumed his journey eastward. It appears that Dias left Bent's Fort with the horse and mule that he had stolen in Taos; but as he began to cross what is now Kansas, he apparently lost one animal, and the other one died. Exactly where he began walking east is not known, but it took him twenty-six days to reach Independence, Missouri. In 1842, what is now Kansas was Indian country; there were no white settlements except Fort Leavenworth, on the Missouri River. Whether or not Dias met any traders bound for Santa Fe is not known. The spring caravan from Independence left for Santa Fe in May of 1842 with sixty-two wagons and about a hundred and twenty men, but there is no record of the caravan's having met Dias.

Aside from reference in one of the Texan's recollections to a Martias or Matias having been with Texas' ill-fated Santa Fe expedition, the only reference to Martias Dias's adventures appears in a newspaper article published by the New Orleans *Weekly Picayune* on June 13, 1842. The unidentified writer reported that Dias had arrived in New Orleans a day or two before the article appeared, and the writer told his readers that he had heard the story of Dias's journey from Dias's own lips. "If this story is correct he is probably the first traveller who has ever 'gone it alone' across the immense prairies of the West; and how he escaped starving to death or being picked up by the Comanches or Pawnees is almost a miracle," wrote the newspaper reporter.

What happened to Dias after he reached New Orleans is not known. It is possible that he returned to Texas. One thing is certain, however: he then faded into history.

# Seth M. Hays and
# Council Grove

Seth M. Hays was a real Kansas pioneer, having come to what is now Kansas even before the territory was organized. He was a grandson of Daniel Boone's and was a cousin of Kit Carson's. From what is known about Hays, he was born about 1811 in Calloway County, Missouri, and not in Kentucky, where some writers have placed his birth. Although much else about his early life is hazy, it is known that Hays was living in Westport, now part of Kansas City, Missouri, from 1839 until about 1844. It was then that Hays, about thirty-three years old, followed the Kansas River west into present-day Kansas to help run a trading post, which was owned by Frederick Chouteau, in what is now the westernmost part of Shawnee County, west of Topeka. The trading post was located on Mission Creek, about two miles from the Kansa Indian mission that Methodist missionaries had founded in 1835.

Hays apparently enjoyed the life of an Indian trader among the Kansa. He got along with the Indians, who had first signed a treaty of peace and friendship with the United States in 1815. Ten years later they signed another treaty, this time giving all of their land to the government except for a large tract along the Kansas River. It was there, along the river that had been named for them, that the Kansa hunted and fished. When the Methodist missionaries arrived, built their mission, and tried to convert the Indians to Christianity and to teach them farming, the Kansa rejected both.

17

In the spring of 1846 the Kansa signed still-another treaty with the government, ceding their land along the Kansas River in exchange for a new but smaller reservation located along the upper valley of the Neosho River, in what is now Morris County, Kansas. Seth Hays, perhaps sensing that Chouteau's trading post would soon close its doors, returned to Westport.

The spring of 1847 found Hays working for his cousin, Albert G. Boone, another of Daniel Boone's grandsons, and for James G. Hamilton, Indian traders in Westport who had obtained a government license to trade with the Kansa on their new reservation. And it was to the crossing of the Santa Fe Trail, located on the Neosho River in a grove of tall trees, that Boone and Hamilton sent Hays. He was to build and operate a trading post among the Kansa, a people he already knew.

The grove of oak, walnut, ash, elm, hickory, and other hardwood trees was the only such grove between Missouri and Santa Fe. It had long been a resting and camping spot on the Santa Fe Trail. Indians had frequented the spot long before William Becknell successfully opened trade between Missouri and Santa Fe, and in 1825 the grove had been the site of a council between United States commissioners and the chiefs of the Osage nations. In signing a treaty, the Indians gave the United States the right to mark the Santa Fe Trail through their land and the free use of the road forever; in return, they were given $800 in cash and merchandise.

George S. Sibley, one of the three United States commissioners who signed the Osage treaty, later recalled that he had named the place Council Grove. He said that he had had "Big John" Walker, a guide, carve the name on a large oak tree standing near their tent. Two years later, according to tradition, Kit Carson cut the name Council Grove on a buffalo hide and nailed it to a tree while camping in the grove. It was to Council Grove that Seth Hays came in April, 1847. He built a small log cabin near the west bank of the Neosho, where the river cut through the grove, and the Santa Fe Trail passed in front of his cabin.

Unfortunately, much of what is known about Seth Hays has been pieced together from accounts left by traders, travelers, and others who traversed the Santa Fe Trail. Hays apparently did not keep a diary, nor did he record his recollections late in life, as so many other Kansas pioneers did. If Hays did write down his recollections, their whereabouts are not known. Traditional stories say that Hays was the first permanent white settler in Council Grove. When he arrived in 1847, he brought with him a Mexican teamster, who also was a handyman and interpreter, and a black slave. Little is known about the slave other than she was Hays's housekeeper. In time she became known as Aunt Sallie.

Soon after Hays built the trading post, George F. Ruxton, a British adventurer who had been touring the West, stopped in Council Grove while heading east with a wagon train. Ruxton met and talked with Hays, and he described Hays's trading post as "a magnificent palace." They talked about the fat and sleek livestock that Hays kept, but Ruxton devoted more space in his account to describing Council Grove:

> On approaching Council Grove the scenery became very picturesque; the prairie lost its flat and monotonous character, and was broken into hills and valleys, with well-timbered knolls scattered here and there, intersected by clear and babbling streams, and covered with gaudy flowers, whose bright colors contrasted with the vivid green of the luxuriant grass. My eye, so long accustomed to the burned and withered vegetation of the mountains, reveled in this refreshing scenery, and never tired of gazing upon the novel view. Council Grove is one of the most beautiful spots in the western country. A clear, rapid stream runs through the valley, bordered by a broad belt of timber, which embraces all the varieties of forest-trees common to the West. Oak, beech, elm, maple, hickory, ash, walnut, &c., here presented themselves like old friends; squirrels jumped from branch to branch, the hum of the honey-bee sounded sweet and homelike, the well-known chatter of the blue jay and catbird resounded through the grove; and in the evening whip-poor-wills serenaded us with its familiar tongue, and the drumming of the ruffed grouse boomed through the grove. The delight of the teamsters on first hearing these well-known sounds knew no bounds whatever. They danced, and sang, and hurrahed, as, one after the other, some familiar note caught their ear. Poor fellows! they had been suffering a severe time of it, and many hardships and privations, and doubtless sniffed in the air the johnny-cakes and hominy of their Missouri homes.

Ruxton probably found Seth Hays's prices for supplies high. Another traveler, E. N. O. Clough, a Missouri volunteer who was heading west to fight in the Mexican War, stopped in Council Grove a few weeks after Ruxton had. Clough observed that Hays was "making money hand over hand. Molasses, $2 per gallon, cheese 35 cents per pound, tobacco 75 cents a plug and rotten at that, shoes, a very coarse brogan, $3.50 per pair. There is also a blacksmith shop here and his prices are just about as reasonable as the trader's," wrote Clough, who apparently was referring to a blacksmith named William Mitchell, who had set up shop in Council Grove to serve wagon freighters and the Indians soon after Seth Hays had arrived. Less than a year after Hays's arrival, the brothers Cyprian and Pierre Chouteau came to Council Grove and opened another trading post.

For those who were following the Santa Fe Trail to California after gold had been discovered there, the two trading posts in Council Grove were the last source of supplies on the plains. By then, about seventeen hundred Kansa Indians—they were often called Kaw Indians—had made their home on their new reservation near Council Grove, and they traded pelts for supplies at the trading posts in Council Grove. In 1850 the government contracted with the board of missions of the Methodist church, South, to establish a mission and school for the Indians in Council Grove. Thomas S. Huffaker, a twenty-five-year-old native of Clay County, Missouri, was placed in charge. After having been schooled in Missouri, he had moved west into present-day Kansas. He had worked at Shawnee Mission, in modern Johnson County, Kansas, before being transferred to Council Grove when the mission and school had opened there.

The mission was in operation in 1852 when Wilson Hobbs, a physician, visited Council Grove. Hobbs recorded in his journal that Seth Hays "carried a considerable stock of goods, which were chiefly supplies for the Indians." Hobbs made reference to the mission and observed that the Indians had a village on the east bank of the Neosho River, while the white settlement was on the west bank. Hobbs wrote:

> The stream was about waist deep to a man at the crossing, and there was no bridge. But there was no hesitation by

An unidentified artist made this drawing of Seth Hays, who was born in 1811 in Calloway County, Missouri, but spent most of his life in Council Grove, Kansas, where he died in 1873.

the Indians at crossing. I was much interested at the sense of shame by the women. To cross, the men disrobed themselves of all clothing except the breech cloth and boldly waded through. But the women were much more modest and careful of the exposure of their persons. They carefully lifted their skirts, as they waded in, to suit the depth, and as carefully dropped them as the water grew shallower toward the other shore. I carefully watched one who approached the crossing with two children in her arms, as her hands and arms were already employed. She stood the little ones in the shallow water near the shore and waded in the deeper water in front of them, where she squatted down in the water and fastened her clothing high up on her shoulders. She then reached for the children and moved on, gradually rising as the water grew deeper. When the water became shallower, near the other shore, she began to squat, and came lower and lower down until she could safely land the children, when she put them down in the water and loosed her skirts and let them drop as she straightened herself up, and waded out without having wet her clothing or exposed her person.

Seth Hays and Thomas Huffaker became close friends, and together they began to guide the development of the settlement. Hays promoted the settlement's commercial interests, while Huffaker quietly paid as much attention to the future prospects of Council Grove as he did to running the mission and school. It was not Huffaker's outside interests, however, that caused the mission and the school to be closed in 1854; it was because the Kansa Indians continued to reject the white man's ways. Huffaker then became an agent for the Westport mercantile firm of Walker, Northrup, and Chick, who had secured a license to trade with the Kansa.

Soon after Kansas Territory was organized in 1854, the government ordered a census of the territory. When census taker James R. McClure arrived in Council Grove the following year, he reported that there were thirty-nine people living there aside from the Indians. He also noted that Seth Hays operated a well-furnished store and "kept for sale all kinds of goods needed by the constant stream of teamsters" who passed through the settlement following the Santa Fe Trail.

From all indications, by the middle 1850s, Hays was making more money from wagon freighters, teamsters, and travelers than from the Kansa Indians. The character of Council Grove was changing: it was becoming a town. The Council Grove Town Company was organized in 1857, with Seth Hays, Thomas Huffaker, the Chouteau brothers, and a few other residents as stockholders; and in 1858 the territorial legislature approved the incorporation of the town.

Although accurate counts of how many freighters passed through Council Grove at any given time are difficult to find, the Kansas State Historical Society in Topeka has in its collection a record kept by Seth Hays for the period April 24 to October 1, 1860, which provides an insight into the amount of traffic passing through Council Grove:

> Passing west—men, 3,519; wagons, 2,667; horses, 478; mules, 5,819; working cattle [oxen] 22,738; carriages, 61; tons of freight, 6,819

These figures include only those humans, animals, and wagons that were involved in wagon freighting, for Hays apparently kept no records of eastbound traffic or of other travelers, including emigrants.

When the Civil War began in 1861, there was much excitement in and around Council Grove. The story of William T. ("Bloody Bill") Anderson's exploits are told elsewhere in this book. A few years after the Civil War had ended, the railroad arrived in Council Grove, and wagon freighting over the Santa Fe Trail began to decline. Seth Hays sold out and started a saloon called the Brown Jug. To attract attention in the growing community, Hays hired a man with a bagpipe to entertain customers. His business prospered, and when members of a church were without a meeting hall, Hays let them use his saloon. When the church held services, he would remove all evidence of his business and would cover some of the walls and the bar with wagon canvas.

Hays's housekeeper, Aunt Sallie, died in 1872. Her funeral was held in Hays's home, a brick house that he had constructed about 1866. Interestingly, when Kansas was admitted to the Union, Hays gave Aunt Sallie her freedom, but she did not leave; she remained with him until her death. As for Seth Hays, he died in 1873 and was buried near Aunt Sallie in the Council Grove cemetery.

A true Kansas pioneer was gone.

# When Horace Greeley Followed Kansas Trails

Horace Greeley is perhaps best remembered by Americans for his advice "Go West, young man, and grow up with the country." Greeley, the founder of the *New York Tribune,* was enthusiastic about the opportunities to be found in the West during the middle of the nineteenth century. But Greeley is also remembered for his stand against slavery and for his support of temperance, a protective tariff, free land for homesteaders, free public education, and a transcontinental railroad. Horace Greeley also helped to found the Republican party.

Born in 1811, the son of a poor New Hampshire farmer, Greeley entered newspaper work at the age of fifteen, serving as an apprentice on a Vermont newspaper. He worked his way up the ladder, and in 1841, at the age of thirty, founded the *New York Tribune,* a low-priced newspaper that was oriented to the politics of the generally conservative Whig party, which had been formed in 1834 to oppose President Andrew Jackson and his policies.

When the Whig party began to falter during the early 1850s over the issue of slavery, Greeley helped to found the Republican party in 1854, the year when Kansas Territory was founded and when the struggle between the Free State and proslavery forces began in the new territory. Five years later, after the issue had been resolved in Kansas Territory, Greeley decided to go west. He wanted to visit Kansas Territory and to attend the first Republican convention in the territory, which was scheduled to be held at Osa-

Horace Greeley, editor and publisher of the *New York Tribune*, who came to Kansas Territory in 1859.

watomie. He also wanted to use the journey to provide his readers in the East with positive reports on the need for a transcontinental railroad. To do this, he announced that he would go to the convention, then cross Kansas Territory and continue west to California. In 1859 the eastern railroads reached only as far west as St. Joseph, Missouri. Greeley came west by rail to St. Joseph; then he took a steamboat to Atchison, in Kansas Territory, arriving there on Sunday morning, May 15. Because Greeley's newspaper was widely read in Kansas Territory and therefore Kansans knew that he was coming, he was welcomed by the town's more prominent citizens and was taken to the Massasoit House, the finest hotel in Atchison. And that night, Greeley witnessed a Kansas thunderstorm. In the first of thirty-four letters that Greeley would write for his newspaper on his western trip, he wrote: "Kansas brags on its thunder and lightning, and the boast is well founded. I never before observed a display of celestial pyrotechny so protracted, incessant and vivid as that of last Sunday night."

At six o'clock the next morning, Greeley left Atchison in a two-horse wagon with his group, which planned to reach Osawatomie by the next evening. They arrived at Leavenworth by late morning and pulled up in front of a hotel before anyone in town realized that Greeley had arrived, because the townspeople had expected him to arrive by steamboat. Greeley planned to remain in Leavenworth only briefly, but because nearby creeks were flooding, his trip was delayed. It was decided to take a steamboat from Leavenworth to Wyandotte, now Kansas City, Kansas, and then to go overland to Osawatomie, about fifty miles farther south.

The party left Leavenworth by steamboat the following morning. The steamboat also carried their horses and wagons, which were unloaded when the boat arrived at Wyandotte. The party found a new wooden toll bridge, and although it was not quite completed, they were permitted to use it in crossing the Kansas River. Once across, Greeley and his party headed south and soon moved onto some high prairies. They passed the village of Shawnee, a settlement of twenty or thirty houses which had a large hotel. South of Shawnee they came in sight of the Santa Fe Trail, which they crossed. After passing near Olathe, they turned due south and soon traveled through Spring Hill, "a hamlet of five or six dwellings, including a store, but no tavern," according to Greeley, and then on to Stanton, where the Marais des Cygnes River was too high to cross.

Greeley and his party stayed the night in Stanton, sleeping on the tavern floor. Other delegates who were heading south for the Osawatomie convention were also there, waiting to cross the river. They were delighted to meet and talk with Greeley. On the following morning, someone managed to repair a ferry across the Marais des Cygnes River, so everyone, including Greeley, made it safely across. They reached Osawatomie at about nine o'clock in the morning. By noon, other delegates had also arrived, and the convention soon began.

Not all Kansas Free-State leaders were present. Some were absent because they opposed forming the Republican party until Kansas had been admitted as a state. The delegates who were there thought it best not to invite Greeley to participate actively, but his presence certainly had an effect on everyone. And when the convention completed its business late in the afternoon and adjourned, everyone gathered in the open to hear him. He was amazed when nearly a thousand people appeared in the crowd. He reviewed the old political parties in the nation and the steady growth of the slave power; then he discussed the origin, history, principles, and objects of the new Republican party. When he had finished, the crowd cheered him.

Greeley left Osawatomie the following morning by stagecoach for Lawrence. The stage crossed the Marais des Cygnes at Bundy's Ferry and traveled north and west to leave the mail at Ottawa Jones, near what is now Ottawa, Kansas. It then headed due north to Prairie City, located near present-day Baldwin City, where he spent the night. Having seen the tiny villages along the route, Greeley later wrote that "it takes three log houses to make a city in Kansas, but they begin *calling* it a city so soon as they have staked out the lots."

On the following morning, Friday, May 20, Greeley continued on his journey to Lawrence, where a warm welcome awaited him and where he spoke that afternoon in front of the Eldridge House. After spending the night in Lawrence, Greeley left Lawrence by stage the following morning and returned to Leavenworth. There he visited the fort and also saw the headquarters of the Russell, Majors and Waddell freighting firm. Greeley was impressed with what he saw: "Such acres of wagons! such pyramids of extra axle-trees! such herds of oxen! such regiments of drivers and other employees! . . . I presume this great firm has at this hour two millions of dollars invested in stock, mainly oxen, mules and wagons. (They last year employed six thousand teamsters, and worked forty-five thousand oxen.)"

On Tuesday, May 24, Greeley left Leavenworth by stage, bound for Topeka and Manhattan. The last three days had been dry, so the once-muddy roads were dusty as the stage crossed the rich valleys of Salt and Stranger creeks and then moved onto the rolling prairie. About noon they had lunch at Osawkie, in a tavern run by what Greeley described as a Pennsylvania Dutchman. From Osawkie they crossed Rock Creek and then Muddy Creek, passed through the settlement of Indianola (now part of Topeka), and reached a ferry on the Kansas River across from Topeka at about sunset. After waiting for a wagon train to complete its crossing on the ferry, one wagon at a time, the stage made its crossing to Topeka, where Greeley spoke briefly.

When his stage finally left Topeka at about six o'clock the next morning—it had been scheduled to leave some two hours earlier—it crossed the Kansas River on the ferry and turned west. At about nine o'clock that morning it began to rain, as the stage pushed on through the Pottawatomie Indian reservation, crossing Soldier Creek, the Red Vermilion River, and Rock Creek before passing St. Mary's mission. When the stage reached the Big Blue River near Manhattan, it crossed on a pontoon bridge. A committee of three Manhattan residents escorted Greeley to a house, where he was to stay, and that evening he spoke to a large gathering in the Methodist church during a thunderstorm. The wet weather detained Greeley in Manhattan a day longer than expected, because Wild Cat Creek, west of the town, was impassable. While waiting for the stream to drop in level, Greeley used his extra time in Manhattan to sum up, on paper, his impressions of Kansas. He wrote that he liked it better than he had expected to. The soil was richer and deeper, the timber was more diffused, and the country was more rolling than he had supposed. He believed that Kansas was well watered, and the limestone underlying the soil was among the chief blessings. But then Greeley wrote:

> An unpleasant truth must be stated: There are too many idle, shiftless people in Kansas. I speak not here of lawyers, gentlemen speculators, and other non-producers, who are in excess here as elsewhere; I allude directly to those who call themselves settlers, and who would be farmers if they were anything. To see a man squatted on a quarter-section in a cabin which would make a fair hog-pen, but is unfit for a human habitation, and there living from hand to mouth by a little of this and a little of that, with hardly an acre of prairie broken (sometimes without a fence up), with no garden, no fruit-trees, "no nothing"—waiting for some one to come along and buy out his "claim" and let him move on to repeat the operation somewhere else—this is enough to give a cheerful man the horrors."

Greeley believed that for the first four or five years the "poor pioneer" should work every hour that he did not absolutely need for rest.

On the following morning, May 27, Greeley caught the Leavenworth & Pike's Peak express coach, bound for the Rocky Mountains. It was drawn by four fine Kentucky mules. The express company, which had been started earlier that spring by the firm of Jones, Russell & Co., had located stage stations from twenty to thirty miles apart, the distance depending upon the availability of wood and water. Fresh animals were provided at most of the stage stops. A few miles southwest of Manhattan the stage passed through Ogden, a town that had a land office; then it passed by the remains of Pawnee City, where the first territorial legislature had met. Pawnee City was located on the Fort Riley military reservation, which Greeley described as having comfortable barracks, a large and well placed hospital, spacious and elegant officers' quarters, and extensive and admirable stables.

On the southwest edge of the post, Greeley's stage crossed the Republican River on a rope ferry. Once across, the stage moved into Junction City, where Greeley spent the night after he had spoken to a crowd that had gathered in an unfinished stone church. The town itself consisted of a store, two hotels, and thirty or forty homes. At six o'clock the next morning, Greeley climbed aboard the stage and said good-bye as the stage moved westward.

All traces of habitation soon disappeared, with the lone exception of what Greeley described as a wretched cabin and an acre or two of broken ground. At Chapman's Creek the stage passed the last settler on the road, a farmer who had settled there two or three years earlier and who had seventy-five acres fenced and broken. Greeley wrote that the farmer had grown "three thousand bushels of corn last year," had a fine stock of horses and cattle, and had a family consisting of at least eight tow-headed children under ten years of age. At Station 8 on Chapman's Creek, about twenty-three miles west of Junction City, the stage stopped to change mules and to give the passengers a chance to dine. Continuing on, the stage stopped at Station 9, located on Pipe Creek in the southeastern part of what is now Ottawa County. There Greeley wrote another letter to the *Tribune*, which said, in part:

I believe I have now descended the ladder of artificial life nearly to its lowest round. . . .

May 12th. — Chicago. — Chocolate and morning newspapers last seen on the breakfast table.

23rd. — Leavenworth. — Room-bells and baths make their final appearance.

24th. —Topeka. — Beef-steak and wash-bowls (other than tin) last visible. Barber ditto.

26th. — Manhattan. — Potatoes and eggs last recognized among the blessings that "brighten as they take their flight," chairs ditto.

27th. — Junction City. — Last visitation of a boot-black, with dissolving views of a board bedroom. Beds bid us good-by.

28th. — Pipe Creek. — Benches for seats at meals have disappeared, giving place to bags and boxes. We (two passengers of a scribbling turn) write out letters in the express-wagon what has borne us by day, and must supply us lodging for the night. Thunder and lighting from both south and west give strong promise of a shower before morning. Dubious looks at several holes in the canvas covering of the wagon. Our trust, under Providence, is in buoyant hearts and an Indian-rubber blanket.

A violent rain and wind storm came up during the night, but little damage was done. Greeley was up before six o'clock the next morning, and after breakfast he climbed aboard the stage and continued westward. He saw his first herd of buffalo — a thrilling sight:

On rising our first ridge this morning, a herd of buffalo was seen grazing on the prairie some three miles, toward the Solomon; soon, more were visible; then others. At length, a herd of perhaps a hundred appeared on the north — the only one we saw on that side of our road during the day. Having been observed, they were heading down the valley of a small creek toward the Solomon. Just then, the tents and wagons of a body of encamped Pike's Peakers appeared right across a little creek; two men were running across the prairie on foot to get a shot at the buffalo; another was mounting a horse with like intent. The herd passed on a long, awkward gallop north of the tents and struck southwest across our road some forty rods ahead of us. . . . Thence nearly all day, the buffalo in greater or less numbers were visible among the bottoms of the Solomon on our right — usually two to three miles distant. At length, about 5 p.m., we reached the crest of a "divide," whence we looked down on the valley of a creek running to the Solomon some three miles distant, and saw the whole region from half a mile to three miles south of our road, and for an extent of at least four miles east and west, fairly alive with buffalo. There certainly were not less than ten thousand of them; I believe there were many more.

When an east bound stage was encountered, its passengers told Greeley that they had seen millions of buffalo within the last two days and that a company of Pike's Peakers had killed thirteen buffalo. When Greeley's stage arrived at Station 13, on Reisinger's Creek in what is today southeastern Phillips County, Greeley learned that eight buffalo had been killed there by simply stampeding a herd and driving them over a high bank of a creek, where they broke their necks. Greeley spent the night at Station 13.

Early the next morning, Greeley was off again, after having written another letter to the *Tribune*. That day he traveled fifty-five miles and stopped for the night at Station 15, on Prairie Dog Creek, a branch of the Republican River. The station, which was located in the west-central part of Norton County, was operated by a former Cincinnati lawyer and his wife, a former actress. On the following day the stage stopped at Station 16, in the north-central part of modern Decatur County, Kansas, where Greeley first saw Indians—a band of Arapahoes which was camped near the station. Most of the Indian men were away from the camp, supposedly on a marauding expedition against the Pawnees; only the women and children were in the camp.

Just before the stage reached Station 17 to spend the night on June 1, the stagecoach turned over as it was descending a steep grade, and Greeley was slightly injured. A woman at Station 17 dressed his cuts, and he was sore and lame for a few days. Station 17 was located just over the northern border of Kansas in what is now Nebraska. The stage route ran slightly northwest to the Republican River and returned to Kansas farther on, cutting diagonally across present-day Cheyenne County, Kansas, before entering what is now Colorado. In 1859, however, Kansas Territory stretched to the summit of the Rocky Mountains. At Station 18, which was located near present-day Benkelman, Nebraska, Greeley wrote another letter to the *Tribune*, which he titled "The Great

American Desert." He described the winds as terrible, the land as being void of any trees and having little grass, and the soil as thin. The sand along the dry creeks and gullies was, he wrote, "as pure as Sahara can boast." And the lack of water was something fearful to Greeley.

At Station 19, in the southwestern part of present Cheyenne County, Kansas, the stagecoach stopped for the night. Nearby was a large village of Cheyenne Indians. Greeley thought the Cheyenne were better clothed than the Arapahoes and seemed to have more self-respect. But Greeley did not like Indians; he considered them all low on the scale of intellectual and moral beings.

On the following morning, June 3, the stage moved into what is now Colorado, and three days later, Greeley reached Denver. His journey across Kansas from Leavenworth had taken about thirteen days. He spent fifteen days in the Denver area and then journeyed to the Pacific Coast. From California, Greeley returned to New York City by way of the Isthmus of Panama.

Nearly eleven years later, in October of 1870, Greeley returned to Kansas, where he lectured in Topeka and Lawrence. Two years after that he was a candidate for president on the Liberal Republican ticket. He lost. Horace Greeley died on November 29, 1872, less than a month after the death of his wife and only a few weeks after Ulysses S. Grant had defeated Greeley in the November elections.

# Lizzie Johnson Williams, the First Cow Woman to Come up the Trail

This is the story of a remarkable woman. Her full name was Elizabeth E. Johnson, and she was born in Missouri in 1843. She moved to Hays County, Texas, soon after her father had established the Johnson Institute there in 1852, two years before Kansas Territory was established. Johnson Institute was the first school of higher learning west of the Colorado River in Texas. And Lizzie, as she was called, began to teach at the institute when she was sixteen years old. Later she left home to teach in schools at Manor, Lockhart, and Austin—all in Texas.

Lizzie saved her money and added to her income by writing short stories for *Frank Leslie's Magazine,* and as she accumulated money she invested it. At one point she purchased $2,500 in stock from the Evans, Snider, Bewell Cattle Company, which had its headquarters in Chicago. She earned 100 percent dividends for three years straight, and she then sold her stock, which was valued at $20,000. On June 1, 1871, she invested the money in cattle and registered her own brand—CY—in the Travis County, Texas, brand book, along with her mark.

Lizzie Johnson's wealth continued to grow, and so did her responsibilities. During the summer of 1879, at the age of thirty-six, she married Hezkiah G. Williams, a preacher and widower who had several children. She continued to teach school in Austin, Texas, to write magazine articles, and to invest in cattle; she also maintained control over her wealth, having had her husband

An eastern artist's conception of a herd of Texas longhorns being driven
north from Texas to the Kansas railhead markets. Beginning in 1879, Lizzie
Johnson Williams bossed such trail drives to Kansas.

sign a paper agreeing that all of her property was to remain
hers.

On his own, Hezkiah entered the cattle business in 1881, but
he was not a good businessman, and he liked to drink; therefore,
Lizzie had to keep pulling him out of financial trouble. But it was
two years before Hezkiah entered the cattle business that Lizzie
became important to Kansas history. Soon after their marriage in
1879, Lizzie and Hezkiah traveled up the trail from Texas to Kansas. Lizzie Johnson Williams, so far as can be determined, was the
first woman to follow the Western Trail north from Texas to Dodge
City, Kansas; and she was the first woman to help drive her own
herd of Texas longhorns north from Texas to the Kansas railhead
cattle markets. She and her husband rode behind the herd, in a
buggy drawn by a team of horses. Lizzie bossed the trail drive, and
she slept out under the stars, just like the cowboys. Although
Lizzie loved silks and satins, on the drive she wore calicos and
cottons, with voluminous skirts, many petticoats, a bonnet, and
a grey shawl. She ate the same grub that the cowboys ate from

the chuck wagon, and she ran the trail drive as well as any man could.

For several years, after coming up the trail and selling the cattle, Lizzie and her husband would take a train east to St. Louis, where they spent the fall and winter months in a nice hotel and where Lizzie made extra money by keeping books for other cattlemen. When Hezkiah died in 1914, Lizzie paid $600 for his casket, a large sum at that time. And when Lizzie died in 1924, at the age of eighty-one, her estate totaled more than $200,000, including large holdings in Texas real estate. Her record in the cattle business was much better than that of many Texas cattlemen.

# Part II

## BURIED TREASURE ON THE PLAINS

*I cannot tell how the truth may be;*
*I say the tale as 'twas said to me.*

—Sir Walter Scott
*The Lay of the Last Minstrel*

# Outlaw's Treasure in Cowley County

The name Bill Doolin once was a household name in southern Kansas and in Indian Territory, now Oklahoma. Doolin was a bank and train robber during much of the 1880s and 1890s. Doolin, whose full name was William M., was born in 1858 in Johnson County, Arkansas, the son of an Arkansas farmer. In about 1881, at the age of twenty-three, he had drifted west into Indian Territory. There he worked as a cowboy, and to bring in extra money, he sold whiskey to Indians. After a serious scrape with the law, Bill Doolin turned into a full-time outlaw. He became a member of the infamous Dalton Gang until that outfit was destroyed while attempting to rob two banks simultaneously in Coffeyville, Kansas, on October 5, 1892. Doolin missed the Coffeyville raid, either because his horse was lame or because he had had an argument with one of the Daltons. He then organized his own gang, and between 1893 and early 1895, Doolin and his "Oklahombres," as they were called, robbed several banks and at least one train.

The train robbery occurred about half a mile west of Cimarron, Kansas, about halfway between Dodge City and Garden City on the major east-west line of the Atchison, Topeka and Santa Fe Railroad. On May 26, 1893, one of his gang flagged down the westbound California Express, and before the train could come to a complete stop, Doolin and another outlaw had swung onto the locomotive from opposite sides and covered the engineer and fireman with their revolvers. Three more outlaws joined the others

39

as they tried to break into the express car. Shots were fired, and the express car's messenger was wounded. Doolin and the others managed to break the door down, and they escaped with a few thousand dollars.

Between 1893 and early 1895, Doolin and his gang made their biggest hauls robbing banks, including those in Spearville and Cimarron, Kansas. According to the best estimates, Doolin and his gang stole about $175,000 in gold and currency during this period. What happened to the loot is the basis for this legend.

Tradition has it that Doolin's gang had many hideouts, one of which was a cave that was said to have been large enough to conceal twenty-five men and their horses. Another is said to have been in the rolling Osage Hills around Pawhuska, Oklahoma; still another was an old trading post at Ingalls, also in Oklahoma. Many treasure hunters, however, believe that Doolin may have hidden much of his stolen treasure in a hideout near Burden, Kansas.

To understand the apparent logic behind this belief, more details about Doolin's life are needed. Early in September, 1893, Doolin and his gang were making their headquarters at Ingalls, Oklahoma. Lawmen soon learned this and moved into the town. A gunfight followed, in which three lawmen were killed. It was perhaps the most exciting gun fight that really happened in the Old West.

Doolin and his gang split up after the Ingalls battle, and Bill Doolin drifted west into New Mexico, where he spent some time on the ranch of Eugene Manlove Rhodes, who became a well-known writer. By early 1895, however, Doolin was moving east again, and by early May he was in south-central Kansas. Two years earlier, in 1893, Doolin had married a preacher's daughter, Edith Ellsworth of Ingalls, Oklahoma, who, less than a year later, had presented Doolin with a son named Jay. By mid May of 1895, Edith and Jay Doolin had joined Bill in the small Cowley County town of Burden, located about thirty-five miles south of El Dorado on what is now U.S. highway 160. Bill Doolin and his family set up a camp a mile and a half west of Burden, near Silver Creek Ford.

As the days passed, Doolin's wife purchased milk, butter, and eggs from a nearby farmer named John Wilson, and she and Mrs. Wilson became friends. When Edith Doolin made up the story that

she and her husband were on their way east to visit relatives but
that they had to stop because her husband was suffering from arthritis, Mrs. Wilson talked her husband into letting the Doolins
move into an old farmhouse with a dirt floor, which was located
on the Wilsons' farm. The Wilsons even furnished an old bed, a
few chairs, a table, and a stove for the house. They told the Doolins
to stay as long as they needed to. The Wilsons even asked their
physician, Henry Manser, to treat Doolin, who was suffering from
arthritis; and the doctor did.

The Wilsons, of course, did not know the real identity of the
Doolins, who used the name Thomas when they went into Burden
to purchase supplies, coal, and feed. Several residents of Burden
would later recall Bill Doolin, his wife, and two-year-old son. John
Tedlie, who operated the feed and seed store, remembered that
the husband would remain in the wagon seat, wearing a long black
overcoat and complaining about his arthritis. Unbeknownst to the
townspeople, Doolin was carrying a short Winchester saddle gun
and a six-shooter under the long coat.

Doolin and his family apparently spent about eight months
living quietly near Burden, Kansas. And because other members
of the gang apparently were not aware of Doolin's whereabouts,
speculation grew that Doolin had his remaining share of the loot
from the robbery with him in Kansas. If so, he may have buried
some or nearly all of it in the vicinity of Burden.

There are other considerations, however. After spending some
time in Burden, Doolin decided that he preferred the peace and
quiet of family life to the life of the outlaw, so he contacted a friend
in Indian Territory and asked that the friend contact the federal
lawmen who had jurisdiction there. Doolin proposed that he would
give himself up provided that he would be allowed to make restitu-
tion for his crimes by serving a short term in the penitentiary. The
lawmen, however, said no, pointing out that Doolin had killed three
lawmen in Indian Territory. The truth was that Doolin's men, not
Doolin, had done the killings.

When Doolin's proposal was rejected, he sent his wife and son
back to Indian Territory. Doolin then traveled east to Eureka
Springs, Arkansas, where he hoped the reputed healing powers of
the baths would cure his arthritis. Unbeknownst to Doolin, William

Matthew ("Bill") Tilghman, a U.S. marshal, had picked up Doolin's trail and had followed him to Burden, Kansas, and then to Eureka Springs, where, on January 15, 1896, Tilghman, disguised in a Prince Albert coat, a black derby hat, and appropriate accessories, surprised Doolin in the lobby of a hotel. Doolin was arrested and taken by train to Guthrie, in what is now Oklahoma.

On May 1, 1896, Doolin pleaded not guilty to charges stemming from the gun battle in Ingalls. He was then returned to the federal jail in Guthrie, whence, on the night of July 5, 1896, Doolin and other prisoners escaped. Doolin hid out near Lawson, Indian Territory; and near there, on August 25 of that year, Doolin was killed by lawmen who were waiting to ambush the outlaw. Doolin's body was taken to Guthrie, and on the morning of August 28, Bill Doolin was buried in the Summit View Cemetery at Guthrie, where his grave may be seen today.

Whether or not Bill Doolin buried any of his outlaw's loot in the vicinity of Burden, Kansas, is not known. There are no records that any of the stolen gold or currency has been recovered. While it is possible that the loot was spent by Doolin, this seems unlikely. It is also possible either that his wife knew where the loot had been hidden or that Bill Doolin had given it to her when she left Kansas to return to Indian Territory in 1896. Her life after Bill Doolin's death does not suggest that she had it, however. Less than seven months after her husband's death, she married Col. Samuel M. Meek, a veteran of the Civil War, who was considerably older than his bride. They lived in Ingalls, Oklahoma, where Jay Doolin took his step-father's last name. In 1901 they moved to Kaw City, Oklahoma, which is south of Arkansas City, Kansas; and in 1902 they moved to Beaver County in the Oklahoma Panhandle, where Colonel Meek died in 1917. Edith Doolin Meek died in 1928 at Ponca City, Oklahoma, where her son, Jay Doolin Meek, spent much of his working life with the Continental Oil Company until he retired at the age of sixty-five.

If Bill Doolin hid his outlaw's loot, it probably remains to be found. If anyone has found it, he or she has kept the fact a secret.

# Entangled Legends about Treasure in Ellis County

When anyone tries to track down a treasure tale, there is the possibility that one yarn may be the result of another or even that two tales have become entangled. This often happens when tales are told and retold and passed along from one generation to another. Such is the case in Ellis County, Kansas, where there is a legend that a missing $22,000 railroad payroll was buried just east of Ellis and just south of modern Interstate 70. In truth, the legend is a distorted blend of two stories, one of which involves a missing $22,000 railroad payroll and the other of which concerns a reported $87,000 in stolen gold that was taken in the robbery of a railroad express train in Nebraska. To understand what appears to be the truth, it is necessary to understand both tales.

The first began about 1870, when the Kansas Pacific Railroad moved its division point from Ellsworth to Ellis. All of the railroad's shopmen and their families were moved to Ellis, which became a new pay center. The method of paying railroad employees was simple. Wells Fargo and Company was responsible for the railroad's express business, and a man named Reddington was the railroad's paymaster. He always paid employees in cash, usually gold. From his office in Lawrence, Reddington would make arrangements to ship the necessary payrolls west via Wells Fargo to various points along the Kansas Pacific line. He would then travel west to Sheridan, in far western Kansas, and start east, paying employees at each pay point until he reached Lawrence.

43

One day in 1870 he sent $22,000 in cash to Ellis, where it was received by Joe Harvey, the Wells Fargo agent. Harvey took the shipment to the express office, which was located in a small general store next door to the Western Hotel. The store was owned by Joe Harvey and by J. K. Hamilton. Harvey used a corner of the store as the express office, but he did not have a safe in which to keep the cash. Exactly where he put it is not recorded, but on the following morning he reported that it was missing. Wells Fargo immediately offered a $5,000 reward for the recovery of the money. Jim Mastin, the express company's agent in Hays, was asked by Wells Fargo to investigate. After being deputized by the Ellis County sheriff, Martin traveled the fourteen miles west to Ellis to interview Joe Harvey and others, including J. K. Hamilton. Mastin was apparently not satisfied with the answers that Harvey gave to his questions, so he arrested Harvey and started for Hays with his prisoner.

Not far from Ellis a group of men — apparently disgruntled railroad workers who feared they would not be paid — forced Mastin to hand over Harvey. The men threatened Harvey and twice went through the motions of preparing to hang him from a railroad trestle in an effort to get him to admit that he had stolen the payroll. Harvey stuck to his first story. The men were about to threaten hanging again when Harvey managed to escape. It was dark by then, and he managed to make his way to Hays, where he surrendered to the sheriff. On the next day he was questioned by Mastin and the sheriff, but he stuck to his story. Having no evidence against Joe Harvey, the lawmen released him.

Harvey returned to Ellis and to his store, but it was not too many weeks later that Harvey and his wife quietly left town. Several weeks later, word reached Ellis that Harvey and his wife were living "high on the hog" in some eastern state. The sudden prosperity meant only one thing to the people in Ellis, who figured that the missing payroll money had been taken east and was being enjoyed.

The second story centers around the robbery of a Union Pacific train at Big Springs, in western Nebraska just northeast of Julesburg, Colorado, which occurred on September 18, 1877. The robbery is a matter of record, but there were only six, not eight, men involved, and the loot was an express shipment of new $20 gold pieces, which was being sent east from the San Francisco Mint. The gold was worth $60,000, not $87,000, the figure that is often quoted in this second tale about Ellis. The legend, as told around Ellis, has also ignored the fact that the leader of the outlaw gang was none other than Sam Bass, a Texas badman. This is documented in Wayne Gard's fine biography of Bass, which was published in 1936.

This second story has long been told around Ellis. It goes something like this: Before leaving Nebraska, the outlaws divided their loot, with each one taking $10,000 in $20 gold pieces. Then they split up into pairs. Two of the outlaws—Joel Collins and Bill Heffridge—were killed at Buffalo Station on the Kansas Pacific line when Ellis County's Sheriff Bardsley and ten cavalry troopers tried to capture them. Some of the gold was recovered. Meantime, two other outlaws—Jim Berry and Tom Nixon—had ridden south-eastward and had made it safely to Missouri with their gold. Berry was killed by lawmen a short time later, near his home, and much of his share of the gold was recovered, but Nixon disappeared with his share.

The two remaining outlaws—Sam Bass and Jack Davis—rode southeastward into Kansas and apparently stopped in Ellis. Old-timers in Ellis recalled that two men dismounted in front of a saloon one day not long after the robbery. While one man went inside for a drink, the other remained outside, watching the horses. When the first man returned, he watched the animals while his partner went into the saloon for a drink. During this time, two or three townspeople who were passing by the saloon heard a jingling noise coming from the horses everytime the animals became restless and moved. According to one account, the jingling sound came from pairs of overalls that were tied just behind the saddle on each horse. The legs of the overalls had been sewed tight, so as to hold whatever was inside.

When the second man came out from the saloon and mounted his horse, both men rode east out of Ellis. It was then that the townspeople reported what they had heard and seen to the sheriff's office. A posse was quickly organized and rode out of Ellis after the two men. When the posse returned, its members reported that they had not been able to find the two men on horseback.

From what can be pieced together, the two men apparently left the trail to Hays and camped in the rugged country just east of Ellis, and the posse had missed them. The two men apparently left on the following day and soon traded their tired ponies for an old horse and buggy. They had then continued southeastward. While driving the old buggy, they encountered a group of soldiers who were looking for the outlaws. One of the outlaws—perhaps Sam Bass—supposedly told the officers in charge that he and his friend were looking for the train robbers in hopes of getting a reward. The two men in the buggy remained with the soldiers for four days without arousing suspicion.

It is known that Bass and Davis returned safely to Texas, and according to most accounts, they carried their share of the gold coins with them in the buggy. The story as told around Ellis suggests, however, that one or both of the men may have buried some of the gold coins in a draw located in the rugged country just east of Ellis.

It was about two years later, in 1879, when a middle-aged couple arrived in Ellis. No one thought much about their arrival after the woman reported that her husband had come west to recover his health. She said he had lung trouble and was unable to work. The woman got a job in a rooming house, while the man soon took up an eighty-acre homestead in the rugged country about a mile east of Ellis. There he built a small stone house some distance east of where another stone house was later constructed by Eli Sheldon. The homesteader found enough flat land so that he could break enough sod to comply with the homestead law, and the couple purchased a few head of cattle. From all appearances they had come to stay.

The man spent a great deal of time wandering over the hills and through the draws; his wife said he walked for his health. The couple stayed to themselves and were downright unsociable to their neighbors, who tried to be friendly. In fact, when the woman saw anyone crossing their homestead, she would usually grab a pitchfork and chase them off, using language that most women did not use.

The couple seemed to have a difficult time making ends meet. Their few cattle were mortgaged to the Ellis bank, and when the couple could not satisfy the debt, the bank's cashier rode out to the homestead to take possession of the cattle. But the homesteader cornered the cashier and threatened to shoot him with a rifle. A neighboring farmer, who happened by, knocked the rifle from the homesteader's hands. The homesteader ran to his stone house and returned with a loaded revolver, but by then the cashier and the farmer had escaped.

Not long after this incident, the homesteading couple, whose names are lost in time, announced that they were going to move to California. They held a public sale, which netted them only a few hundred dollars after they had paid off their debts. A few months later, however, word was received from California that the couple was doing very well. In fact, they were wealthy.

It was then that the people in and around Ellis concluded that the homesteader was really one of the two men who had stopped in Ellis in 1877 after the Big Springs, Nebraska, train robbery. They believed that the men had hidden some or all of their shares of gold coins in the rugged country just east of town. And the townspeople believed that the couple had posed as homesteaders to give them time to recover the buried gold. The couple had waited until the time seemed ripe for them to leave the neighborhood without exciting suspicion.

Whether the man who homesteaded east of Ellis was really one of the six outlaws who had robbed the Union Pacific train in 1877 is not known. Four of the six outlaws died violent deaths within a year after the robbery. Joel Collins and Bill Heffridge died at Buffalo Station, as has already been related. Sam Bass died of gunshot wounds in Texas, and Jim Berry was killed in Missouri. Only Jack Davis and Tom Nixon would have been alive in 1879 when the homesteaders arrived in Ellis. Nixon, however, was then reported to have been living in Canada. If the homesteader was one of the outlaws, he must have been Jack Davis, the only surviving outlaw whose whereabouts in 1879 are not known. And if Davis and his wife had gone to California from Kansas, it would have been an easy voyage to Nicaragua, where Davis was reportedly living a comfortable life early in this century.

It is rather easy to see how these two separate stories might become entangled: both involved railroads, both involved a treasure, and both occurred within a few years of each other. But there seems to be little basis in fact for the belief that the missing payroll or part of the gold that was taken in the train robbery may still be hidden in Ellis County. In fact, the evidence suggests that the treasures were never really lost. Still, it is human nature to wonder if perhaps the stories are in error and that just maybe the treasures, one or both, are still lost and waiting to be found. Such wishful thinking makes the treasure hunter keep hunting.

# The Treasure Legend
# That Wasn't

**O**ccasionally, while searching for legends about buried treasure, a tale does not ring true. Something tells you that it is highly unlikely that events that are linked to the tale ever occurred, and careful research may confirm such suspicions. Such is the case of a buried-treasure legend that is set in southeastern Wabaunsee County, Kansas, long before Kansas Territory was established.

One day, while I was looking through old books containing county histories, among the vast holdings in the library of the Kansas State Historical Society in Topeka, a story in Matt Thomson's 1901 book titled *The Early History of Wabaunsee County* caught my attention. Thomson relates a story, which he heard from an old-timer, about $75,000 in gold, supposedly buried near Harveyville in southeastern Wabaunsee County. The story is fascinating; in fact, it has all of the ingredients that are usually found in a Hollywood Western.

The story goes something like this. There is a large mound or hill near what is now Harveyville. During the early 1840s, outlaws used the mound as a lookout. South from the mound ran the Santa Fe Trail, and close-by, a branch trail from Fort Leavenworth ran into the Santa Fe Trail. From atop the mound, outlaws carefully observed all travel on the two trails. If they saw a wagon train that appeared to be carrying valuables, they would send one or two men after the wagons. The men would pretend to be looking for mules or oxen that had strayed away or stampeded from another train.

49

The men would ask permission to travel with the wagons until they reached their camp. Permission was usually granted, and as the outlaws traveled along, they would carefully look over the wagons, the teamsters, and their arms to determine which wagons, if any, were carrying gold. In those days, wagon trains that were returning east from Santa Fe usually carried their profits in gold. And Mexican freighters that were bound for Missouri to buy merchandise also carried much gold. These were the wagon trains that the outlaws wanted to raid.

Once the outlaws had learned what they wanted, they would quietly leave the wagon train, sometimes while the teamsters were making camp. The outlaws would then return to the lookout mound. On the far side of that mound, out of view from anyone who might be passing along on the trails, there was a log cabin, apparently constructed during the early 1840s. It was located on the bank of Dragoon Creek, near the mouth of Bachelor's Branch.

During 1842 and 1843, several wagon trains were robbed by this gang as they followed the Santa Fe Trail between 110 Mile Creek, in present Osage County, and Big John Springs, just east of Council Grove. Soldiers who had been sent out from Fort Leavenworth searched for the outlaws after each raid but without success. And the military warned freighters to be on their guard against the robbers.

Late on a spring afternoon in 1844, a mule-drawn train of forty-three wagons made camp about two hundred yards west of Log Chain Creek, near the present-day Wabaunsee County line. The wagon train, which was owned by an American but was manned by Mexican teamsters, was suddenly surprised by a band of twenty-one outlaws, who killed twenty-seven of the forty-three teamsters. The American who owned the train managed to evade the outlaws and thus escape.

While some of the outlaws were holding the surviving teamsters, some of whom had been wounded, other outlaws rummaged through the wagons, going first to a wagon that contained an iron box 18 by 12 by 8 inches. Inside the box was $75,000 in gold. The outlaws took the box and then made off with about five hundred mules that had been used to pull the train's wagons.

Exactly what happened next is hazy, but the American owner of the train returned after the outlaws had left. He made a survey of the dead and wounded teamsters and told one Mexican to take charge. The American then rode to Fort Leavenworth, a journey that took him two days. At the fort he told about the attack, and a company of cavalry accompanied him to the scene of the raid, a return trip that also took two days.

After burying the dead teamsters, the soldiers tried to follow the outlaws' trail, but the herd of mules had been split up and driven in different directions. The soldiers followed one trail, which led them west; and after a few days they arrived at the Little Arkansas River, about midway between present-day Lyons and McPherson, Kansas. There the soldiers met an old trapper and plainsman, H. B. Hobbs. When the officer in charge informed Hobbs about the wagon-train raid and murders and the search for the outlaws, Hobbs agreed to act as a guide. He knew the country, and he soon concluded that the outlaws would not dare to take the mules to Missouri or to New Mexico. He said the only safe market was in Oregon.

With this in mind, Hobbs led the soldiers in a northerly direction, and a few days later they came upon the fresh trail of the outlaws and the mules. It appeared that the split herd had been brought together. The trail headed west, following the Smoky Hill River. The soldiers followed, and somewhere in present-day Logan County, near Russell Springs, Kansas, the soldiers came upon the mules and the outlaws. A battle followed, in which fourteen of the outlaws were killed; but if any soldiers were killed or wounded, it was not reported. The five surviving outlaws were taken to Fort Leavenworth, where they were tried and sentenced to life in a prison at Alton, Illinois. The mules were returned to their owner, but the iron box that reportedly contained $75,000 in gold was not recovered. It became evident that two missing outlaws — twenty-one had attacked the wagon train, only nineteen of whom were accounted for — had not traveled with those who were herding the mules. The soldiers returned to the scene of the raid and searched for but did not find the iron box, so the matter became history.

In 1857, as the story continues, a man named Allen Hodgson settled in the vicinity of the mound that had once been used as a lookout by the outlaws. Nearby he found the ashes and outline of a 14-by-16-foot log cabin. Hodgson's son Ira, who seems to have been the primary source for this tale, recalled that he learned about the story, as thus far related, from an old plainsman named Tom Fulton. Ira met Fulton in about 1861, while the latter was crossing the plains, and when Fulton learned about Hodgson's home, he related the account of the robbers and claimed that the outlaws had selected the site because it was too far west of settlements for white men to molest them and was not far enough west to be bothered by Indians.

Ira Hodgson also recalled that during the late 1850s, there was much talk among the employees of the Overland Mail Company about a treasure's being buried somewhere between 110 Mile Creek and Big John Springs. Some of the employees reportedly searched for it but did not find anything. Hodgson also recalled that in 1867, after the Civil War, a man who said that his home was Alton, Illinois, where five of the outlaws had been jailed for life, had spent the summer months searching for the treasure along Big John Springs and along Rock, Bluff and 142 Mile creeks. He did not find it, but before he left the area, he supposedly told a few people that the treasure was located on the south side of a creek that had a big bluff where another creek came into the main creek from the north. On the bluff south of the creek, according to the information, there were many big flat rocks. On one of the rocks was cut the figure of a compass, pointing to the place where the box was buried. And under the compass was cut the number of rods to the buried box. Where the man got this information is not reported.

According to Matt Thomson's account, the matter had been forgotten, but during the summer of 1895, an old Englishman had arrived in Harveyville. He was a preacher, but in addition to his occasional preaching in the neighborhood, he did a great deal of fishing. His favorite spot for fishing was near the mouth of Bachelor's Branch, close to where the outlaws had had their cabin. Some people wondered why he fished there, since it was one of the poorest fishing holes in Wabaunsee County. Then, on one September day, the man disappeared, according to Thomson's account. Within days, someone discovered a hole in the ground north of the Harveyville cemetery, on the site of the old log cabin that had been used by the outlaws. The hole was about four feet deep, and on the sides of the hole, people said they had seen the imprint of an iron box 18 by 12 by 8 inches. Iron rust supposedly was still visible sticking to the earth, so the people concluded that the old Englishman, the preacher, had found the iron box containing $75,000 in gold that had been taken during the reported wagon-train raid fifty-one years earlier.

That's the tale told by Matt Thomson in his 1901 book. Efforts to confirm the story have been unsuccessful, however. Missouri newspapers contain no reference to the 1842 wagon-train raid, and no military records exist of the cavalry's involvement. But tucked away in the manuscript section of the Kansas State Historical Society in Topeka there are two letters relating to the tale. One, dated February 10, 1903, was written by S. B. Harvey, the man for whom Harveyville was named. The other letter was written later, in 1903, by Stephen Jackson Spear, a Wabaunsee County pioneer. Both letters reflect upon the story that Matt Thomson related in his book.

Harvey, who settled on Dragoon Creek on August 4, 1854, wrote: "I was all over the neighborhood with my gun dozens of times before Hodgeons [Hodgson] came. . . . I was, I believe, on every rod of timber above the llworth [Leavenworth] road with my gun hunting and I never saw a vestige of a former 'Robbers Roost' and I do not think such a place ever existed in the neighborhood."

Spear's letter is even more revealing. He explained that the treasure tale was a hoax:

> In the fall of 1891, William Wetzel, Jr., made a fishing trip on Dragoon Creek, near its confluence with Bachelor Creek. On his return trip he crossed the southeast quarter of Section 28, Town. 14, Range 13, George M. Harvey's original preemption claim, and at a point at about 50 rods north of the south line and an equal distance from the east line, he discovered what he thought was an Indian grave. Some days later he took a spade and went unobserved to this place, hoping by digging to uncover some Indian relics. He dug a hole about six feet long north and south, and two feet wide, and about three feet deep in the center. Not finding any signs of Indian relics he then dug another hole about 18 inches long, 12 inches wide and 8 inches deep in the bottom of the larger excavation, but discovered nothing. He returned home without having refilled the hole. A short time after this he happened to be in Harveyville one evening and proposed to some boys to go coon

hunting. The plan met with approval and a short time later a gang of about eight or ten men, William Wetzel at the head and armed with a lantern, were on their way. . . . After leading the boys around through the woods for awhile, William at length brought up at the scene of his recent digging. Feigning surprise at finding such a hole he exclaimed: "I wonder what this is?" The story of the hole soon went the rounds of the community, and during the next few days there were several investigations to find if some treasure had not been taken away. William Wetzel some time later gave the writer the particulars of the above.

Spear recalled that not long after Wetzel had perpetrated his joke, Ira Hodgson recalled the story that he had heard from the old plainsman named Tom Fulton. It was then that people in Harveyville began to tell the tale of the buried treasure. Who embellished it by suggesting that the old Englishman — the preacher — had found the treasure and disappeared is not known. But Spear, in his account, observes that the preacher did not disappear; in fact, he was taken to Burlingame, Kansas, to preach. Spear concludes his account thus: "My object in writing this account is to show that Samuel B. Harvey and others who had a chance to know would have heard or known of a report if money had been buried there. I believe the man described as Tom Fulton by Ira, did tell him about the Log Chain robbery and the burial of the iron box on Dragoon Creek, but that is no evidence of the truth of the account. This statement is written with no feelings of unkindness towards those who differ with me."

The statements by Spear and Harvey, plus the total lack of factual evidence relating to the wagon-train raid, leave little doubt that the legend of buried treasure near Harveyville is fiction, not fact.

# The Missing
# Indianola Treasure

**I**ndianola is one of the lost towns of Kansas; it no longer exists. Indianola was located on the banks of Soldier Creek in what is now northwest Topeka; but in 1854, the year in which both Topeka and Indianola were founded, several miles separated the two settlements. While the sentiments of early Topeka residents were antislavery, Indianola was largely made up of proslavery settlers, many of whom had come into the area as squatters even before Kansas Territory was opened for settlement in 1854. During the early years of Kansas Territory, Indianola was considered to be a more prosperous community than Topeka.

Indianola's location was its attraction: it was situated on the old government road or military trail that linked Fort Leavenworth and Fort Riley. The trail was established in about 1852, the year that Fort Riley was founded. And during the ensuing years, hundreds of government wagon trains followed the trail west to Fort Riley and to other posts beyond. It was also common practice for government paymasters to follow this trail, bearing military payrolls to Fort Riley and other western posts. One such payroll is the basis for the legend about Indianola treasure.

Much of what is known about the legend is contained in an 1893 Topeka newspaper clipping in the files of the Kansas State Historical Society in Topeka. The article in the *State Journal* relates how one government paymaster was robbed of $75,000 in gold near St. Mary's mission, now St. Marys, Kansas, in 1853. The mission

This photo of Samuel J. Reader's 1861 watercolor painting shows the settlement of Indianola, near where the treasure supposedly was buried. Indianola, which is now extinct, was located northwest of Topeka. The road to the right in the illustration linked Indianola to Topeka.

was then about twenty miles west-northwest of Indianola. The paymaster was heading toward the west from Fort Leavenworth at the time of the robbery. He was not harmed, so after the robbers had fled, he went for help.

A posse, which tracked the robbers eastward towards Indianola, found the empty paymaster's chest, but the gold was gone. Because of the quantity and weight of the gold, squatters in the area figured that the robbers probably had buried the gold. The posse failed to locate the robbers or the gold, and in time the robbery was forgotten by many. But on a Sunday morning in 1893, some freshly made excavations were found near the old town site of Indianola by J. Q. A. Peyton, a long-time resident of the area. He contacted the sheriff, who investigated and found the stump of a large old tree on a farm that was then owned by W. W. Phillips. The tree had been a huge elm, the largest in the area. It once had served as a landmark, but it had died and had been cut down some years earlier, so that only the stump remained. Close to the stump, four large holes had been dug into the earth. A Topeka newspaper reporter wrote:

> The holes were five feet deep and nearly as many square. In one of them were the imprints of a metal kettle and a very

large demijohn [a large earthenware bottle with a narrow neck, wicker casing and handle] as if they had been buried there a considerable time and had recently been removed. To all appearances some person had measured a certain distance from the tree and dug to find something. He dug four of the holes before the right spot was located. The imprints of the kettle and the jug are perfect, and there can be no doubt as to the nature of the articles removed from the hole.

The reporter interviewed several old-timers in the area, including Orren A. ("Jack") Curtis, the father of Charles Curtis, the thirty-first vice-president of the United States. Orren Curtis recalled the robbery. Although Curtis had not arrived in Kansas until 1856, he related stories he had heard about the robbery from men who were in the area at the time. And J. Q. A. Peyton, the man who discovered the holes, told the reporter that he was living in the area near Indianola at the time when the robbery had occurred. Peyton recalled that two notorious gamblers from Leavenworth had set up their operations at Indianola at the time of the robbery. According to Peyton, a man named Sam Harper had hauled an enormous demijohn filled with whisky from Leavenworth to Indianola for one of the gamblers, a man named Farrell. Sometime afterwards, Harper had gone to Farrell and asked to buy the demijohn. Farrell told him that he didn't have it, that he had buried it. This was sometime after the robbery.

The sheriff and others in the neighborhood had come up with the theory that the two gamblers probably had had a hand in the robbery and that they had buried the gold in the demijohn and in the old kettle. Either the gamblers had returned forty years later to recover the gold, or someone else had learned where it was buried and had dug it up. According to Orren Curtis, the gamblers had left Indianola sometime after he had moved there in 1856.

Whether the demijohn and the iron kettle actually contained the missing government payroll in gold is anyone's guess. There is the possibility that the missing gold is still buried somewhere along the old government trail between St. Marys and the site of old Indianola.

# Legends of Treasure in Morton County

**M**orton is the southwestern-most county in Kansas. Its western boundary borders on Colorado, and its southern boundary borders on Oklahoma. To the north is Stanton County, and to the east is Stevens County. The Cimarron Cut-off, or Dry Route, of the Santa Fe Trail once cut across the southeastern portion of Morton County, following much the same route as U.S. highway 56 does today. After Kansas Territory was established, a military road or trail was developed through the area, running from the northwest to the southeast. Called the Palo-Duro Trail, it was primarily a military road, connecting Fort Lyon, in what is now eastern Colorado, to Fort Elliot, in Texas. The trail was also used for a time during the nineteenth century as a cattle trail. There was also the O-X Trail, which linked the O-X Ranch, on Beaver Creek just south of modern Guymon, Oklahoma, to what is today called Point of Rocks Ranch, located northwest of present-day Elkhart, Kansas, along the Cimarron River.

Point of Rocks Ranch took its name from the high sandstone bluffs along the river. Travelers over the Santa Fe Trail called the bluffs simply Point Rocks. The Spaniards referred to them as Mesa Blanca, meaning white mesa. For people who were traversing the Santa Fe Trail, Point Rocks was an important landmark. It was five hundred miles to the Missouri River or, if you were traveling in the opposite direction, about two hundred and fifty miles to Santa Fe.

58

This aerial photograph shows Point of Rocks in modern Morton County, the site of two legends about treasure in Kansas.

Two legends about treasure are set in Morton County; both are tied to the area around Point of Rocks, as that landmark is called today. The first legend seems to have little basis in fact. At least, no evidence has been found to support the tale that is told by old-timers in and around Morton County. The tale goes something like this. Point of Rocks was far from any settlement during the early days of the Santa Fe Trail, and since it was often used as a campsite by travelers who were following the trail, it was a good spot for bandits to rob unsuspecting travelers. This was particularly true after the California gold rush in 1849, when many successful gold-seekers began to return east with their gold.

Exactly when the following incident is supposed to have occurred is not known, nor has it been confirmed by newspaper accounts or other documents of the period. However, tradition has it that robbers took more than $90,000 in gold from one party of gold seekers who were returning east. Before the robbers could escape with their loot, they saw another party of travelers approaching. Because the gold was quite heavy and because the robbers could not flee the area rapidly, they reportedly buried the gold in the vicinity and then fled, intending to return to dig up the gold. But according to the legend, they never returned, and the gold supposedly still remains buried for anyone to find.

The second tale about treasure in Morton County contains a few more details; but like the first one, it lacks confirmation. It concerns a man named Alexander and four other men who, during the early 1850s, left their homes in Illinois with three wagons full of dry goods. These men intended to go overland, following the Santa Fe Trail to New Mexico, where they planned to sell the dry goods. According to tradition, they arrived safely in Santa Fe and sold their calico for $2 a yard. They received their profit in silverware, silver bars, and silver bullion, and then they started back up the trail, intent upon returning to Illinois.

Near Point of Rocks in modern Morton County, which is close to the later site of Point of Rocks Ranch, the successful Illinois traders made camp, only to be surprised during the night by Indians, who drove off their animals. Exactly what happened next is not clear, but apparently the men, fearing that the Indians would return at dawn, buried their silver and then pulled and pushed their wagons over the spot where the silver was buried. Next they set fire to the wagons. The men fled the scene, took cover some distance from camp, and watched their wagons burn, the flames licking into the night sky. There were only a few coals remaining as the first rays of sunlight appeared at dawn. The men waited several hours for the Indians, but there was no sign of Indians anywhere. By early in the afternoon the men began to walk eastward, toward Missouri. How many days they were on the trail is not known, but they eventually reached Independence. They were discouraged and weak from hunger, but they were alive. When they recovered their strength, the men returned to Illinois. According to the legend, they never returned to recover their silver, which they had buried somewhere in the vicinity of Point of Rocks along the Cimarron River.

# Abram B. Burnett's Treasure

Some tales about treasure are based more on wishful thinking than on solid facts. One such tale concerns Abram B. Burnett, a Pottawatomie Indian chief. Burnett, whose Indian name was Kah-he-ga-wa-ti-an-gah, was born in Michigan about 1811. He was given the name Abram Burnett while attending mission schools in Indiana, Michigan, and Kentucky. In 1821, when Abram was only ten years old, he served as an interpreter for Rev. Isaac McCoy, a Baptist missionary, who later operated the Shawnee Mission in present-day Johnson County, Kansas.

When Burnett grew to manhood, he became an important figure among his people. His name appears on the treaty that ceded Pottawatomie lands in Indiana to the United States; he also signed the treaty in 1846 that ceded Pottawatomie land along the Osage River in Missouri in exchange for land along the Kansas River in what is now Kansas.

When the Pottawatomie Indians moved to Kansas about 1848, the government opened a trading post for them at what became known as Uniontown, which was located about a mile south of the Kansas River in what is now far-western Shawnee County, west of Topeka. And it was there that Abram Burnett and his family moved. His wife was a native of Germany who had come to the United States at the age of eight. She was described as a very good woman, stocky in build, and a fine cook. The Burnetts had one daughter when they moved to Uniontown, and Abram's

This photograph of Abram Burnett, a Pottawatomie Indian chief, was taken during the late 1860s, before his death in 1870.

wife gave birth to another daughter less than two months after they arrived.

The Burnetts remained and witnessed the start of Kansas Territory in 1854. By then they had four children. A fifth child arrived in April, 1854, and by 1865, two more children had been born. Altogether, they had five girls and two boys. By 1865, Abram Burnett was in his middle fifties. He had become a very large man, weighing about five hundred pounds. The only way that he could get into a wagon was by means of a pair of steps, which he carried for that purpose. The Burnetts' home was then in Mission Township, on the southwest edge of what is now Topeka.

One day, Burnett visited a store in Topeka. The storekeeper had just returned from a trip to Leavenworth, and among the items that he had purchased was a bladder of putty. In those days, putty was put up in bladders. The storekeeper placed the bladder on a keg of nails. Burnett came in shortly thereafter and sat down on the bladder of putty, all five hundred pounds of him. Burnett did not notice that anything was wrong until he tried to stand up:

he could not rise. The storekeeper had to cut the seat out of Abram's pants in order to free him. Abram's rear end was exposed for all the world to see, but the large Indian was not concerned. He simply conducted his business and then left.

During the late 1860s, Burnett became quite well-to-do as a cattle buyer. He conducted his business in the family cabin, which was located about a hundred and fifty yards north of Shunganunga Creek and about a hundred yards east of the west line of the southeast quarter of section 9, township 11, range 15 east, in Mission Township. When he was engaged in a cattle trade, he followed the practice of getting a jug of whiskey, which he kept in a small cupboard at the east end of his cabin. After he had taken a drink, he would pass the jug to the person with whom he was doing business.

Most of his neighbors knew that Burnett made good money in the cattle business, and because most business was conducted by using gold coins, people suspected that he had accumulated much wealth. Yet he did not seem to spend his money, and he reportedly did not trust banks. This speculation is the basis for the belief that Burnett buried his gold somewhere in the vicinity of his cabin. When Abram Burnett died on June 14, 1870, his wife told no one until she had had time to hide her husband's guns, saddles, bridles, and other possessions. She did this because it was a Pottawatomie custom to visit the home of a dead chief before his burial and to take away some memento that had belonged to the dead man.

If Abram Burnett had buried his gold in or around his cabin, it seems likely that his wife would have known of its whereabouts. Yet through the years, people have searched the property for the gold. Whether it has been found or whether it even existed is not known.

Burnett's widow remarried, and in 1879 the property was given to a daughter, Clarissa Bell Burnett Yott. She and her husband eventually sold the property to a man named Little. In about 1907 the cabin was torn down by W. C. Little, who then owned it. No treasure was found.

# Legends about Treasure
# in Lincoln County

**B**uried treasure really did exist in Lincoln County, northwest of Salina. This is a matter of public record. In fact, on November 22, 1930, the Associated Press reported from Sylvan Grove, which is located on Kansas highway 181, that a treasure had been recovered. In that year a pioneer woman, Mrs. W. H. Meyers, had died; her husband had preceded her in death. They had been early settlers in Lincoln County. Mrs. Meyers' two sons—Skinney and Rudolph—set about the task of dividing the family property. They were the only heirs. As they reviewed everything, they had the feeling that there should have been more wealth. Their parents had been thrifty; they had good saving habits; and the sons knew that their parents had owned much property.

The two brothers began a careful search of the family farm home. First they found a can containing a large amount of silver; soon they came upon another container, which was filled with gold coins. In the farmyard and in the fields near the house they located more containers, which were filled with cash and a few mortgages on neighbors' property. In all, they had uncovered more than $20,000 in cash by late November of 1930.

While this treasure tale is well documented, another Lincoln County story is not. No facts can be found to substantiate the traditional claims that a fortune in gold remains buried along a creek that is probably south of present-day Sylvan Grove. The tellers of this tale claim that a young man named McGee and his partner were traveling across Kansas, heading for a military fort in New Mexico, perhaps Fort Union. Although there is no reference to their being military officers, it seems likely that they would have been government paymasters. In the vicinity of modern Sylvan Grove, the men saw an Indian war party in the distance. The Indians, who had spotted the white men at about the same time, charged toward them. The two men quickly took the payroll chest and threw it over the bank of a small stream, which is identified in the tale as Cow Creek, though early maps of Lincoln County do not show a Cow Creek. Aside from the Saline River, the closest streams to Sylvan Grove are the Twin Creeks—East Twin Creek and West Twin Creek. It is possible that the chest was thrown over the bank of one of these streams. The two men then covered the chest with loose dirt and grass. The chest contained about $20,000 in gold, according to one account, or about $90,000, according to another.

The two men were attacked by the Indians. McGee was wounded, though not seriously. At nightfall, both men were able to escape and head southwest toward Fort Larned. The post was about seventy miles away, but after a day or two they reached it and told the post commander where the payroll was hidden. While McGee's wounds were being treated, a troop of cavalry was sent northeast to recover the gold, but the troopers did not find it. Other parties later searched for it, but according to tradition, it has never been found.

# The Devil's Den Treasure

In southeastern Rooks County, about twenty-five miles north by northwest of Russell, Kansas, there are some high hills. Natoma, in southwest Osborne County, is the closest community to these hills. According to tradition, long before the white man arrived in the area a huge landslide had created a series of deep caves in the rolling chalky hills. Flowing from the cave were currents of air that supposedly frightened Indians who passed that way. The Indians regarded the caves as the homes of evil spirits, and it was the Indians who apparently named the caves the Devil's Den.

The history of the caves is rather hazy. There are unconfirmed accounts that early white settlers had hidden in the caves to escape marauding Indians who avoided the area. And for many travelers, the caves have served as something of a landmark. Perhaps the first notice of the Devil's Den outside of Kansas came in 1923, when a reporter for a Chicago newspaper wrote a story in which he said that the sign of the cloven hoof had been found in the depths of one of the larger caves: "Hundreds of small goatlike hoof tracks were found imprinted in the solid rock. The tracks formed a circle and in the center, fully six inches deep in the rock appeared prints of two large distinct cloven hoofs. Many people believe that the tracks are of the fiends dancing in satanic worship of their master, the devil."

When a copy of the story found its way into Natoma, many residents were indignant, so a few Natoma men decided they would

66

prove that there was nothing sinister about the Devil's Den. They got into a car and drove out to the canyon, where they parked the car on the edge of the creek that runs through the canyon below the caves. Moving on foot, they slowly climbed to the caves, reaching them about dusk. As they entered one of the larger caves, the men were met with strange shrieks; later, they claimed that they were suddenly surrounded by flickering lights.

The men then ran down from the caves toward where they had parked their car, only to find it sitting in the middle of the creek. They hurriedly pushed the car out of the shallow creek onto the low bank and started the motor. Again, shrieks echoed through the canyon, lights flickered, and the car's engine sputtered and died. Each time that they tried to start the engine, there was a repeat performance of the shrieks and the flickering lights, so they started to push the car away from the Devil's Den. About half a mile away, they got the car started and hurriedly drove back to Natoma. The flickering lights may have been nothing more than lightning bugs, and the shrieks may have been only the sounds of night hawks or other wildlife; but the men who visited the Devil's Den that afternoon and early evening apparently thought otherwise.

Someone in Osborne County supposedly then began to do some research and learned that in 1849 in Mexico City, some bandits had escaped with jewels and $300,000 in Mexican gold. The bandits' trail led the Mexican authorities to Kansas, near where the Devil's Den is located. There the Mexican authorities lost all trace of the bandits, who may have been Americans.

Early in this century, according to the story, a man who was then living in the mountains near Juárez, Mexico, produced a map on his deathbed. The map showed that the jewels and gold had been buried in one of the caves in southwestern Rooks County. In the spring of 1916, Mexican authorities came to Kansas in hopes of locating the missing gold. When they arrived at the Devil's Den, they found that nine of the caves on the south side were inhabited by outlaws, who were using them as a hideout. A gun battle followed, during which some of the Mexicans were killed or wounded and the outlaws apparently escaped. A search of the caves by the Mexican authorities failed to locate the missing gold or any sign of the stolen jewels.

Whether or not the jewels and gold were ever buried in one of the caves is not known, though the tale is fascinating. Also, a search of Kansas newspapers has failed to turn up a single account of such a gun battle in 1916. If such a shoot-out had occurred, it undoubtedly would have been reported. Furthermore, no other documentation can be found confirming other aspects of the tale. One thing is certain, however: the caves do exist in the chalky hills west of Natoma, Kansas, not far from Kansas highway 18; and many local residents still refer to them as the Devil's Den.

# The Mysterious Iron Box
# in Sedgwick County

As a writer of tales about buried treasure in Kansas, I occasionally receive letters from readers who have their own treasure tales to tell. Early in 1985, I received one such letter from Brady DeVore of North Platte, Nebraska. At the time, DeVore was spending the winter in sunny Pasadena, California, where he had read the story about the "Du Pratz Gold Mine Legend" in one of my earlier books.

Brady DeVore wrote that my story reminded him of another tale, set in Sedgwick County, Kansas, which had been told to him in about 1921 by an uncle, Jacob Elbert ("Ebb") DeVore, who was born on October 8, 1869. Ebb lived with his parents, John and Esther DeVore, and several brothers and sisters in Sedgwick County, outside of Wichita. One day in about 1880, Ebb and another boy, probably his brother, were roaming over the countryside, "out a long way from any place," as Ebb later told Brady DeVore. There had been heavy rains a few days before, and the two boys came upon an iron box that was partially buried in the earth. The recent rains had apparently washed away the soil that had covered the top of the box.

The two boys dug up the box. It was either 14 or 16 by 12 by 10 inches deep. The iron box was quite heavy, and it was locked. As Ebb later recalled, he believed the iron box contained coins. The two boys were trying to get the box open when a rider appeared in the distance. Not wanting the stranger to see the box, Ebb and his friend carried it to a nearby lake or pond and threw it in. They intended to return later, retrieve the iron box from the water, and open it; but they never did.

The family soon moved north to Nebraska, where the children grew up near Nelson and Angus. When Ebb DeVore had grown up, he and his brother, James B. DeVore, drove down to Sedgwick County in Kansas, thinking they could easily find the lake and recover the box. But when they arrived in the Wichita area they could not find any sign of a lake having ever been where they thought it was.

Ebb DeVore never did find the iron box. He became a subcontractor in the dirt-moving business, making railroad grades in the Nebraska and Dakota region and working on the Mississippi River levee. He quit that business in 1906 and became a farmer just east of Angus, Nebraska, where he died on April 8, 1933.

Whether or not the mysterious iron box really did contain coins, perhaps a farmer's life savings or the loot from a robbery, is not known. And whether the iron box was later found by someone else is anyone's guess. In telling the story, Brady DeVore concluded, "I am the oldest of any member of our family and am no doubt the only living person who ever heard the story."

# Part III

# THE LAWLESS AND THE LAWMEN

*A strict observance of the written laws is doubtless one of the high duties of a good citizen, but it is not the highest. The laws of necessity, of self-preservation, of saving our country when in danger, are of higher obligation.*

—Thomas Jefferson

# Bloody Bill Anderson

His real name was William T. Anderson, and through the years, most Kansans have ignored the fact that he once called Kansas his home. Anderson was born at Palmyra, in northeastern Missouri, about 1840. His father was a hatter by trade, but apparently not a very good one. Late in 1847 or early in 1848, the Anderson family moved to Huntsville, which is located seven miles west of Moberly in north-central Missouri. When word reached that area that gold had been discovered in California, young Bill's father left the family and headed west, to strike it rich. He did not return to Missouri until 1854, and he apparently returned a poorer man than when he left, for he had found little if any gold.

After Kansas Territory was established and opened to settlement in 1854, the Anderson family moved west, seeking greener pastures in the new territory. Exactly when they arrived in Kansas Territory is not known, but by 1857 they were living near Agnes City, a tiny settlement located at the Rock Creek crossing of the Santa Fe Trail in what is now far northwestern Lyon County. Agnes City, a community that began to fade into obscurity late in the nineteenth century, was about twenty-five miles north of modern Emporia and about nine miles east of Council Grove. One of the first settlers on the site of Agnes City was Arthur I. Baker, who built a general store near the Rock Creek crossing. Other settlers included Henry Closing, a man named French, and two or three other men. They arrived soon after Baker and most of them brought their families. A few months before the territorial legislature approved the incorporation of Agnes City in February, 1857, Arthur I. Baker was appointed postmaster, and he operated the post office in his general store.

The Anderson family apparently settled south of Agnes City, where they built a dugout. One man who knew them, O. F. O'Dell, later recalled that the family included the father and mother, four sons, and three daughters. But two of the sons died soon after the family moved to Kansas Territory, and on one spring afternoon, either in 1858 or 1859, the mother was killed by lightning while standing in the door of their dugout during a thunderstorm.

Some residents of the area recalled that after Mrs. Anderson's death, the father and two sons — Bill and Jim — became hard characters. They had no visible means of support, which led to speculation that the Andersons were responsible for stealing from freighters and settlers who camped along the Santa Fe Trail. The thefts are a matter of record, but whether or not the Andersons were responsible is not known. What is known is that when the Civil War began in 1861, Bill Anderson, aged twenty-one, and his younger brother, Jim, announced that they were supporting the South. They joined a few other Southern sympathizers who were living on Bluff and Rock creeks in Lyon County. Among the group was Arthur I. Baker, Leander ("Lee") Griffin, and William Reed. Griffin and Reed were cousins of the Andersons.

A few weeks later, these men rode east to near the Missouri border and raided two or three farms that belonged to Free Staters. The Andersons and the others, elated with their success, hurried back to Lyon County. Soon they started on another raid, but as they were riding their horses across some open country north of Fort Scott, they were chased by a squad of home guards. All of them escaped and returned to Lyon County, except for Arthur Baker, who was captured, taken to Fort Scott, and put into the guardhouse. But when he identified himself as the postmaster at Agnes City and was identified by some influential friends, Baker was released. He returned to Agnes City, where he apparently decided to give up bushwhacking and to settle down to running his general store and the post office.

Baker tried to convince the Anderson brothers, Leander Griffin, and William Reed to also give up such raids. But they refused, and Baker stopped associating with them. A few weeks later, Baker observed Griffin riding past his general store with two large iron-gray horses that belonged to a German by the name of Seigar, who lived nearby. Baker, when he learned from Seigar that the latter's horses had been stolen, went with Seigar to Council Grove and filed charges against Griffin. A warrant for Griffin's arrest was issued, and Baker returned to his store at Agnes City.

When word reached the Andersons that a warrant had been issued for Griffin's arrest, Bill Anderson and his father rode to Baker's store, and young Bill Anderson threatened to kill Baker if he did not have the warrant withdrawn by ten o'clock the following day. Baker, knowing that Bill might make good on his threat, returned to Council Grove and charged young Bill Anderson with threatening his life. When word reached the Andersons, Bill saddled his horse and fled, but Bill's father took his shotgun and headed for Baker's general store. What happened next is told in the words of O. F. O'Dell, a witness:

> At or about 10 the next day, Anderson's father went to Baker's house and inquired the whereabouts of Baker. Some one of the family about the kitchen told him that Baker was up stairs over the sitting room. Anderson passed through the kitchen into the sitting room, where there were quite a number of men collected for the purpose of trying to arrest Bill Anderson. Old man Anderson made straight through the crowd to the foot of the stairway, with the double-barrel gun, both locks at full cock. Baker, hearing the rumpus below and being on his guard, ran to the head of the stairs, and seeing Anderson coming up with a gun, fired down on him with a double-barreled shotgun and killed him in his tracks.

The news of the killing quickly spread as the body was being removed to 142 Mile Creek, where O. F. O'Dell lived. (The creek was 142 miles from Independence on the Santa Fe Trail.) Bill Anderson, learning of his father's death through friends, went to 142 Mile Creek. He was arrested but was permitted to attend the funeral of his father. Afterwards he made arrangements to hire an attorney named Rugles, from Emporia, to defend him. But when the warrant was found to be defective for some reason that is not known, Bill Anderson was released. Before a new complaint could be filed, he had fled the area. A few weeks later, a stranger with a team and wagon came to the Anderson home near Agnes City and moved Jim Anderson, his sisters, and their belongings to somewhere in Missouri.

Two weeks passed, then a month. Nothing was heard of the Andersons. No one reported having seen them in the area. Some residents believed that the Andersons, especially Bill, had left the region for good, but then, on the morning of July 2, 1862, someone saw Bill, Jim, and a third man lurking near Baker's home and store. Learning that Baker had gone on a trip to Emporia, the Andersons, leaving their friend to watch for Baker's return, rode off some distance and set up camp. Late the next afternoon, Baker and his wife returned from Emporia. Anderson's friend watched them enter their home and then hurried to where Bill and Jim Anderson were camped.

It was after dark when Bill and Jim Anderson, their friend, and three other men went to the store where Baker and his thirteen-year-old brother-in-law were working. One of the strangers who was with the Andersons went inside and asked for a pint of whiskey. Baker took a lamp and, with his brother-in-law, opened the cellar door and went into the basement to get the whiskey. When Baker and the boy started up the stairs, Bill Anderson and perhaps one or two other outlaws fired their revolvers at Baker. The bullets struck him and the boy, and both fell down the stairs into the cellar. Thinking they were dead, the Andersons and the others began to help themselves to tobacco and other merchandise in the store. But in the cellar, Baker and the boy were not dead, though both were wounded. While the boy hid, Baker took a revolver, which he kept in the cellar, and crawled up the stairs. Near the top, seeing Bill Anderson, Baker fired his weapon. The bullet struck the fleshy part of one of Anderson's legs. Jim Anderson and the other men rushed Baker and kicked him down the stairs, shut the cellar door, and rolled a barrel of sugar up to the door, thus blocking it. The Andersons and the other men then set fire to Baker's store, and they did the same thing to his nearby home. Baker's wife, at the first sign of trouble, had fled from the house and was in hiding outside when the structure was set on fire.

Meantime, smoke began to fill the cellar of the store. Baker told the young boy to escape through a small cellar window. Wounded

Photograph of William T. Anderson, better known as "Bloody Bill" Anderson, after he left Kansas and became a Confederate guerrilla leader in Missouri. Anderson was killed near Albany, Missouri, in October, 1864.

in the abdomen and the thigh, the boy tried several times before he was able to squeeze through the small opening and crawl away from the burning store to the safety of some brush. He was found an hour or two later by neighbors, who were attracted to the scene by the fire, and he told them what had happened. Efforts to save the boy's life failed, and he died the following day. As for Baker, he knew he could not squeeze through the tiny window, and not wanting to be burned alive, he shot himself through the head after the young boy had made it to safety.

Not satisfied with what they had done, the Andersons and the four other men decided to make a night of it. Although Bill Anderson's leg was causing him pain, it had been bandaged, and whiskey had taken away much of the pain. He could ride, and as the six men rode east along the Santa Fe Trail, they surprised O. F. O'Dell, who operated a combination general store and saloon at the crossing of 142 Mile Creek. O'Dell recalled that the men were Bill and Jim Anderson, Leander Griffin, William Reed, and two other men whom he did not know. One of the strangers remained outside on guard, watching their horses. Inside, the five men helped themselves to tobacco, whiskey, and other merchandise. As they did, they talked with O'Dell and described what had happened at Baker's store. And before they emptied the money drawer, one of them identified the man outside as William Clarke Quantrill. Whether he really was Quantrill is not known.

When the members of the Anderson gang were ready to leave, they marched O'Dell and the others who had been in the store to a small log stable a few yards away. Leaving a man to guard the O'Dell group, the rest of the Anderson gang set fire to O'Dell's store and saloon. As the building began to burn, members of the Anderson gang helped themselves to the best horses they could find. As O'Dell later recalled, "They then mounted them, set us at liberty, bade us good night very politely, and rode off at full speed."

Riding east along the Santa Fe Trail, the Anderson bunch next stopped at the Chicken Creek crossing, where O. F. O'Dell's father, Benjamin G. O'Dell, operated the stage station. The gunmen again helped themselves to fresh horses, told O'Dell what they had done, and rode on to 110 Mile Creek, twenty miles to the east. They arrived there about sunrise and ordered a man named Harris to get breakfast for them. After eating, they exchanged horses again and went on. At nearly every stage station along the trail, except for Burlington, they stopped and exchanged horses at gunpoint. They avoided Burlington because there were too many people there. In this manner they were able to ride from near Council Grove to Missouri—142 miles—in less than sixteen hours.

About six weeks later, in August, 1862, Bill Anderson and two other men rode across the western border of Missouri and into Olathe, Kansas, in Johnson County. They hitched their horses in front of Charlie Tillotson's hardware store and walked inside. According to one account, they placed a revolver to Tillotson's head and asked the shaking man how they could find the road to De Soto, another Kansas town about eleven miles northwest of Olathe. Tillotson gave them directions, and the three men left. Just outside of Olathe, they met a deputy sheriff named Weaver. They took the lawman's revolver and rode on. Weaver, still on his horse, rode into Olathe and told Sheriff John Janes what had happened. Janes set out after the three men. Exactly what happened next is not clear, but Anderson and the two other men robbed the sheriff and then let him go. Weaver started for Olathe to get help, and en route he ran into John and Ben Roberts, both of whom were armed with Spencer carbines. They joined Sheriff Janes and rode after the gunmen.

There was a gun battle when the sheriff and the Roberts brothers found Anderson and his two friends. One of Anderson's men was wounded and soon died. Anderson and the other man were arrested and were taken to Olathe. On the following morning a mob elected a jury of twelve men to try the outlaws. The jury, which was anything but legal, sentenced Bill Anderson and his friend to hang. But Sheriff Janes closely guarded his prisoners in the Johnson County jail. A few days later, both outlaws were turned over to military authorities at Fort Leavenworth, but before leaving Olathe, Anderson reportedly said, "Gentlemen, I will visit your town again."

Anderson escaped from army custody at Fort Leavenworth and returned to Missouri. On the evening of September 6, 1862, he was one of perhaps a hundred and fifty men, under the command of William Clarke Quantrill, who rode into Olathe, killed six men, broke windows, tore out building fronts, and loaded everything of any value onto stolen wagons and rode back to Missouri.

Anderson, who went on to become a guerrilla leader in Missouri, earned the nickname Bloody Bill. On August 21, 1863, Anderson was with Quantrill when Lawrence, Kansas, was raided, at least 143 persons were killed, many were wounded, and much of the town was burned. According to tradition, Anderson killed more men in Lawrence than did any other man in Quantrill's command.

Bloody Bill Anderson also killed and looted elsewhere; he led the guerrilla raid on Centralia, Missouri, on September 27, 1864. But about a month later, on October 26, he was killed near Albany, Missouri, by some militia and was buried at Richmond, Missouri.

# Dutch Henry, Horse Thief

He was called Dutch Henry. During the 1870s he gained quite a reputation in Kansas, western Nebraska, Texas, and Indian Territory as a horse thief and outlaw. His real name was Henry Born (sometimes spelled Borne or Bourne), and he was born in Manitowoc, Wisconsin, in 1849 to German immigrant parents. He was also educated in Wisconsin. According to tradition, just after the Civil War, Born was in Michigan, where he was accused of killing a man. Whether Born was guilty is not known, but at that time he fled west.

By the spring of 1867 Born was serving as a scout for the United States Cavalry and George Armstrong Custer on the plains of central Kansas. Custer, then a twenty-eight-year-old field commander of eight companies of the newly formed Seventh U.S. Cavalry, was pursuing Indians who were fleeing from Maj. Gen. Winfield Scott Hancock's so-called western peace mission. Custer's command included a band of fifteen Delaware Indian scouts under Fall Leaf and a small detachment of white scouts, including Born and James Butler ("Wild Bill") Hickok.

When buffalo hides were found to be a good source of leather, Henry Born turned to buffalo hunting. This was probably in the early spring of 1872. Born had good success killing the shaggies and selling their hides, but by the fall of 1873 the number of buffalo in western Kansas had declined. Too many had been slaughtered. It was then that Born and other hunters looked south toward

Dutch Henry as he appeared in his late twenties or early thirties.

Indian country, the region that today forms the panhandles of Oklahoma and Texas. The Medicine Lodge Treaties of 1867 had provided that white hunters would not hunt south of the Arkansas River: this was Indian land, and the buffalo and other wild game were for the Comanches, Cheyennes, Arapahoes, and Kiowas.

Born and other hunters had avoided the region south of the Arkansas, out of respect more for the Indians than for the treaties. But early in 1874, several buffalo hunters decided to move south. Dodge City merchants, not wanting to lose the hunters' business, decided to head south with the hunters and to establish a branch trading post. They selected a spot just north of the Canadian River, about 160 miles south by southwest of Dodge City. Only ten years before, Col. Kit Carson, commanding U.S. troops, had fought a band of Kiowa and Comanche Indians at the site. Much earlier, before 1840, William Bent had built an adobe trading post in the same area, but it had been abandoned sometime in the 1840s.

Henry Born traveled south from Dodge City and joined the other hunters and merchants in establishing Adobe Walls. The post had two stores, a blacksmith shop, and a saloon. And the little community was ready for business by late May, 1874. By early June, buffalo hunters were finding many buffalo and were making Adobe Walls their headquarters. Because Indians began to cause some problems, many of the hunters frequently came to Adobe Walls to spend the night, believing that there was strength in numbers.

Henry Born was at Adobe Walls early on the morning of June 27, 1874, when more than five hundred Indians attacked the twenty-eight men and one woman in the settlement. The Indians — Cheyennes, Kiowas, and Arapahoes — killed three white men and numerous horses and oxen before they were driven off. Henry Born was in the store during the attack, and he fired at the Indians with his rifle from an opening in the adobe wall.

After the Indians had left, Born and the others deserted the trading post and returned to Kansas. He soon headed west into Colorado, to hunt buffalo there. But one day a party of Cheyenne Indians stole Born's stock from his hunting outfit. Born made it safely to Fort Lyon, which is located on the Arkansas River in eastern Colorado, and reported what had happened. When an army officer refused to aid him in capturing the Indians and in recovering his stock, Born became angry and stole some army horses to replace the ones that had been taken by the Indians. On that day Henry Born began his career as a horse thief and an outlaw.

During the months that followed, Born stole no less than fifty horses and mules between the Arkansas and Saline rivers in Kansas. When some horses and mules were stolen near Dodge City in Ford County, and the evidence pointed toward Born, the Ford County sheriff telegraphed Kansas sheriffs to be on the lookout for Born. But by then he had gone.

Born's whereabouts during 1875 are not known, although the theft of many horses and mules during this period was credited to Born. On June 13, 1876, however, Born calmly rode into Russell, Kansas, tied his horse to a hitching rail, walked into a saloon, and ordered a drink. Some of the customers recognized him but did not say anything. When he had finished drinking, Born walked out of the saloon and down the street to a tailor shop, which was owned and operated by David Auer, Sr. Inside, he told the owner that he wanted to buy a suit of clothes.

Meantime, Russell County's Sheriff J. C. Weakly, on his rounds, stopped in at the saloon. When he learned that Born had just left the saloon, he hurried outside and ran into David Auer, Jr. He asked the young man if he had seen Born. After the sheriff had described the wanted man, young Auer told the sheriff that the man had gone into his father's tailor ship. Born asked young Auer if he would help him arrest Born, and Auer agreed to do so.

Sheriff Weakly and young Auer went quickly to the tailor shop but waited outside. Presently, Born walked outside, and the sheriff drew his revolver and pointed it at Born. According to the newspaper account, Sheriff Weakly said, "You are my prisoner." What happened next was reported by the paper.

> Born made no reply, but grasping the Sheriff's pistol with his left hand, with his right he attempted to draw his own revolver. As he made the attempt to draw his revolver, and after he had got it about half way out of the scabbard, young Mr. Auer sprang to his left side, and catching hold of his right arm with his right hand, threw his left arm in front of him to hold him. The sheriff, afraid to fire for fear of shooting some of the by-standers (several of whom had congregated around the

door), put up his revolver and drew his knife (a long bladed one, by the way), with which he made a pass at "Dutch Henry," and, missing him, cut Mr. Auer very severely in the left arm, near the elbow. He then made a second pass, and striking "Dutch Henry" in the left side, stabbed him to the depth of four inches, cutting the lining of the stomach and penetrating the bowels.

According to the newspaper account, Dutch Henry exclaimed, "I am dying," and sank to the ground. Born was taken to the sheriff's office in the courthouse, where his wounds were dressed by Dr. H. A. Ellis, who said the wounds were not as serious as Born had believed. At about 11:30 that night, while Born was sleeping under heavy guard in the courthouse, someone fired four or five shots through a window, toward the bed on which Born was sleeping. Born was not injured, and the person who fired the shots was not located. What happened next is not clear, but Born did recover from his wounds. Several weeks later he managed to escape custody and fled. Born returned to horse stealing.

Late in August, 1876, Sheriff Beardsley of Ellis County received word that recent horse thefts in Ness County apparently were the work of Henry Born and his gang. Beardsley advised residents of Ellis County to be on the lookout for the stolen horses; he sent the same warning to people along the Kansas Pacific line. One man who received the warning was James Thompson, who ran the Buffalo Station depot on the Kansas Pacific, about sixty miles west of Hays City. A day or two later, several parties of men visited Thompson in the depot, one or two at a time. Each of them purchased a few provisions and then left. Their actions and talk convinced Thompson that they were together and that they were not on the right side of the law.

About noon that day a man wandered into the station, claiming to be a tramp, and asked for food. Thompson recognized the man as a known horse thief, arrested him, and telegraphed Hays City for an officer to come and get him. H. C. Allen was deputized and sent west on the next train. But before he reached Buffalo Station, the men who had come into the railroad depot earlier in the day returned. They demanded that Thompson turn over his prisoner. Thompson, considering discretion to be the better part of valor, turned the man over to them, and the men left.

At that time, Thompson realized that the men probably were the horse thieves from Ness County. He telegraphed Sheriff Beardsley at Hays City, but the latter was in Abilene, Kansas, on business. The message was forwarded to Abilene. When the sheriff received it, he telegraphed to his deputy, Charles Zaun, in Hays City and ordered him to get a posse and to go west by train to Buffalo Station.

Zaun organized a posse and left Hays City about midnight on a freight train going west. The posse consisted of ten men — six soldiers and four civilians. At Ellis, Kansas, their freight train was overtaken by the westbound passenger train, which was carrying Sheriff Beardsley, who had taken the next westbound train from Abilene. Beardsley took charge of the posse, which traveled by freight train to Buffalo Station. There the men rested until dawn, when they set out after the horse thieves.

The posse soon located and took into custody six men, three women, and thirty-six head of horses and mules along the South Fork of the Solomon River, about sixteen miles from modern Hoxie, Kansas. The men, women, and horses were in a camp. One of those who were arrested said that other men had headed north.

Sheriff Beardsley left all but three members of the posse to guard the six men and three women; then he started north after the others. Near the North Fork of the Solomon, in what is now northern Sheridan County, Kansas, Beardsley's group met a man named Levi Richardson, who was looking for horses that had been stolen from his employer, a Mr. Sitler of Dodge City. Richardson told Beardsley that he had seen one of the men whom the lawmen were looking for. In fact, he said, he had just left the man and was riding to check some stock on the South Fork of the Solomon, to see if any of the stolen horses were there.

The sheriff told Richardson that the horses and men and women had been located and were being held by other lawmen. Sheriff Beardsley then asked Richardson if he would help, which Richardson agreed to do. The sheriff and his men hid nearby. Richardson rode a short distance and then signaled to the man to come to Richardson. The man soon appeared, and when he got within thirty yards of Richardson, the lawmen rode out of hiding on their horses with their guns drawn. They demanded that the man surrender. The man, however, drew his gun and fired at

Beardsley. The lawmen returned the fire, and the man fell from his horse, badly wounded.

The sheriff soon learned the man was a well-known character called Big Ike. He was the same man whom James Thompson had arrested at the Buffalo Station depot. The sheriff and his men took Big Ike to a ranch a few miles away, where he was treated for his wounds. The man thought he was going to die, so he told everything that he knew about the horse thieves, including where the stolen horses were hidden.

After spending the night at the ranch on the North Fork of the Solomon, Sheriff Beardsley and his men left the wounded outlaw under the rancher's guard and headed north toward Prairie Dog Creek in modern Decatur County, Kansas. The lawmen soon found the stolen animals—twenty horses and mules—and captured two men in the camp. It was then that they learned that three other men, including Henry Born, had left the camp and headed north only the day before.

The sheriff and his men took their prisoners and the stock and retraced their steps to where Big Ike was being held. And then, with Big Ike, the lawmen returned to where the first group of men and women were being held. Together the posse took everyone to Buffalo Station, including the stolen stock. As it turned out, only Big Ike and the two men who had been captured with the stolen stock on the North Fork of the Solomon were part of Dutch Henry's gang. The four men and three women were released. They had been traveling north from Dodge City when Dutch Henry and his gang overtook them and proposed to drive their stock together. One of the four men recognized Henry Born and decided that the outlaw and his men might rob them if they refused Born's proposal. But Dutch Henry and his men had taken their stolen stock and separated from the other party only a few hours before Sheriff Beardsley and his posse had arrived on the scene.

As for Dutch Henry, he and two other members of his gang surfaced again in late September. Someone saw them camped on Hackberry Creek, in modern Grove County, Kansas. The *Hays Sentinel* reported this fact, adding:

> We are nightly expecting a raid. Our citizens have organized
> a vigilance committee; and woe be unto him who steals a rope

with something on the end of it. "Dutch Henry" tried to get off with some horses owned by a cattle man in the west side of the county, one night last week; but his attempt was frustrated, and he barely escaped with his life. His party also went through Mr. Johnson's house, while the family were out picking plums, and stole a pair of pants, a pocket-book, and other things—coolly riding off in plain sight of the family.

Dutch Henry was next reported crossing the Santa Fe Trail at Lakin, Kansas, in late November, 1876. Reports indicated that he was en route to Indian Territory. The *Hays Sentinel* noted: "It will behoove the citizens of Southwestern Kansas to sleep with their horses."

The subsequent exploits of Henry Born went unreported until early July, 1877, when the *Hays Sentinel* reported that Born had been captured by the Fourth U.S. Cavalry while he was traveling from Red Cloud, Nebraska, to the Hays City area. Born was arrested and charged with horse stealing. The newspaper account noted that Born was behind bars in Nebraska, but it added, "Judging from the past, however, we believe his escape to be only a matter of time." The newspaper was not correct. Born did not escape; the charges were simply dropped for lack of evidence, because he had not been caught with the stolen animals.

Henry Born was not heard from again until the following spring, in 1878. He had made the acquaintance of a young man named Hulett from Gloversville, New York. Hulett had just arrived in Kearney, Nebraska, when he met Born, who proposed that they become partners and catch wild horses. Born said there was good money in horses. Hulett liked the idea, and both men headed southwestward from Kearney until they reached what is now Rawlins County in northwestern Kansas. There Born, apparently without Hulett's knowledge, stole some horses belonging to a rancher. Born told Hulett that the horses were strays and therefore public property.

Returning to Kearney, Nebraska, with the stolen horses, Born and Hulett were met by the local sheriff, who had been alerted about the stolen horses. When the sheriff, whose name was Anderson, tried to arrest the two men, Born drew his revolver. The sheriff pulled his gun and wounded Born in a leg. A deputy U.S. marshal, W. B. Rogers, with the help of other lawmen, took Born and Hulett to Norton, Kansas, where authorities who had jurisdiction over what later became Rawlins County were located.

Born and Hulett were held in the courthouse, because there was no jail in Norton. It was from there, on June 7, 1878, that Born and Hulett escaped. Where they went and what they did after that is not known. Lawmen throughout Kansas, Nebraska, Colorado, and other nearby states were alerted that Born had escaped. A reward of $500 was offered for Born's capture.

Hulett vanished. But Henry Born was arrested in late December, 1878 by Las Animas County lawmen in Trinidad, Colorado. By then, his fame as an outlaw had spread far and wide. While his fame never reached the extent of that of Frank and Jesse James or the Dalton Gang, Born was considered one of the most successful horse thieves, escape artists, and all-around outlaws on the plains.

Ford County's Sheriff Bat Masterson of Dodge City went to Colorado and brought Henry Born back to Kansas. Born was wanted in Dodge on charges of grand larceny. Masterson and Born arrived by train in Dodge City early in January, 1879, and Born's trial began late in the month. After two days, the jury brought in a verdict of not guilty. A Dodge City newspaper reported: "Insufficient evidence and barred by the statute of limitations, though the latter point was negatively decided by a jury, probably led to the prisoner's acquittal."

Henry Born was therefore free again. He left Dodge City soon after the trial and headed east by train. At Wichita, Deputy U.S. Marshal C. B. Jones arrested Born before he could get off the train. Born was still wanted on federal charges. According to one account, he had escaped from jail in Fort Smith, Arkansas, much earlier. And he reportedly was taken back to Arkansas to serve out his sentence. From what is known, however, Born spent little time in jail. He probably escaped, because in the early 1880s he appeared in Colorado. By then he was in his early thirties, and he turned to a new line of work. He became a prospector.

About 1885, Henry Born discovered gold east of West Willow Creek, north of what was the settlement of Creede, Colorado. Born's mine became known as Happy Thought, and he shared in its initial wealth enough to retire from his outlaw ways. In the 1890s he homesteaded 160 acres on the West Fork of the San Juan River in Mineral County, Colorado. His claim was jumped by a druggist from

Pagosa Springs, but the Land Commission awarded the homestead to Born, and the patent was issued to him in 1903.

Henry Born married Ida Dillabaugh from Montague, Michigan, in July, 1900. They had four children—two boys and two girls. They lived beside a beautiful trout lake in the San Juan Mountains about twenty miles above Pagosa Springs during the spring, summer, and early fall. They spent their winters in town.

In the summer of 1920, one of Born's friends, David Hirsch, gave Born a copy of the book *A Lone Star Cowboy*, written by Charles Siringo, who then lived in Santa Fe, New Mexico. Born wrote to Siringo, inviting him to come to Colorado and fish. Born added:

> We might hark back together over old times. I was one of the buffalo hunters, was at the battle of the "Adobe Walls." Have been over the Chisholm Trail. Have been at White Oaks and knew Pat Garrett. Knew about the Lincoln County War. . . . I am about ten years older than you are so was on the stage of action earlier. . . . My home is twenty miles from town up in the mountains. Every one in town knows Henry Born, so you would have no trouble in finding me. I make weekly trips, usually on Wednesday and back home Thursday.

Born added a postscript: "Known to some as Dutch Henry."

There is no record of Charles Siringo's having visited Born in Colorado. If he had, we would probably know more about Born's life as an outlaw. On January 10, 1921, about six months after Born wrote to Siringo, Henry Born died at the age of seventy-two. The once-famous Kansas horse thief died a respected man in his community.

# The Rescue of John Doy

The experience of settling in the West seemed special for many Kansas pioneers who came west during the nineteenth century. Many of them apparently believed that helping to settle the American West was truly important, and perhaps this was the reason that countless pioneers kept diaries or wrote about their experiences late in life. While many such recollections do little more than relate the pioneers' experiences, which seem dull and uneventful to some people, there were pioneers who participated in significant events and recorded them for history. John Doy, a surgeon, was such a man.

Doy was born in England in 1812. About 1850, at the age of thirty-eight, he emigrated to Canada and later to Rochester, New York. After Kansas Territory was organized in 1854, Doy came west and settled in what is now Lawrence, where he became an active Free State fighter. And as the underground railroad was organized to help conduct slaves along its route to the North and to freedom, Doy acted as a conductor.

On January 25, 1859, Doy, who was then about forty-seven years old, and his son Charles, who was twenty-five, left Lawrence with thirteen slaves. Doy had agreed to conduct them as far north as Holton, where someone else would take over the escort. About twelve miles north of Lawrence, on the road to Oskaloosa, Doy was riding his horse in front of a large wagon, which was carrying his son and the slaves. Suddenly they were stopped by a party of armed border ruffians, led by Jake Hurd, who lived near Lawrence. Several of the other armed men, all of whom supported slavery, were from the Lawrence area.

The armed men took Doy, his son, and the slaves to Weston, Missouri, which is just across the river from Leavenworth. Doy and his son were locked up in the Platte City jail, a few miles from Weston. Later they were moved to St. Joseph, Missouri, where Doy and his son were tried. The son was freed, but the jury could not agree on whether or not Doy was guilty of kidnapping a slave. That was on March 24, 1859. Another trial was scheduled during the month of June, and John Doy was convicted. He was sentenced to a term of five years in the Missouri Penitentiary. Doy appealed, but since he could not find a bondsman in St. Joseph, he was kept in jail.

Doy's friends in Lawrence had followed the developments in St. Joseph closely. When word reached Lawrence that Doy had been found guilty and had been sentenced to prison, a group of Free State men decided to rescue Doy. Theodore Gardner, the son of one of the Lawrence men, later recalled that the group included his father, Joseph Gardner, James B. Abbott, Joshua A. Pike, Jacob Senix, Thomas Simmons, John E. Stewart, S. J. Willis, Silas Soule, George Hay, and Charles Doy, the son of the imprisoned man.

On about June 23, 1859, the Lawrence men climbed aboard a large freight wagon and traveled from Lawrence to Elwood, in northeastern Kansas Territory, just across the Missouri River from St. Joseph. There the teamster parked his wagon; the men crossed the river on the ferry and then separated. St. Joseph was busy, so the Lawrence men had no difficulty in fitting in with the Missourians and with the many travelers who were coming from or going to the Kansas gold fields in what is now Colorado.

At about dark, a note was passed to Doy by a young man who had gained entrance to the jail. The note read: "Be ready at midnight." At about nine o'clock that evening, a violent rainstorm began. The streets of St. Joseph were soon deserted, and sometime after midnight, the Lawrence men moved to the front door of the jail and knocked loudly. A jailer soon appeared in his nightshirt at a second-floor window. On the ground, one of the Lawrence men yelled to the jailer that the group was a sheriff's posse from Kansas and that it had succeeded in capturing a notorious horse

Dr. John Doy (seated) and his rescuers posed for this photograph, taken by A. G. DaLee, a Lawrence photographer, soon after Doy was returned to Lawrence from St. Joseph, Missouri, in late June, 1859. Although the other men in this photo are not identified, they probably are Theodore Gardner, Joseph Gardner, James B. Abbott, Joshua A. Pike, Jacob Senix, Thomas Simmons, S. J. Willis, John E. Stewart, Silas Soule, and George Hay.

thief after a long chase. The posse was worn out, he added, and they wanted to have the horse thief locked up for safekeeping.

The jailer believed the men, so he dressed and soon opened the first-floor door into the jail. Once inside, the Lawrence men confronted the jailer with their weapons and released John Doy. Warning the jailer not to move for half an hour, the party quietly left and walked to the river through the rain. The Lawrence men located some small rowboats, in which they crossed the Missouri River to Kansas Territory where they climbed into the waiting freight wagon and headed back to Lawrence in the rain.

Within a day or so, the party posed for A. G. DaLee, a pioneer Lawrence photographer. DaLee produced a daguerreotype of Doy and his rescue party, which is reproduced with this story. Later,

Doy wrote of his experiences in a little book titled *The Narrative of John Doy of Lawrence, Kansas,* which was published in 1860 in New York City. His recollections preserved a piece of early Kansas history that might otherwise have been lost.

# The Most Violent Town
## in Kansas

A few depressions in a pasture located in Logan County in far-western Kansas are the only visible reminders of what was once the most violent town in Kansas. Officially called Phil Sheridan, it was named after the Civil War general who later came west to chase Indians. But during its short life, everyone called it Sheridan.

The story of Sheridan began in the summer of 1868, when a construction camp was established on the east bank of the North Fork of the Smoky Hill River, about thirteen miles northeast of Fort Wallace. The camp was for the railroad construction gangs who were building the Union Pacific Railway, Eastern Division, across Kansas. Tents and crude shacks constituted the town's first structures, and like so many other railroad construction camps, it was to be temporary. But then came word that the railroad would not continue to build beyond that point, because the company had used up its government subsidies and had to wait until it could find more money. Almost overnight Sheridan boomed; within two weeks it had about sixty-five businesses and two hundred residents. Because it was at the end of the railroad, Sheridan became a major transfer point for freight and passengers.

The railroad brought people and freight from the East. The people would transfer to stagecoaches at Sheridan for the thirty-hour ride to Denver or Pueblo or the three-day ride to Santa Fe. And the freight that had been brought west by rail either was stored temporarily in Sheridan or was transferred immediately from railroad cars to ox-drawn wagons for the much-slower journey to Denver or Pueblo or Santa Fe. Returning east, the wagon trains hauled wool, hides, ore, and lumber to the railhead at Sheridan, where these shipments were either sold or transferred to rail cars and then were taken to eastern markets. Much of the lumber that was brought from Colorado was sold in Sheridan, where a thousand board feet of pine cost $100.

Other goods were just as expensive in Sheridan. A reporter for the *Junction City Union,* who visited Sheridan in late July, 1868, reported that a hundred pounds of winter-wheat flour was selling for $14, a bushel of corn for $2.50, butter for 75 cents per pound, and eggs for 60 cents per dozen. Milk cost 25 cents a quart, while whiskey was 24 cents per drink. At the same time, ordinary laborers were being paid only $2.50 a day.

Most of the larger business houses in Sheridan were constructed of wood; these included a few hotels and several buildings that belonged to the railroad. There were also tents, crude shacks, and even sod houses, made of sod cut from the nearby prairie. A flat-shared plow cut the sod two inches thick and about two feet in length. The sod was then laid up into walls that were two to three feet thick. Timbers were laid across the top, and sod was placed on the timbers to form a roof. Such a sod building was cool in the summer and warm in the winter, unlike the many tents that dotted the Sheridan town site.

An eastern newspaperman, Nathan Meeker, described the town as having "two half streets, some 300 feet apart, the railroad track being in the center. There are large commercial houses engaged in the Santa Fe trade having heavy stocks of stable goods, representing capital ranging from $20,000 to $500,000. Some of the stores are as much as 150 feet long and wide in proportion, and I saw one where many tons of Mexican wool was stored awaiting shipment." Meeker said the rest of the buildings in the town were "saloons and gambling establishments, more than 50 in number, all open and apparently doing good business. In almost every one there are women. Fiddles and accordions are playing, glasses jingling and there are billiard and roulette tables and other gambling devices." Meeker also made some vivid observations about the men in Sheridan, who were able-bodied and strong; few are more than 35; the majority are less than 30 years old; their faces are flushed, their necks red and thick and they speak good English as any people in the United States. But they have a restless, uncertain look and a quickness of movement both strange and suspicious and this more so because they are connected with much that is homelike and familiar. Of course, they are well armed and very offensive or aggressive, although I have every reason to believe that they would commit murder on what we would call the slightest provocation for they have been so audacious and bold that men of property have been obliged to resolve themselves into a Vigilante Committee and hang 15 or 20.

Just when the vigilante committee was formed is not known, but it was apparently formed by late summer 1868. A Lawrence newspaper reported in late July of that year that the "customs and ways of the town are rather on the free and easy, high-pressure order and there is but little danger of the citizens dying from ennui. Whiskey, tents, gamblers, roughs, and 'soiled doves,' are multiplying at an astonishing rate and all things are lively indeed."

There was no law and order in Sheridan. The new town seems to have been under the jurisdiction of the legal machinery in Ellis County at Hays City, more than a hundred miles to the east on the Union Pacific Railway, Eastern Division. But when the law did not arrive, the merchants and businessmen started the Committee for Safety. The committee sent letters to a number of local characters, telling them to leave town within forty-eight hours. Then, before the deadline was up — perhaps to issue a warning to others — the committee hung three of the town's worst characters from the railroad trestle just east of town. Apparently four men had been singled out as examples by the committee, but one of them had slipped the noose from around his neck and had escaped in darkness as the three others were being prepared for hanging.

A post office was established at Sheridan in late September, 1868, and Cornelius W. N. Ruggles became postmaster. He served perhaps a thousand residents in the growing town. The population was approaching two thousand by the spring of 1869, when Sheridan was visited by De Benneville R. Keim, an eastern newspaper correspondent, who wrote:

Ten o'clock in the evening I discovered was the regular hour for the public entertainment to begin, which consisted of a skirmish with pistols, or a series of pugilistic encounters, in which it rarely happened that both parties come off with their lives, or at least without receiving a damaging and indelible remembrance of the contest. I had already heard fearful stories of the "quiet and orderly" town of Sheridan, and, as much as possible, kept clear of the streets from fear of some stray pistol ball, by mistake, finding a lodgment in my own person.

The week before Keim arrived in Sheridan, six men had been shot in drunken brawls. And on the Sunday night before he arrived, two men got into a fight. One was mortally wounded, and the other one then tried to escape. Keim recalled that the latter

was closely pursued. The pursuers fired repeatedly, which was responded to by the fugitive. After a lively chase and considerable firing the pursued was overtaken. He fought desperately, but without avail. A rope was procured; one end was fastened around the victim's neck, the other to a cross-tie in the tressel railroad bridge at the town. The victim was then forcibly ejected between the ties into the space below, and was there left to shuffle off the coil which had been prepared for him by his perculiarly justice-loving fellow citizens.

Exactly how many men were hung by vigilantes in Sheridan is not known, but most accounts suggest that as many as thirty men died at the end of a rope on the railroad trestle, located just east of town, that spanned the North Fork of the Smoky Hill River. Perhaps fifty or more men died from fights with other men in the town; thus Sheridan's cemetery became well populated.

One killing in Sheridan was witnessed by Col. Homer W. Wheeler, a military man who, in his 1925 book titled *Buffalo Days*, wrote:

I went down to Sheridan once with some of the scouts. Sharp Grover, the post [Fort Wallace] guide and interpreter, went into a barber shop with me. While there, we heard shooting outside. Grover and I went to the door and saw a discharged soldier of the Fifth Cavalry running amuck and shoot-

ing in the street. Grover shouted, "Stop that shooting." The man taun-
tingly yelled back, "Hunt your hole or I'll kill you!" At the same time
he fired upon us. Grover drew his revolver and shot the soldier dead. He
then returned to the barber shop and sat down in the chair, remarking,
"I don't believe that man will do any more harm."

Wheeler recalled that on another occasion a former army scout
named Hank Whitney was running a dance hall in Sheridan. One
night he was shot in a drunken carousal. The man who did the
shooting was immediately arrested by members of the Committee
for Safety and was taken into a nearby saloon for trial. While the
court was in session, Hank Whitney entered the courtroom. He
had his wound dressed. He walked to where the prisoner was sitting, placed a pistol against the back of the prisoner's head, and
fired. The prisoner jumped up, then fell dead; and Whitney was
immediately escorted to the railroad trestle and hanged. Next morning, a brief funeral service was held over the bodies, and both
men were buried in the same grave. Wheeler added that in about
two years, nearly a hundred men had been buried in the Sheridan
cemetery. With only one or two exceptions, the men had died violent
deaths.

Another visitor to Sheridan told the story of a bad character
who had been arrested on some charge by the vigilante committee. When he was brought before their court in some saloon, he
yelled at the judge and called the court names. The visitor, W. E.
Webb, who was known to embellish his stories, wrote that the judge
replied: "This yere court feels herself insulted without due cause
and orders the prisoner strung up for contempt." According to
Webb, the man was promptly hung from the railroad trestle.

Webb wrote about another incident which involved two noted
bullies, Gunshot Frank and Sour Bill. One day they had a quar-
rel. Each man got a revolver and a spade, and then with a few
friends, started for a spot just outside of town. The plan was for
each man to dig a grave for the other and then to have a duel.
But before the digging had been finished, Gunshot Frank made
an impudent remark to Sour Bill, who shot Gunshot Frank through
the abdomen, killing him. The dead man's friends at once fell upon
Sour Bill, and one of them broke Sour Bill's skull with a spade.

That night, according to Webb, two men slept in the graves that their own hands had helped to dig.

Another incident that occurred in Sheridan should perhaps be included under the part of this book that contains tales of buried treasure, but because the information is so slim, I have included it here. It involves a gambler who one night won an entire pot of money in a card game at one of Sheridan's gambling halls. The gambler took his winnings, excused himself from the table, and went outside. When he returned a few minutes later, the men with whom he had been playing cards decided that he had cheated them. They immediately took him to the railroad trestle and hung him, but they never found his winnings. To this day, treasure hunters believe that he went outside the saloon and buried the money somewhere nearby. Treasure hunters have continued to search the town site even in recent years, much to the anger of the present owner, who discourages such trespassing.

The beginning of the end for Sheridan occurred early in 1869, less than a year after the town had been established. Congress authorized the railroad to mortgage the road and its land located between Sheridan and Denver at $32,000 a mile. This enabled the railroad to resume construction. But in the meantime, the Union Pacific Railway, Eastern Division, had changed its name to the Kansas Pacific. The route west of Sheridan was surveyed in the spring of 1869, and the actual construction began. Sheridan remained the line's western terminal until the tracks reached Kit Carson, Colorado, in March, 1870. Then the buildings, shacks, and tents of Sheridan were dismantled and shipped west over the road to Kit Carson. By early July, 1870, Phil Sheridan, Kansas, had a population of only eighty people, most of whom were railroad employees. The post office ceased to exist on January 20, 1871, by which time Sheridan had become almost a ghost town. It was not until 1882 that a county was organized around what had been Sheridan. First called St. John, the county had its name changed to Logan in 1887, by which time the most violent town in Kansas was only a memory.

# James M. Daugherty's
# Kansas Journey

James M. ("Jim") Daugherty was born in Texas County, Missouri, early in 1850, but soon after his birth, his parents moved to Texas, where young Jim grew up. Times were hard, and after his basic schooling in the three Rs, he went to work as a cowboy. He learned the occupation quickly during the Civil War, when most of the men had gone off to fight for the South. By the time the war ended, young Jim was an experienced cowboy, determined to make good.

In 1866, at the age of sixteen, Jim Daugherty decided to take a herd of Texas longhorns north to Missouri, where good prices were being paid for cattle. There were no good markets in Texas because cattle were so numerous. With five other cowboys, Daugherty started to drive his cattle north, and they crossed the Red River at Rock Bluffs, near Preston in present-day Grayson County, Texas. After crossing the river, they started northeast through Indian Territory, now Oklahoma.

Several days later they were met by Cherokee Indians, who demanded a tax for crossing their land. Daugherty refused to pay and turned his herd east. Crossing into Arkansas near Fort Smith, he and his men drove the cattle north. They may have stopped at Elkhorn Tavern in northwest Arkansas, near the summit of Elkhorn Hill. The hill is also known as Pea Ridge, the scene of a bloody Civil War battle. The tavern had developed as a rest stop for cattlemen who were driving their herds north. From there, Daugherty and his men turned their herd northwest, returning to

Indian Territory and what was then known as the Neutral Strip, a piece of land about twenty miles wide which ran across the northern edge of Indian Territory and the southern border of Kansas. South of Baxter Springs, Kansas, Daugherty told his cowboys to watch the herd, while he headed north into Kansas to "investigate conditions." What happened next is told in Jim Daugherty's own words:

> On arriving at Baxter Springs I found that there had been several herds ahead of me that had been disturbed by what we called . . . Kansas Jayhawkers, and in one instance the Jayhawkers had killed the owner, taken the herd, and ran the rest of the cowboys off. This herd belonged to Kaynaird and was gathered in the southern part of the Chocktaw Nation in Indian Territory.
>
> I rode as far as Fort Scott, Kansas, and there I met a man by the name of Ben Keys, whom I told I had a herd on the Neutral Strip I would like to sell. He agreed to buy them if I would make deliverance at Fort Scott. I returned to the Neutral Strip and we started driving the herd north along the Kansas-Missouri line, sometimes in the state of Kansas and sometimes in Missouri. From the information that I had received regarding the big risk we were taking by trying to drive through, we were always on the lookout for trouble.
>
> Some twenty miles south of Fort Scott, and about four o'clock one afternoon a bunch of fifteen or twenty Jayhawkers came upon us. One of my cowboys, John Dobbins by name was leading the herd and I was riding close to the leader. Upon approach of the Jayhawkers John attempted to draw his gun and the Jayhawkers shot him dead in the saddle. This caused the cattle to stampede and at the same time they covered me with their guns and I was forced to surrender. The rest of the cowboys stayed with the herd, losing part of them in the stampede.
>
> The Jayhawkers took me to Cow Creek which was near by, and there tried me for driving cattle into their country, which they claimed was infested with ticks which would kill their cattle. I was found guilty without any evidence, they not even having one of my cattle for evidence. Then they began to argue among themselves what to do with me. Some wanted to hang me while others wanted to whip me to death.
>
> I being a young man in my teens and my sympathetic talk about being ignorant to ticky cattle of the south deseasing any

This illustration from Joseph McCoy's classic book *Historic Sketches of the Cattle Trade of the West and Southwest,* published in Kansas City in 1874, supposedly shows James M. Daugherty being whipped by what he called Jayhawkers, or border ruffians, south of Baxter Springs, Kansas, in 1866. Daugherty's recollections, however, make no mention of his having been whipped; and Kansas artist Henry Worrell, who made the drawing, makes Daugherty appear to be an old man, instead of a boy of sixteen.

of the cattle in their country caused one of the big Jayhawkers to take my part. The balance were strong for hanging me on the spot but through his arguments they finally let me go. After I was freed and had joined the herd, two of my cowboys and I slipped back and buried John Dobbins where he fell. After we had buried him we cut down a small tree and hewed out a head and foot board and marked his grave. Then we slipped back to the herd.

This being soon after the close of the Civil War, the Jayhawkers were said to be soldiers mustered out of the Yankee army. They were nothing more than a bunch of cattle rustlers and were not interested about fever ticks coming into their country but used this just as a pretense to kill the men with the herds and steal the cattle or stampede the herds. After re-joining the herd I found that during the stampede I had lost about one hundred and fifty head of cattle, which was a total loss to me.

I drove the balance of the herd back to the Neutral Strip, and after resting a day or two, went back to Fort Scott, and reported to Mr. Keys what had happened. Mr. Keys sent a man back to the herd with me to guide us to Fort Scott. On my return to the herd with the guide we started the drive to Fort Scott the second time. The guide knew the country well, which was very thinly settled. We would drive the herd at night and would lay up at some secluded spot during the day. After driving in this manner for five days and five nights we reached Fort Scott about day-break of the fifth night and penned the cattle in a high board corral adjoining a livery stable, which completely hid them from the public view. . . . As soon as the cattle were penned Mr. Keys paid me for them. Then we ate our breakfast and slept all day. When darkness fell we saddled our horses and started back over the trail to Texas.

James Daugherty returned safely to Texas. Later he made many other trips up the trail to Kansas, but none that was filled with as much excitement. He became a well-known Texas cowman. In 1923, at the time when he put his experiences on paper, Daugherty owned a large ranch in Culberson and Hudspeth counties of Texas and was known as "Uncle Jim" Daugherty.

# Gunfights and Gunfighters

The swinging doors at the saloon slowly open. The town marshal walks onto the boardwalk in front of the saloon, steps down to the dusty street, and walks to meet the gunfighter. A distance of about twenty feet separates the two men when they stop in the center of the street. For a moment they stare at each other; not a word is spoken. In a flash they reach for their guns, and the quiet is broken with the thunderous roar of shooting. When the blue smoke clears, the marshal stands alone. The bad gunfighter is dead — shot through the heart. From the protection of the buildings, the townspeople emerge to shake the marshal's hand. He is the hero.

This scene, reenacted on television, in Western films, and in countless Western novels, is often the climax of many Western stories. The gunfighting marshal or sheriff is perhaps the most enduring legend of the Old West; he is also the most overrated. Such gunfights, especially in Kansas, rarely occurred. In the fifteen years between 1870 and 1885, only forty-five homicides were reported in the cattle towns of Abilene, Wichita, Ellsworth, Dodge City, and Caldwell. Of these killings, most were of the shot-in-the-back variety.

Few gunfights in Kansas cattle towns even resemble the mythical shoot-outs of modern Western stories and movies. The first such gunfight occurred in Abilene on Thursday evening, October 5, 1871; it involved the town marshal, James Butler ("Wild Bill") Hickok. In that year, Abilene was really two towns in one. The railroad tracks divided the town. North of the tracks was the

104

James Butler ("Wild Bill")
Hickok late in life.

literary, religious, and commercial "Kansas Abilene," while south
of the tracks was "Texian Abilene," which contained hotels for the
Texas cattle drovers; saloons; railroad cattle pens for the Texas
longhorns that had been driven north over the Chisholm Trail; and
the places where the "dealers in cardboard, bone and ivory"
operated.

Abilene's saloons, most of which had Texan or bovine names,
included the Bull's Head, the Lone Star, the Long Horn, the Applejack, the Old Fruit, the Trail, and the Alamo. Of these, the
Alamo had the most splendor: it had three double glass-front doors
and a large bar, which had brass mountings and colorful bottles
of liquors that were reflected in large imposing mirrors. There were
green gaming tables and paintings — imitations of feminine nudes
by Titian, Tintoretto, and Veronese.

Wild Bill Hickok made the Alamo his headquarters while he
was serving as marshal for eight months from April to December,
1871. And Hickok was at the Alamo on the night of October 5,
when several Texans, who were about ready to return home, went
on a spree. They compelled several citizens, whom they found on
Texas Street outside, to buy them drinks at the saloons. Hickok,

who was more than six feet in height, muscular, athletic, and had long black hair—a fine figure of a man—treated the men to drinks at one of the saloons. But he told them to keep within the bounds of order or he would stop them.

For a time the Texans were orderly, but at about 8 P.M. they began to gather on Texas Street, near the Alamo Saloon. Suddenly, one or more shots rang out. Hickok, who was in the Alamo, drew his guns and rushed outside. There he confronted Phil Coe, a half-owner of the Alamo. Hickok asked who had fired the shot, and Coe told him that he had fired at a dog. Coe still had his revolver in his hand. If the two men said anything else, it is not recorded. Both men raised their weapons toward each other and fired. They were not more than eight feet apart. Hickok's first shot hit Coe in the abdomen, and Coe's first shot went through Hickok's coat, grazing his right side. Coe, staggering, fired again, and the ball passed between Hickok's legs.

Mike Williams, a policeman who was stationed around the corner at the Novelty Theater, heard the firing and ran around the corner and down the boardwalk to help Hickok. But according to an Abilene newspaper account, Hickok thought that Williams was a Texan, so the marshal fired two shots, killing Williams. Because of the darkness, Hickok had not recognized his friend.

Although Williams had died instantly, Coe was still alive. He was taken to his frame cottage on the southwestern side of Abilene, where a doctor tried to save his life. Coe lived in agony for three days before he died. One or two bystanders were wounded, but not seriously. J. B. Edwards, a pioneer Abilene businessman, later wrote:

> Coe was a gambler by profession and a bully by nature. He had been in the Confederate Army and shared feelings of hatred against "Wild Bill" Hickok who had been a Union scout.
>
> The trouble between Bill and Coe had started when the former took occasion to reprimand Coe as to a charge of cheating in his gambling with some men who had complained to Bill. The Abilene citizens were of the opinion that the whole fracas was from the beginning intended to dispose of Bill, but it failed.

This photo shows "Wild Bill" Hickok (upper left) in late 1867. The man in the upper right who is holding a pipe is H. C. Lindsay, a captain in the Fighteenth Kansas Regiment. The other men are not identified. Hickok was a government scout. The men probably were celebrating the end of the Hancock Indian War in Topeka, Kansas, where this photo was taken about four years before Hickok became marshal of Abilene.

The other Kansas shoot-out that resembled those of the Hollywood variety occurred in Dodge City on April 5, 1879. The main characters were Levi Richardson and "Cockeyed Frank" Loving. Richardson, a native of Wisconsin who was about twenty-eight years old, had lived on the frontier for several years. In 1879 he was a well-known freighter around Dodge City. Loving, who was about twenty-five years old, was a gambler; little else is known about him. The shooting took place in the Long Branch Saloon on a Saturday night. Richardson had been in the saloon and was about to leave when Loving walked in. Richardson decided to stay, and he sat down near Loving. What happened next was reported by a Dodge City newspaper:

> One said, "I don't believe you will fight." The other answered "Try me and see," and immediately both drew murderous revolvers and at it they went, in a room filled with people, the leaden missives flying in all directions. Neither exhibited any sign of a desire to escape the other, and there is no telling how long the fight might have lasted had not Richardson been pierced with bullets and Loving's pistol left without a cartridge.
>
> Richardson was shot in the breast, through the side and through the right arm. It seems strange that Loving was not hit, except a slight scratch on the hand, as the two men were so close together that their pistols almost touched each other. Eleven shots were fired, six by Loving and five by Richardson.
>
> Richardson only lived a few moments after the shooting. Loving was placed in jail to await the verdict of the coroner's jury, which was "self-defense," and he was released.

Dodge City's town marshal, Charles Bassett, recalled that when he heard the shooting and ran to the Long Branch, he saw Loving and Richardson "dodging and running around the billard table." Bassett grabbed Loving's revolver while another man, William Duffey, disarmed the dying Richardson.

Again, as in the Hickok and Coe shootout, bad feelings apparently were the cause for the Loving-Richardson gunfight. A Dodge City newspaper pointed this out:

> For several months, Loving has been living with a woman toward whom Richardson seems to have cherished tender feelings, and on one or two occasions previous to this . . . they have quarreled and even come to blows.
>
> Both, or either of these men, we believe, might have avoided this shooting if either had possessed a desire to do so. But both being willing to risk their lives, each with confidence in himself, they fought because they wanted to fight.

William L. ("Billy") Brooks's clothing is a far cry from that of gunfighters in modern western movies and on television. This photo of Brooks was taken about 1873, a year before he was apparently hanged in Sumner County, Kansas, as a horse thief.

Television and western movies to the contrary, most early-day killings were of the ambush variety. Few Kansas gunmen gave their victims an opportunity to defend themselves. Most killings were nothing more than bushwhackings; the victim was rarely given an even break. And this was true elsewhere in the West. Two well-known examples are the killings of Jesse James, who was shot in the back by Bob Ford at St. Joseph, Missouri, on April 3, 1882, and of Wild Bill Hickok, who was shot in the back by Jack McCall at Deadwood, Dakota Territory, on August 2, 1876. An examination of the old newspapers in five Kansas cattle towns has shown that killings were not as frequent as contemporary writers of westerns would have us believe. Of the forty-five homicides between 1870 and 1885 in Abilene, Wichita, Ellsworth, Dodge City, and Caldwell, thirty-nine of the victims died from gunshot wounds. Of these, only about fifteen were given the chance to return the fire; many of the victims were not even armed.

One such account involves William L. ("Billy") Brooks — sometimes called Bully — a former stage driver and cattle-town lawman, who is believed to have been hanged as a horse thief in Sumner County, Kansas, in 1874. Two years before he is supposed to have died, Brooks was blamed for the killing of Dodge City saloon keeper, Matt Sullivan. Sullivan was in his saloon working when someone pointed a gun through a window and shot and killed him.

Another Dodge City shooting occurred early on the morning of July 25, 1878, as three or four herders — cowboys — were preparing to leave Dodge after a night of drinking. This shooting is noteworthy because of the lawmen who were involved. A Dodge City newspaper reported that the cowboys

> had buckled on their revolvers, which they were not allowed to wear around town, and mounted their horses, when all at once one of them conceived the idea that to finish the night's revelry and give the natives due warning of his departure, he must do some shooting, and forth with he commenced to bang away, one of the bullets whizzing into a dance hall near by, causing no little commotion among the participants in the "dreamy waltz" and quadrille.

Two Dodge City lawmen, Wyatt Earp and James Masterson — Bat Masterson's brother — gave chase and exchanged shots with the Texas cowboys. In the shooting, either Earp or Masterson hit one of the cowboys, named George Hoy or Hoyt. Hoy was taken to a physician, but he died a few weeks later. If Earp did kill Hoy, it is the only known killing by Earp in Kansas. Wyatt Earp, however, became a legend as a gunfighter the following year, when he went to Arizona. There, about two years later, Wyatt Earp and his brothers took part in the legendary gunfight at the OK Corral.

Another Dodge City lawman who gained a reputation as a gunfighter was William Barclay ("Bat") Masterson, who had hunted buffalo before becoming a member of what was called the Dodge City Peace Commission. Masterson, who was perhaps as legendary as Earp, Hickok, and other early Kansas lawmen, was credited by a New York City newspaper in 1882 with having killed twenty-six men. In truth, his only known victim was Sgt. Melvin A. King, at Sweetwater Creek, Texas, in 1876. King supposedly surprised Masterson and a young woman in an after-hours meeting and tried to shoot Masterson. The young woman, who threw herself in front of Bat to protect him, was killed; and Masterson then shot the soldier.

While no single shoot-out appears to have been responsible for the "gunfighter myth," the Hickok and Coe, Richardson and Loving, and other Kansas gunfights did add to the growing legend that has since been enhanced by writers of western movies, television shows, and novels.

# Part IV

# THE FAMOUS AND THE OBSCURE

*We are all omnibuses in which our ancestors ride, and every now and then one of them sticks his head out and embarrasses us.*

—Oliver Wendell Holmes

# The Saga of Lew Cassel,
# Trapper

The year was 1860. It was autumn in north-central Kansas, then Kansas Territory. The leaves of trees and bushes that grew along Elk Creek, which runs close to the eastern border of what is now Cloud County, were changing colors, and the crisp cool air hinted that winter was approaching. Few white settlers had pushed as far west as Elk Creek. In fact, few white people had settled west of the Blue River, which runs south from near Marysville to modern Manhattan, Kansas, before emptying into the Kansas River.

In that fall of 1860, however, Lew Cassel, who was then about thirty years old, crossed the Blue River and made his way west to Elk Creek. He had ridden his horse for many days, having come south from Minnesota into Kansas Territory and then west to trap beaver. As he reached a high ridge just east of Elk Creek, a ridge that overlooked the valley of the Republican River, he spotted a small cabin. As Cassel soon learned, the cabin had been built by Moses Heller, one of the first white men to settle that far west in northern Kansas Territory.

Cassel started to ride toward Heller's cabin, but then he noticed a small stream of smoke ascending from a wooded area about a mile north of the cabin. Cassel investigated, and from some distance he saw a large body of Indians in camp, preparing their evening meal. Without being seen, Cassel turned his horse, which was named Raven, and rode to Heller's cabin, where he was welcomed and invited to stay the night. Cassel immediately told Heller about the presence of Indians nearby, and he offered to help Heller defend the cabin, should the Indians attack.

Heller did not seem to be alarmed. He told Cassel that he knew the Indians were in the area, that they had been hunting during the day along the Republican River. Heller also said he had heard the reports of their guns, but he did not think the Indians would molest him. Yet Heller seemed pleased that Cassel had arrived and that he was armed with two large revolvers, a rifle, and plenty of ammunition.

After supper the two men talked and then prepared to go to bed. Cassel, however, did not accept Heller's invitation to bunk inside the cabin; instead, he took his blankets outside and rolled up under the stars, near where his horse was tied. Cassel said he did not want the Indians to steal his horse during the night.

At the first light of dawn, Cassel awoke to find his horse still tied nearby. He moved into the cabin, where Heller was fixing breakfast. The two men carried their food and coffee outside and began to talk about the country around them, the streams that flowed into the Republican and Solomon rivers, and the prospects for trapping beaver. Suddenly they realized that a band of Indians had surrounded the cabin and was slowly moving toward the two white men. One Indian gave the peace sign, and another, in broken English, said they wanted to talk with the "big man," meaning Heller. As they talked, it became clear that the Indians wanted Heller to tell all white men that the country west of a certain line was the hunting ground of the Indians and that the whites must not hunt or extend their settlements beyond that line. Cassel asked the Indian who spoke broken English where the line was. From what the Indian said, the line appeared to cross the Solomon near the mouth of Pipe Creek, and it ran over the divide to the head of Wolf Creek, in what is now Cloud County, and then down to the Republican River and north to the mouth of the Big Sandy, in what is now Nebraska.

Heller nodded his head as though he understood, but Cassel told the Indian that he, Cassel, was an American citizen. In so many words he told the Indian that his father had fought under Andrew Jackson in the battle of New Orleans and that he intended to trap beaver and hunt on the Republican and Solomon. Accord-

ing to tradition, Cassel then added that he did not propose to be
"hemmed in by any deadlines, guide-posts or other Ingen humbugs!"

Heller tried to stop Cassel from making such a strong statement, but to no avail. The Indians looked at Cassel carefully. Until he spoke, they were more concerned with Heller. It was then
that one of the Indians moved toward Cassel's horse and began
to examine the beaver traps that hung from the saddle. When Cassel
saw what the Indian was doing, he whistled. Cassel's horse kicked
and tried to bite the Indian, who quickly backed away, shaking
his tomahawk and bow at Cassel. It was as if the Indian had said,
"I'll meet you sometime." Then the Indians left.

Cassel remained at Heller's for a few days before setting out
to trap and hunt. During the winter of 1860 and 1861 he trapped
and hunted along the Republican and Solomon rivers. He frequently stayed at Heller's and at the cabins of two other white settlers who had moved into the area east of Heller. One settler, named
Haines, had built his cabin on the site of modern-day Clifton,
Kansas.

In the fall of 1862 Cassel was joined by a trapper from Illinois
who brought his traps and outfit from the east. Little Tim, as the
other trapper was called, had the same interests as Cassel, and the
two men became partners. In the meantime, other whites had
moved into the area. Several families had settled on Elm Creek, a
few miles west of Heller's cabin and on the south side of the stream.

Before the trapping season began, Cassel and Little Tim were
hunting for buffalo on Pipe Creek, near the southern boundary
of Cloud County. Cassel, who was riding his horse named Raven,
and Little Tim, atop his mule, brought down a buffalo. The two
men, however, soon became separated while trying to kill a second
shaggy. Little Tim started to chase the animal, but when he fired
his rifle at the buffalo from close range, his mule stopped abruptly
and threw Tim over his head to the ground. The wounded buffalo turned and charged Tim, and one of his horns ripped some
of Tim's clothing. According to the account, Tim grabbed the buffalo by the tail and pulled his hunting knife out in order to cut
the animal's ham-strings, but the buffalo reared and plunged, trying
to shake Tim loose. Cassel, seeing what was happening, raced to
the scene and killed the animal with two shots from his rifle. The

two hunters then signaled to a friend, who had been following in a wagon. When the friend pulled up, all three men skinned the buffalo, loaded the meat onto the wagon, and returned to what is now the Clifton area with the meat of two dead animals.

On another occasion, Cassel and Tim were trapping on the Republican, some miles below the mouth of White Rock Creek, when they discovered that their traps had been robbed of beaver. The trappers knew that a band of Otoe Indians had been seen camped to the northwest on White Rock Creek a few days earlier. Cassel and Tim figured that the Indians were the thieves, so early the next morning the two trappers headed for their traps before dawn. Just as the sun was coming up, they saw an Indian robbing one of their beaver traps. Nearby was the Indian's horse.

Cassel tied his own horse and moved quickly and quietly to where the Indian's horse was tied. Unfastening the reins, Cassel detached the rope reins from the bridle, made a slipnoose at one end, and then secreted himself behind the horse. When the Indian who was carrying the beaver returned to his horse, Cassel threw the rope around the Indian's neck, drawing it tightly, then passed it around the Indian's body and tied the Indian's hands behind him. The Indian struggled, but Cassel was a strong man, and he made the Indian mount his horse. Cassel then tied the legs of the Indian together, passing the rope around the body of the horse in such a manner that the Indian could not dismount. Cassel then gave a whistle, and Little Tim ran to where Cassel was standing next to the Indian, who was mounted on the horse. Tim held the horse while Cassel finished tying the Indian firmly to the animal. When Tim asked Cassel what he was doing, Cassel supposedly replied, "This 'ere redskin has been sowin' his wild oats in our trappin' ground, and I propose now he shall harrow them in."

At that, Cassel cut a bush and fastened it to the horse's tail. The horse did not like this, so it began to kick and to try to bite the bush. Cassel told Tim to point the Indian's horse toward the northwest, in the direction of the Indian camp. A moment later, Tim released the Indian's horse. The animal reared and plunged like a bucking bronco and soon took off toward the northwest, with the Indian swaying to and fro, like a cottonwood sapling in a hurricane.

Tim and Cassel laughed and yelled as the horse and rider disappeared over the horizon, but then Cassel told Tim that they had better pack their beaver traps and leave. They did, and the two men headed down river. Near where Concordia, Kansas, now stands, they killed an elk in some timber, butchered the animal, and carried the meat back to the settlement that was located on the site of present-day Clifton.

The winter of 1863/64 was not good for trapping, so Cassel and his partner, Tim, had little luck catching beaver. Tim soon decided to look for greener pastures; he gave his traps to Cassel and headed east. At one of the towns located on the Missouri River, perhaps Leavenworth, Tim got a job as a teamster with a wagon freighting company.

Cassel, however, remained in north-central Kansas, hunting and acting as a scout for settlers during the summer and autumn of 1864. When fall came, he returned to trapping and apparently had good luck. During the summer and autumn of 1865, he returned to hunting and scouting before returning to trapping in the fall, when he set his traps along the Republican River below the mouth of White Rock Creek. One day he discovered that his traps had been molested, so he kept a sharp watch on them, and two days later he saw an Indian pulling one of his traps from the river. Cassel moved in, fired his rifle, and killed the Indian. Since much of the river was covered with ice, Cassel rolled a large log from the bank out onto the ice. The log fell with such force that it broke through the ice; then Cassel dragged the Indian's body to the opening and pushed it into the water. He then placed the Indian's gun in such a position on the ice near the log to make it look as if the Indian had been sitting on the log and that the log had broken the ice.

Cassel hastily packed his traps, and after covering his tracks, he headed down the river to the settlements. In a few days, some Indians came down the river, searching for their missing comrade. They asked the settlers, including Cassel, if they had seen the Indian whom they described. Cassel said nothing. Whether the Indians found their missing friend is not known.

Cassel continued to make his living by scouting, hunting, and trapping; and in May, 1866, Cassel agreed to guide some friends

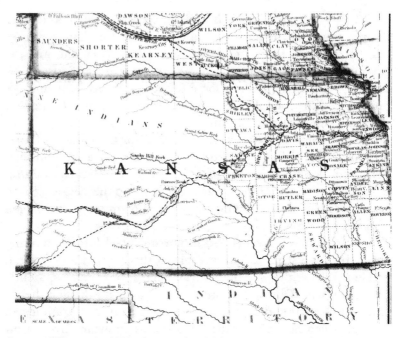

A map of Kansas in 1866, the year in which Lew Cassel was killed by Indians west of modern Concordia, Kansas. The location of organized counties reflects the westward line of settlement in Kansas.

on a buffalo hunt. Their goal was what is known now as the Brown's Creek area, just across the western border of Cloud County in modern Jewell County. Early one morning, Cassel, Walter Haynes, John C. Roberts, T. B. Tallman, and John and William Collins started west. The Collins brothers had a wagon, which was drawn by two oxen; the others rode in a wagon drawn by horses. Their friends bid them goodby as they rode west.

When one week had passed, then two weeks, and the hunters had not returned, G. D. Brooks, a settler in the area, organized a search party of about thirty settlers. Late on their first day out they met a party of friendly Otoe Indians, who were hunting on Buffalo Creek. The Otoe told the searchers that they had not seen the buffalo hunters but that there had been Cheyenne Indians in the area. And the Otoe pointed in the direction where the Cheyenne had been camped. The search party went in that direction and soon found an abandoned Indian camp near the head of Brown Creek. There they found some harness buckles, and one searcher found the pocketbook that had belonged to Walter Haynes. Another searcher discovered land-filing papers that had belonged to Lewis Cassel. The searchers began to suspect the worst.

All signs in the abandoned Indian camp suggested that there had been forty or fifty Cheyenne. There were only thirty men in the search party, so the decision was made to return east to get reinforcements. They did so, and less than two days later, fifty armed men, with plenty of supplies, started west again. They found where the buffalo hunters had camped, and from there they followed the tracks of their wagons to Buffalo Creek. On the third day they came upon the wagon that had been owned by the Collins brothers. Nearby lay the dead oxen, which had been shot with bullets and arrows. The two animals were still yoked together. The searchers concluded that it was at this spot that Indians had attacked the hunters. Some yards away the grass had been wallowed flat, and blood was on the ground, which suggested that an Indian had been shot.

The wagon trail then led in a southwesterly direction toward Cheyenne Creek, about twelve miles away. The searchers started over the trail. The wagon's tracks showed that the vehicle had changed its course several times. This suggested that the Indians had attacked the hunters in the wagon several times. Soon the searchers found a dead dog, with two arrows sticking in its body, which someone identified as having belonged to one of the hunters.

As the searchers neared Cheyenne Creek, they followed the wagon's trail up a narrow ridge that provided something of a smooth road to the creek bottom ahead. There was a ravine on both sides of the road. And up ahead the searchers soon found the missing wagon, with the bodies of the six hunters scattered about. It was obvious to the searchers that the Indians had ridden ahead of the wagon, had hidden in the ravines, and then had attacked the hunters as they passed.

From the position of the bodies, it appeared that Lewis Cassel and Haynes had broken through the Indian lines. Haynes's body was found lying on the bank of Cheyenne Creek, and Cassel's body was found in the creek bed. There was an empty revolver in one of Cassel's hands. The other hand held several cartridges, suggesting that he was trying to reload his weapon when he was killed. All the bodies had been scalped.

The searchers dug graves and buried the six men; then one of the searchers, R. P. West, offered a prayer. The searchers returned to their settlements and reported the sad news. During the following spring, the bodies were removed and interred near Clifton, Kansas. The scene of the battle was about twelve miles west of present-day Concordia, Kansas. Early in this century, some conductors on the Central Branch Union Pacific Railway used to point out the grove of trees where Lew Cassel and the others had been killed, for the railroad passed near the grove. But the railroad and its passenger trains are now gone, and only a few old-timers in the area remember having heard the story of what happened to Lew Cassel.

# The Jordan Massacre

It was a clear, warm spring day in 1872 when Dick Jordan, his wife, Mary, and their dog, Queen, arrived by wagon in the tiny settlement of Park's Fort, which was located twenty miles west of Ellis, Kansas. Park's Fort was a stop on the Kansas Pacific Railroad. Jordan was a buffalo hunter, and he was moving west so as to be closer to the buffalo range. Jordan and his wife had come from Ellis, where his mother and father lived, and where Mary's widowed mother ran the railroad's boarding house, with the help of her six other children.

At Park's Fort the Jordans found a boxcar, which had been placed next to the railroad tracks. It housed the telegraph office. Nearby were two empty dugouts, constructed about five years earlier by soldiers who had been stationed there as the railroad was being built westward. The soldiers had moved west with the construction crew, thus providing protection from Indian raids. The dugouts had been deserted since the soldiers had left.

Dick Jordan wasted no time in constructing a small frame house on the south side of the track with lumber that he had brought from Ellis. He had the help of his nineteen-year-old brother George and a friend named Fred Nelson. George and Fred had driven another wagon from Ellis to Park's Fort; it was loaded with lumber and supplies. When the house was finished, the Jordans moved their belongings inside, and Mary Jordan set up housekeeping.

The Jordan men and Nelson then repaired the two dugouts, in which Dick Jordan planned to store and dry buffalo meat until it was ready to be shipped east by railroad. There was a good market for buffalo meat in 1872, especially in eastern cities, and Jordan hoped to make a good profit. But first he needed to find buffalo. About July first, Dick Jordan decided that it was time to go buffalo hunting. His brother George and Fred Nelson were anxious to join him, and Mary Jordan announced that she wanted to go along. She said she could do the cooking, and her husband did not object.

While the three men were getting their equipment ready, Mary Jordan took the train east to Ellis to visit her mother, sisters, and brothers. Mary's sister Jeannie, who was eighteen, later recalled that her mother had not wanted Mary to go buffalo hunting; but Mary insisted and was quoted as having said: "Don't worry, mother. We will come back. There are no Indians near here."

By July 15, Mary had returned to her husband at Park's Fort, and a few days later the three men and Mary headed south in two large wagons with canvas covers. They took with them a cooking outfit, bedding, and everything that would be needed for a three-week hunting trip. Their dog Queen went along.

Back in Ellis, no one worried until two weeks had passed and no word had been received from the hunting party. Other hunters and travelers, as they crisscrossed the plains, would usually carry word that they had seen so-and-so and then would deliver any messages. But no such word had been received in Ellis, and by the end of the second week of August, Mary's family and the parents of the Jordan brothers were very worried.

Then one morning the father of the Jordans found Queen, Dick Jordan's dog, at the back door of his home in Ellis. He thought that his sons had returned from the hunt, but their wagons were not in town. And from the way Queen was acting, Jordan soon realized that the dog was alone, so he became even more concerned and told Mary's mother. She and the Jordans and other townspeople tried to get the dog to take them to her master. The dog would start for a hill on the edge of town, go to the top, lie down, and whine; but it would not go any farther. People tried many many times, but the dog would only go so far and then stop.

By then, everyone in Ellis was fearing the worst. Some men from Ellis rode their horses out across the plains for many miles from town in hopes of finding the buffalo-hunting party, which no one did find. Then, one morning in late August, a message was received by telegraph from Buffalo, Kansas (now Dodge City). A buffalo hunter named Coffey said he had come across a camp where there had been a terrible Indian massacre. Coffey reported that he had found a flour sack with the name R. Jordan, Ellis, Kansas, printed on it. He had also found a dead man, lying by the ashes of a campfire, face down, with a woman's sunbonnet close by. Coffey said he laid the bonnet on the body and then quickly had covered the body with dirt before riding as fast as he could to Buffalo with the news. He advised that he would wait in Buffalo for soldiers and would help to guide them to the camp site.

As word of the discovery spread across Kansas, two railroad cars loaded with horses and soldiers of the Sixth Cavalry at Fort Hays were moved toward Ellis. Meantime, several Ellis men got their horses, arms, and supplies and awaited the soldiers' arrival. One Ellis man, T. K. Hamilton, who later became sheriff of Ellis County, promised the relatives that as soon as the party had found out anything, it would return to Buffalo and send a telegram to Ellis.

Two and a half days later, a telegraph message was received at Ellis from Hamilton, but no one wanted to deliver it. J. C. Henry, the young man who received the message, asked nearly twenty-five people to deliver it, but all of them refused. Finally a woman named Walker said she would deliver it if a few other women would go with her first to Mary Jordan's mother and then to the parents of the Jordan brothers.

Mrs. Walker, when she reached the Kansas Pacific Railroad's boarding house, which was run by Mary's mother, opened the front door and announced who she was. Jennie Smith Martin later recalled the scene:

> I answered her and started for the middle door, but she got there first and sat right down in the doorway. She tried to read the message, but could not. So I took the message out of her hand and looked at it. Mother began screaming "Read It." I got the words out at last. It was short:

> Buffalo, Kansas. Reached ground of
> massacre. Have found the three boys,
> Mary missing. Suppose she has been
> carried off by the Indians.
>
> Signed T. K. Hamilton

Mother stood up straight for a moment, then threw her hands over her head and, giving a piercing scream, fell to the floor in a dead faint. By this time our house was full of people. My sister never moved out of her chair, until some one helped her up. I managed to get out of the house and went to the east side and laid down on the ground, face as near the house as I could get. I was not unconscious, just stunned. Some of our friends asked me if I wanted anything and urged me to get up. I laid there about two hours, then let my friends take me in the house.

Soon the parents of the Jordan brothers decided to have their sons' bodies and the body of Fred Nelson returned to Ellis for burial, but no coffins could be found in Ellis. The boss carpenter at the Kansas Pacific Railroad shops said he could make them if the railroad would let him have the lumber. It did, and everyone offered to help the carpenter. It took him three days to build three nice-looking black coffins. These were loaded into wagons, and several men started south to retrieve the bodies. It was several days before the Ellis men returned with the bodies in the coffins, which were placed in the living room at the boarding house. After two days the funerals were held, and the coffins were buried on a nearby hill as everyone cried.

Meantime, the soldiers were searching for Mary Jordan and were trying to piece together what had happened. The site of the massacre was a sheltered place in a bend of the south fork of Walnut Creek about fifty miles south of Park's Fort. The three men and Mary had evidently been cooking a meal when they were surprised by the Indians. Dick Jordan had been shot twice with rifle bullets, one in his breast and the other in the shoulder. He had fallen by the campfire. Fred Nelson had been shot in the head and breast and had fallen about twenty feet away. George Jordan had been killed with arrows. Eighteen were found in his body, and he had fallen on his back, with an arrow between his teeth. He was about a half-mile from camp, on higher ground. It appeared that there had been a running fight between George and the Indians, and he had gotten that far away before being killed. The three men had been scalped.

There was no sign of Mary Jordan, however. She had a storm cloak that was as long as her dress and was fastened down the front with little straps of the same material as the cloak. The soldiers found a few pieces, torn in strips, from the straps of this coat. They thought she had left a trail, and this suggested to them that she had been alive when the Indians had taken her from the camp. But the trail lasted only a short distance from the camp. The Indians may have observed her dropping the cloth and then stopped her.

The government soon intensified its search for Mary Jordan. Soldiers and government men visited reservations in Indian Territory, and the government offered a large reward for information as to her whereabouts. Early in the fall of 1872, soldiers returned to the site of the massacre and burned the tall dry grass in a wide area around where the attack had occurred; but they found nothing.

It was many months later when Dick Jordan's gun was found in the possession of an Indian. What kind of weapon it was is not known, but according to one account, Jordan had ordered some special shells, which were quite different from the ones that were used by buffalo hunters in the West. The shells were in the gun when the Indian was found with the weapon. The Indian, a northern Cheyenne, eventually admitted that he had participated in the massacre. He told how Mary Jordan had been taken about ten miles from the scene of the massacre and then killed. The area was carefully searched, but no body was ever located.

The Indian said he was a member of a small party of northern Cheyenne who were returning north after visiting kinsmen in Indian Territory, now Oklahoma. He said the killings of the three men and Mary Jordan were in revenge for the killing of a member of his party a few days earlier. It was learned that about two days before the Jordan massacre, two buffalo hunters—Bob and Jim Carter—had encountered the same Indian party between the Arkansas and Pawnee rivers, many miles south of the massacre site. Bob Carter had climbed up onto his wagon bed and had motioned for the oncoming Indians to go away; but they did not. They kept riding hard toward the two hunters. The Carters, fearing for their lives, began to fire at the Indians, killing one. The Indians had then turned and fled. The next whites whom the Indians had encountered were the Jordans and Fred Nelson, camped on the south fork of Walnut Creek. Then the Indians had their revenge.

# John O'Loughlin,
# Trader and Town Builder

John O'Loughlin was an Irishman who came to Kansas after the Civil War. Born in county Clare, Ireland, in 1842, he came to America with his mother and her other two children in 1850 and settled at Dubuque, Iowa. About the time that the Civil War began, he came to Kansas and entered government service at Fort Leavenworth. O'Loughlin became a teamster in the department of quartermaster, and during the war years, he hauled military freight across the plains.

The year 1867 saw O'Loughlin hauling military supplies from Fort Hays southwestward to Fort Dodge, over a new trail that had been laid out by the military. Fort Hays, which was established in 1865, was a supply point, and from there the new trail to Fort Dodge crossed Ellis, Rush, Ness, and Hodgeman counties before reaching Fort Dodge in present-day Ford County. In 1867, however, most of these counties had not yet been established.

O'Loughlin's job was demanding as he crisscrossed the plains in all kinds of weather. It was not the weather that bothered him, however, it was the crossing on Pawnee Creek, about twenty-five miles west of present-day Larned, Kansas, that gave him the most trouble. The creek banks were very steep at the crossing, and O'Loughlin found it very difficult to get his wagons across Pawnee Creek. Other teamsters had the same problem.

On December 1, 1869, O'Loughlin quit his military freighting and settled at the troublesome crossing on Pawnee Creek, where he constructed a bridge out of logs that had been cut from trees growing along the stream. As soon as it had been built, he began charging a dollar for each government team that used his bridge. All others paid fifty cents to cross the bridge. Teamsters who followed the trail between Fort Hays and Fort Dodge used the bridge and gladly paid the toll. Near the bridge, O'Loughlin also built a log cabin and surrounded it with a log stockade, constructed by setting poles in the ground on end. Inside the stockade he dug a well, so that he would not be without water should Indians attack his compound.

Soon O'Loughlin was stocking goods and merchandise in his cabin, and the spot became known as O'Loughlin's trading post. He did a thriving business with governmental freighters, soldiers, buffalo hunters, travelers of all sorts, and even a few Indians. Tradition has it that General Custer and some troopers camped near the trading post in November, 1868, and that Wild Bill Hickok, among other frontier notables, stopped there.

O'Loughlin sold or traded staple groceries and dry goods, feed, rifles, ammunition, saddles, spurs, boots, and other things that were needed on the frontier. But his business began to fall off abruptly when the Atchison, Topeka and Santa Fe Railroad was built into Dodge City in 1872. No longer did the government ship supplies by wagon from Fort Hays to Fort Dodge; such things were now transported by rail. O'Loughlin had anticipated the change, so he sold his interests to George Duncan in the spring of 1873. The trading post and the crossing then became known as Duncan's Crossing.

O'Loughlin loaded his merchandise and belongings onto his wagon and started southwestward, looking for a new opportunity to do business. He stopped for a while in Dodge City but decided, for reasons that apparently have been lost in time, not to settle in Dodge. Instead, he continued and found opportunity about sixty-five miles west of Dodge City at a stop on the newly built Santa Fe line. This location was forty miles from the Colorado border, in a region that was not yet settled; and the only building at the railroad stop was a small frame structure that housed a telegraph office. Nearby, using railroad ties, O'Loughlin built a corral for his animals.

John O'Loughlin, the Irishman who came to Kansas after the Civil War. This photograph was taken after he had helped to found Lakin, Kansas.

O'Loughlin's trading post became the first store between Dodge City and LaJunta, Colorado. And since the Santa Fe Trail passed close to O'Loughlin's store, his business was good. The railroad had not yet reached Santa Fe, New Mexico, and wagon freighters were still hauling freight between the end of the railroad tracks and Santa Fe. Freighters, teamsters, buffalo hunters, and a few cowboys frequented the trading post. And because there was little money in the area, O'Loughlin often traded provisions from his stock for buffalo meat, and later for buffalo bones. These he shipped east to wholesalers, who accepted them in trade for provisions, clothing, and ammunition. These things were then shipped west on the railroad to O'Loughlin. In this manner he built an inventory that included just about everything that anyone on the frontier might need. He also traded worn-out oxen from passing freighters for fresh animals in his corral. O'Loughlin would reshoe the tired oxen, keep them, and feed them until they were in con-

The main street in Lakin, Kansas, early in the twentieth century. John O'Loughlin died there in December, 1915.

dition to travel again. He would then hold them until passing freighters needed fresh animals. He made a good profit in this manner.

By early 1874 O'Loughlin had secured a post office for the settlement. The post office was named Lakin, in honor of a director of the Santa Fe line. O'Loughlin was appointed postmaster, and the post office was established in his dugout store. When the railroad platted the town site in 1882, the post office's name was given to the town. In that year, O'Loughlin was married, and in the following year he built a new, a more modern, store. Soon a hotel was built, and then a restaurant and other businesses. The area was being settled by farmers and ranchers. O'Loughlin began to prosper, and he and I. R. Holmes formed a bank. Holmes was president, and O'Loughlin was vice-president. As the years passed, O'Loughlin increased his holdings, which by 1900 included farms and ranches in southern Kansas, Oklahoma, and Texas. The hardships of pioneering had paid off. When John O'Loughlin died on December 9, 1915 at his home in Lakin, his business interests were taken over by his sons.

# Hugh Cameron,
# the Kansas Hermit

**M**any old-timers may recall the stories about an old hermit who once lived in a tree and slept in a box near Lawrence. He was a colorful character who wore buckskins and a stocking cap and carried a staff, like that of the old hermit of Biblical times. During the late 1880s and early 1890s, young men and women who were attending the University of Kansas often went to see him. Most of these young people viewed him as something of an oddity, a freak, and something that every student should see.

During the late 1880s and early 1890s most of the students at KU made at least one pilgrimage to his hermitage, which was located about three miles north by northwest of Lawrence, on the south bank of the Kansas River. During this time, most of the students were ordered off the land by the hermit, who waved a shotgun in their faces. By the late 1890s, however, he had become more sociable. From time to time he would permit students to sit around his campfire as long as they respected his property. The young people, usually only a handful of them, would listen to the stories that he told. And his stories were viewed as just that—stories. He would relate how he had known Daniel Webster, Henry Clay, Stephen A. Douglas, and other prominent men in the nation's capital, how he had worked in the government in Washington, how he had helped to found the city of Lawrence, and how he had become a brigadier general after the Civil War.

Most people in Lawrence, then a town of about ten thousand, scorned the old hermit. He was not held in high esteem by most, and they criticized him for turning his back on society. Others accused him of shrouding himself in the mystic glory that his imagination fancied, and still others labeled him as an outcast. In truth, few people seem to have known the facts or even sought them. The Kansas Hermit, as he was called, was one of the founders of Lawrence in 1854, and he had known many famous people.

The old hermit's name was Hugh Cameron. He was born in Perth, Fulton County, New York, about ten miles east of Saratoga Springs, on October 29, 1826. His parents were Allen Cameron and Catherine Frazier, and Hugh grew up on their farm. As a boy he helped his father with the chores, and he educated himself without going to school. By the age of eighteen, however, he had a strong desire to learn, so he entered a normal school and received a formal education. Soon after the election of Zachary Taylor as president in 1849, young Cameron, then twenty-three years old, traveled south, where he soon became employed as a teacher of mathematics in the Rittenhouse Academy in the nation's capital.

In 1849, Washington, D.C., was not a large city. Cameron soon became acquainted with such prominent men as Daniel Webster, Stephen Douglas, and Henry Clay; he also became friends with Gen. William L. Chaplain, an abolitionist from Albany, New York. Three months after Cameron began his teaching job, Chaplain was arrested while trying to sneak several slaves, who belonged to two southern lawmakers, north to Pennsylvania. The city marshal in the capital arrested Chaplain a few miles north of the city and placed the abolitionist in jail.

After learning that Chaplain had been jailed, Cameron visited him behind bars. The administrators of the Rittenhouse Academy soon learned about Cameron's visit and promptly fired him. A day or two later Cameron was attacked by a mob of proslavery men on the streets of Washington, who handled him roughly. When it appeared that Cameron might be killed, Henry Clay, then a United States senator from Kentucky, stepped in and saved Cameron's life.

How Cameron made a living in Washington during the weeks and months that followed is not known, but later, Thomas Corwin, secretary of the Treasury, offered Cameron a job as a clerk. Cameron accepted the position and worked at the Treasury Department for six months. It was then, however, that he suffered a lung hemorrhage. Cameron was given a sixty-day furlough from his job to recuperate; but when it came time for him to return to work, he resigned from his government job.

Doctors apparently had told Cameron that he needed much exercise to strengthen his lungs. It was then that Cameron, about twenty-five years old, "took a subscription agency for *Harper's Monthly* magazine." Selling subscriptions gave Cameron more exercise as he walked around the city. He did well, but his health did not improve. How long he sold magazine subscriptions is not known, but by 1853, Cameron had decided to go west.

Determined to strengthen his lungs, Hugh Cameron walked westward from Washington, D.C., to St. Louis. The journey must have taken nearly a year. In St. Louis he met the first Emigrant Aid Society party from Massachusetts, which was bound for Kansas Territory and what would become Lawrence. Cameron was voted a member of the party; he even served as chairman during a meeting in St. Louis, when the party passed resolutions "of confidence and thanks for the services of the Aid Company." But Cameron had to pawn his overcoat in St. Louis to obtain enough money to pay his boat fare to Kansas City, Missouri. After arriving in Kansas City, Cameron reportedly walked to the spot where Lawrence, Kansas, stands today. Cameron was then about twenty-eight years old.

On November 29, 1854, when the first formal election was held in Kansas Territory, Hugh Cameron was one of eleven men of the pioneer party to vote; his name appears on the voting list. By then, Cameron had staked a claim north-by-northwest of Lawrence. Later he would call this claim Camp Ben Harrison.

A biographical sketch that appears in A. T. Andreas's *History of Kansas,* which was published in 1883, contains much information on Cameron. Most of such sketches that appear in the book were provided by the subjects and were published only after the individual had agreed to purchase a copy of the book. The volume was something of a vanity publication insofar as the biographical sketches are concerned. Because of this, it is likely that the information on Cameron's early years in Kansas was written or at least provided to a writer by Cameron. His biography reads in part:

He denounced the lawlessness of the Free-State men on the one
hand, and the outlawry of the slavery party on the other, for
which he was at times mobbed and robbed by the Free-State
men, because he would not inforce all their acts; and also by
the border ruffians, because he condemned their infamous conduct. His property was freely taken by both parties and his life
was constantly in danger. Gov. Reeder appointed him a judge
at the first Territorial election, and when the polls were surrounded by more than 1,000 ruffians [most were from
Missouri], he did not abandon his post, although others fled.
In making out the returns, he secured a certificate from the
two judges (elected by the ruffian invaders), that the votes cast
at his precinct were not all by legal resident voters; and the
returns being made in this form, furnished the Governor valid
grounds on which to declare the election void, which he did.

Governor Wilson Shannon next appointed Hugh Cameron as
a justice of the peace in Douglas County. Cameron issued only one
warrant during the term of his appointment; this was for the arrest of Jacob Branson, a Free State man. For issuing the warrant,
Cameron was "menaced and threatened" by the Free State forces,
but he did not leave Lawrence. Cameron was arrested and taken
before James H. Lane and Charles Robinson. Lane demanded that
Cameron resign as justice of the peace, but Cameron refused to
do so. He was freed, only to be taken prisoner soon after by another
mob and "subjected to many and gross indignities," according to
Cameron's biographical sketch in *History of Kansas.*

In 1857 the territorial legislature granted Cameron a charter
to establish a ferry across the Kansas River opposite his land. He
was given a ten-year privilege of landing on the north side of the
river on the Delaware Indian reserve. Cameron probably built the
ferry and operated it, although I cannot locate any proof of this.
The ferry—called Cameron's ferry—does appear, however, on an
1857 map of Douglas County, which was produced by J. Cooper
Stuck. The ferry was located about two and one-half miles up the
Kansas River from Lawrence. Cameron, however, apparently abandoned his ferry soon after the Civil War had begun. After the battle of Wilson's Creek, west of Springfield, Missouri, early in the
war, Cameron volunteered for service in the Union Army and
became a first lieutenant.

His military record in the *Official Military History of Kansas Regiments* (1870), which was produced by the adjutant general, relates that Cameron later became a captain and was placed in charge of Company G, Second Kansas Cavalry, on December 27, 1861. In the following April the unit designation was changed to Company F, and by August, 1862, the Second Kansas Cavalry, with Cameron and his unit, were moving south into Indian Territory. There they secured the archives and the treasure of the Cherokee Indian Nation at Tallequah, the Cherokee capital. The unit returned to Kansas, escorting John Ross, the principal chief of the Cherokee Nation, his family, and other Indians, as well as the archives and the treasure.

In the fall of 1862 the Second Kansas Cavalry moved south again, this time into northwestern Arkansas, where they engaged the enemy on several occasions. In one instance, Cameron is credited with having checked the enemy's advance by racing with his company to aid other units of the Second Kansas Cavalry that were about to be overrun.

There is one mystery concerning Cameron's military career. On January 12, 1862, he was sent on a scouting expedition to Huntsville, in northwestern Arkansas. He did not return until January 20, but the reason for this is not known. No written account was ever made of that scouting trip, according to official records, but on the day when Cameron returned, a first lieutenant named J. C. French preferred charges against Cameron, who was then arrested. What the charges were is not known, and they seem to have been dropped soon after Cameron was arrested.

Cameron's career is otherwise spotless. And on February 8, 1864, he was promoted to lieutenant colonel of the Second Arkansas Cavalry. In the late summer of 1865, Cameron received an honorable discharge at La Grange, Kentucky. Later, as copies of documents that are on file at the Kansas State Historical Society show, Cameron was brevetted as a colonel and then as a brigadier general of volunteers for his meritorious service.

Cameron returned to his land along the Kansas River north by northwest of Lawrence and resumed farming. He held the southeast quarter of section 14, tier 12, range 19, in Wakarusa Township; he called his farm Glen Burn. According to postal records, Cameron applied for a post office at Glen Burn. His request was granted, a post office was established there on March 12, 1875, and Cameron was appointed postmaster. For reasons that are not known, however, the post office was discontinued less than nine months later, on December 8, 1876. It may have been closed because of a lack of business.

It was at Glen Burn that Cameron established a journal "devoted to sobriety, equality and equity" for the working man. Titled *Useful Worker,* it reflected Cameron's longstanding beliefs in the value of the working man. The journal, however, was not successful. Its failure may have been tied to Cameron's broken romance with a woman named Mary Phelps from Missouri. Soon Hugh Cameron, who had once been boldly outspoken and aggressive with his fellowmen, turned away from civilization and began to live the life of a hermit. He gave up living in a house, he moved his belongings into the out of doors, and he gave up the luxuries of organized society.

"The out-of-doors and fresh air were his two hobbies and perhaps never has a mortal in the past century lived in queerer places than the old hermit," wrote one Lawrence newspaper editor, who described Cameron's method of housekeeping as follows:

> Cleanliness was not one of the Hermit's virtues and he would live in one spot until so much trash had gathered as to almost crowd him out. Then instead of having a general house cleaning day he would have a house moving. He would move his papers and other valuables and set fire to his habitation and pitch camp anew. This process was kept up for years . . . and during the time he lived the lonely life of a hermit he had more than a half dozen homes on his camp site.

Early in this century a Lawrence newspaperman went to Cameron's camp, which was located on some bluffs, called Cameron Bluffs, north by northwest of Lawrence. It was a crisp October evening as the reporter sat on a fallen log before a campfire, with the hermit standing silhouetted in the glow from the dying embers of the fire. The reporter listened as Cameron related the following story:

Hugh Cameron, the Kansas Hermit.

You read in the Bible of the prophets of old. . . . How to become a seer, a prophet, one had to bury himself alone in the woods. Your old Scotch bards would often bury themselves in the mountains. [At this point Cameron began to sing a quaint and weird Scotch ballad. The reporter had to stop Cameron and bring him back to the subject at hand.] I wanted to become a seer so I buried myself here in my woods. Some day the vision may come.

Cameron was eighty years old in 1906, and his health was beginning to fail. His last camp on Cameron Bluffs was visited by a Lawrence newspaper reporter, who described it as "a kind of tepee of logs" located in a grove of trees. Inside, Cameron kept an old trunk, which contained his valuable papers. His bed was a couch, and from his bed at night he could view the stars through gaps in the logs.

As Cameron got older he became more sociable. He often talked with visitors, and he encouraged people to visit him. This continued when he moved into Lawrence in about 1907, as he began to spend more time with people. Cameron, with his long white hair and beard, rode in most parades after he moved to town. He rode a mule, with the stars and stripes draped gracefully around him.

Cameron's move into Lawrence did not change his living habits, however. His city home was just as unusual as his country home: his bedroom was a wooden platform, constructed in a large maple tree at the corner of Louisiana and Penn (Fifth) streets. Below the tree there was a creek. Cameron dug out a wide area in the creek bank, roofed it over, and established his kitchen and dining room there. He placed his old trunk in the makeshift room. Soon, Cameron had a telephone installed in his cave. Whether or not he used the phone much is not recorded, but it was there, and it worked. And in the spring of 1908 he sought to have electricity installed in his Lawrence home.

On Monday, December 7, 1908, Cameron learned about the death of an old friend, A. H. Case, of Topeka. Cameron appeared at the Case home the following afternoon. He wanted to attend the funeral, but he was disturbed to learn that it would be on the following day. Cameron visited with the widow and other friends until about 9 P.M.; then he said his feet were cold, so he asked to be allowed to sit near a gas stove in a bedroom. He remained by the stove for several minutes; then he returned to the sitting room and lay down on a lounge. Mrs. Case awakened him an hour later and insisted that he stay the night. He did not object, so she led him to a bedroom on the second floor, and he went to sleep.

On Wednesday morning, December 9, 1908, Cameron did not come downstairs for breakfast. Thinking that he wanted to rest, Mrs. Case did not disturb him. When he had not come downstairs by lunchtime, a friend of Mrs. Case's went upstairs to arouse him and remind him of the afternoon funeral. Cameron did not answer the knock on the door, and when a hired man entered the room, he found Cameron unconscious. Cameron was then taken to a Topeka hospital, where he was pronounced dead. Doctors said that he had suffered a stroke of apoplexy. It was ascertained that Cameron had two sisters living in Lawrence, and they were informed of his death.

The Kansas Hermit was no more. Hugh Cameron never did see his vision, and fate did not will another wish — to die in the out of doors that he loved so much. But history will remember Hugh Cameron as a man who chose to be different.

# John Baxter and the Town
# That Was Named for Him

The southeastern Kansas town of Baxter Springs is located in southern Cherokee County, only a mile north of the Oklahoma line. It is a picturesque community in a part of Kansas where much of the rolling woodlands resemble the Ozarks. Like many other Kansas communities, the town was named for an early settler and what he found there.

This settler's name was John L. Baxter. He was of English stock; his ancestors had been liberals in their day, emigrants who came to America in the latter half of the eighteenth century and took part in the American Revolution. Baxter was born near Springfield, Illinois, on July 17, 1809, and he grew up in Illinois. He was in his thirties when he moved to Missouri during the 1840s and settled on Big Lost Creek, west of Neosho in southwestern Missouri. There he mined lead in what became known as the Baxter mines, and he secured the title to his property.

After Kansas Territory was opened for settlement in 1854, Baxter decided to move west and look for new opportunities. In 1855 he found them just across the western border of Missouri. He staked a squatter's claim (homestead preemption) on the west side of the Spring River about four miles southwest of what later became Lowell, Kansas. Baxter claimed a strip of land about three miles wide, which extended five miles from the Spring River to what later became known as Blue Mound. The claim was then part of a disputed strip of land that lay north of the as-yet-unsurveyed line

142

between Kansas Territory and Indian Territory. The claim was only about thirty miles west by northwest of his property in Missouri.

Baxter took his wife, four daughters, and four sons into Kansas Territory and built a cabin on his claim. The cabin was near two springs and was located on the northwestern corner of Seventh Street and Cleveland Avenue in modern Baxter Springs. John Baxter was an impressive-looking man: he stood six feet seven and one-half inches tall and had a massive frame that was well proportioned. His hair was dark, and he sported a well-trimmed mustache and beard. His eyebrows were also black and heavy enough to cast a pleasant shadow over his massive features.

The Baxter cabin was not far from a military road that linked Fort Leavenworth and Fort Scott, in Kansas Territory, to Fort Gibson in Indian Territory. But Baxter soon laid out a new trail from the military road. This trail passed close to his cabin and then followed a route south for about three and a half miles. Baxter marked the trail, or road, with a large turning plow, and he made a cut down the banks of Brush and Willow creeks to make them crossable. His new road was actually a shortcut for travelers who were following the military road: it shortened the distance, and it also saved travelers from having to ford the Spring River.

Baxter's real purpose in laying out the new road, however, was to bring travelers past his cabin. Soon after he had completed the new road, his cabin became something of a trading post and tavern. He stocked staples and a few supplies and notions, and he offered accommodations for a few travelers. He had soon built a good business, and as it grew, Baxter constructed corrals to accommodate stock that belonged to the travelers. He also attracted Texas cattle drovers who were driving their longhorns up from Texas. Many drovers stopped at Baxter's en route to Missouri, where their cattle could be sold for much higher prices than in Texas. The plentiful supply of cattle enabled Baxter to establish a small tannery, where he made leather from the hides of the Texas longhorns.

Baxter was an honest man. People liked to do business with him. He never allowed himself to get into debt, and he never allowed anyone to owe him a cent for long. From what is known, Baxter had a remarkable influence over his family. They worshipped him, and his daughters and his wife kept him neatly dressed in homespun clothing. Store-bought clothes did not fit him; even his boots had to be made specially for him.

Baxter was also a religious man. In fact, he joined the Baptist Church and was publicly ordained a minister in 1843, though he never called himself reverend. He liked to write religious songs and to play them on a violin. All of his family played the violin, and on cool evenings, they would sing and play. Baxter also was a medium, and he occasionally presided over spiritual seances in which the spirits of the dead supposedly appeared and tapped out messages to the living. Although religious, Baxter usually was armed. He liked to wear two navy Colts in plain sight. His massive frame, plus the two weapons, no doubt served to discourage troublemakers.

Between 1855 and late 1858, Baxter and his family prospered in their new Kansas home. Two of his daughters married and took claims nearby. By late 1858, one of his son-in-laws had died and left a claim on the east side of Spring River. The claim had a cabin and several acres in cultivation. Baxter's daughter rented the cabin to a man named Commons, and she moved in with her parents. Commons, however, soon claimed the daughter's claim and refused to move. John Baxter, on behalf of his daughter, demanded that Commons vacate the claim. Baxter told Commons to leave by January 26, 1859, or he would eject him. On the morning of that day, Commons still had not moved. Later in the day, Baxter, along with his son William T. Baxter and his son-in-law Pink Killebrew, went to the cabin to eject Commons.

The cabin was located in the middle of a field. It had been barricaded by Commons, his young son, and a man named Morris, who reputedly was a hired gunman. As Baxter, his son, and his son-in-law started to walk across the field toward the cabin, Commons pushed a double-barreled shotgun through a crack and fired. Commons killed Baxter instantly. Baxter's son and son-in-law then opened fire and killed Morris and the Commons boy, and Commons fled.

Baxter's family and friends were shocked by his death. They buried him about a hundred yards east of the springs that still bear his name. John Baxter, who was fifty years old at the time of his death, did not live to see the town of Baxter Springs established.

That occurred just after the Civil War, in 1866, when it became something of a cattle town. By then the springs were well known and were called Baxter Springs. It was only appropriate to name the town after the springs. John Baxter's family did not remain to see the town established, however; they moved to Bonham, Texas, in 1860, just before the Civil War. Two of John Baxter's sons— Cyrus and John A.—joined the Confederate Army. Another son— William T.—joined the Union Army. The fourth son—Manford— apparently remained in Texas to care for his mother, who died in Texas in 1871 at the age of sixty.

# Eugene Fitch Ware,
## "Ironquill"

There was a time when every Kansan knew the name Ironquill. His poems were read by school children, were recited during programs of women's clubs, and were published by newspaper editors who praised them: even men read his poetry.

Ironquill was the pen name of Eugene Fitch Ware, who claimed Kansas as his home, even though he had been born in Hartford, Connecticut, on May 29, 1841. He was only a few years old when his parents moved to Burlington, Iowa, where he grew to manhood and was educated in the public schools. In April, 1861, he enlisted in the First Iowa Volunteer Infantry for three-months' service, a period that many people thought would be enough for putting down the rebellion. When the war continued, Ware reenlisted in the Fourth Iowa Cavalry and, later, in the Seventh Iowa Cavalry. He had climbed to the rank of captain by the time he was mustered out in June, 1866, at the age of twenty-four.

Ware then returned to Burlington, Iowa, where he contributed a few editorials to the *Burlington Hawkeye*. The editor of the newspaper liked Ware's writing and offered him $75 a month to work full-time for the paper. Ware accepted the position, but in May, 1867, less than a year later, he resigned his job and headed for Kansas. As a soldier, he had been in the state and liked what he had seen.

Ware traveled through much of eastern Kansas, looking over both the country and the opportunities. Returning to Iowa in

Eugene Fitch
Ware as he
appeared in 1866,
at about the age
of twenty-five.
This photograph
was taken less
than a year before
he came to
Kansas.

August, 1867, he convinced his father, mother, and two brothers
to move the family's harness business to Fort Scott, Kansas; and
by late October the move had been made.

Meantime, Ware apparently took two claims, totaling three
hundred and twenty acres, in Cherokee County. Although the
records are hazy, Eugene Ware seems to have taken the claims in
the name of his father, his two brothers, and himself. He lived in
Fort Scott during the fall and winter months, but he returned to
the claims in order to farm during the spring and summer. This
continued until the fall of 1870, when his parents and two brothers
moved from Fort Scott in order to farm the claims.

Eugene Ware, however, remained in Fort Scott, where he had
a job. While farming, he had contributed prose and poetry to the
*Fort Scott Monitor.* When the editor offered Ware a full-time position with the newspaper in late September, 1870, Ware took the
job and moved permanently to Fort Scott. By 1871, Ware had added
the study of law to his newspaper work. Ware became editor of

the paper in 1872 during the presidential campaign, and he supported Horace Greeley in his unsuccessful campaign for president.
Soon after the election, however, Ware left the paper and opened
his own law office in Fort Scott early in 1873. He continued to write
poetry.

According to Ware's own recollections, he began to write
rhymes in advertisements to help the family's harness business in
Fort Scott. That was in 1867. "I sort of tumbled into it," Ware told
C. H. Matson, of *Leslie's Weekly,* in a 1903 interview. "I had never
written any poetry that I know of at the time I was thirty years
old. . . . I had advertised my harness shop in the local papers, and
to make people read what I said I tried putting it in rhyme. My
competitor wrote versified advertisements and I did the same thing
to meet his competition."

Ware continued to contribute poems to the *Fort Scott Monitor*
after he had left the post of editor in November, 1872. His accept-
ance as a poet in Fort Scott and throughout Kansas did not come
overnight; it was gradual. From the time when his poems started
to appear in the Fort Scott paper, editors across Kansas read them,
because nearly all Kansas newspapers regularly exchanged papers.
After Ware was invited to read a poem before the meeting of the
Kansas Editors and Publishers Association in Fort Scott in 1874,
the editors began to call him the poet laureate of Kansas.

His reputation truly began to grow in 1876 when the *Fort Scott
Monitor* published his poem "The Washerwoman's Song." It seems
to have "struck a responsive chord among men of his religiously
disturbed generation," wrote James Malin, a professor of history
at the University of Kansas, in the late 1960s. Malin spent several
of his retirement years in researching and studying Ware's life and
in reading his prose and poetry.

### The Washerwoman's Song

In a very humble cot,
In a rather quiet spot,
    In the suds and in the soap,
    Worked a woman full of hope;
Working, singing, all alone,
In a sort of undertone,

"With a Savior for a friend,
    He will keep me to the end."
Sometimes happening along,
I had heard the semi-song,
    And I often used to smile,
    More in sympathy than guile;
But I never said a word
In regard to what I heard,
    As she sang about her friend
    Who would keep her to the end.

Not in sorrow nor in glee
Working all day long was she,
    As her children, three or four,
    Played around her on the floor;
But in monotones the song
She was humming all day long,
    "With a Savior for a friend,
    He will keep me to the end."

It's a song I do not sing,
For I scarce believe a thing
    Of the stories that are told
    Of the miracles of old;
But I know that her belief
Is the anodyne of grief,
    And will always be a friend
    That will keep her to the end.

Just a trifle lonesome she,
Just as poor as poor could be,
    But her spirits always rose,
    Like the bubbles in the clothes,
And though widowed and alone,
Cheered her with the monotone,
    Of a Savior and a friend
    Who would keep her to the end.

I have seen her rub and scrub,
On the washboard in the tub,

Fort Scott, Kansas, around the turn of the century.

> While the baby, sopped in suds,
> Rolled and tumbled in the duds;
> Or was paddling in the pools
> With old scissors stuck in spools;
> She still humming of her friend
> Who would keep her to the end.

> Human hopes and human creeds
> Have their root in human needs;
> And I would not wish to strip
> From that washerwoman's lip
> Any song that she can sing,
> Any hope that songs can bring;
> For the woman has a friend
> Who will keep her to the end.

Ware met Jeanette P. Huntington of Rochester, New York, in 1871. They were married in 1874 and lived in Fort Scott. As an attorney, Ware concentrated on constitutional law, and later he dealt with insurance law and revision of it. Toward the end of his

Eugene Fitch Ware at about the age of sixty-three. This photograph was probably taken in Topeka in 1904, a few years before his death.

legal career he became actively involved in stressing the public's interest in preserving natural resources for public enjoyment. Ware maintained that beauty of nature possessed a value that should be preserved and protected under law.

As a Republican in his politics, he was elected state senator from 1881 to 1883, and later, from 1902 to 1904, he was appointed

United States commissioner of pensions. But Ware is best remembered as a Kansas poet, writing most frequently under the pen name Ironquill and occasionally using other pseudonyms, including Paint Creek. By the time his poems had become well known, most Kansans knew the identity of Ironquill, especially after his verses were collected and published in book form in 1885 under the title *Rhymes of Ironquill*. Eventually, fifteen editions of the book were issued, three of them in England.

Some of his lines became minor classics during Ware's lifetime. For instance, the political collapse of Senator John J. Ingalls elicited the following from Ware's pen:

> Up was he stuck
> and in the very upness
> of his stucktitude
> He fell

Another poem was to Adm. George Dewey's victory over the Spanish fleet at Manila during the Spanish-American War. Ware supposedly scribbled the following lines on a napkin in a Topeka restaurant:

O Dewey was the morning upon the first of May,
And Dewey was the Admiral down in Manila Bay,
And Dewey were the Regent's eyes, them orbs of Royal Blue,
And Dewey felt discouraged? I Dew not think we Dew!

Still another was Ware's poem that was simply titled "Politics":

> Ever so many the childhood friends
>     That started ahead of me,
> With fearless ignorance, fearless hope,
>     To sail on the vitriol sea;
> Little they knew of the depth or the scope
>     Of the treacherous vitriol sea.
>
> Some of them sailed in boats of wood—
>     Think if it! sailed with glee,
> In boats of wood—yes, painted wood!
>     Out on that vitriol sea;

It eat them right up--wood was not good
> To sail on a vitriol sea.

Many tried brass, and some tried glass,
> To sail on the vitriol sea;
Mindless alike of corrosion or storms,
> They sailed with a fearless glee;
Happy to-day, but to-morrow, in swarms,
> To be wrecked in the vitriol sea.

"Where were they going," I hear you ask,
> "That sailed on the vitriol sea?"
Well, that is a something I do not know,
> A mystery even to me;
But still they did go, and determined to go
> And sail on the vitriol sea.

Although Ware gained national prominence as a poet, he also became well known for the prose that he wrote after he had become a successful poet. His published books include *The Lyon Campaign and History of the First Iowa Infantry* (1907) and *The Indian Campaign of 1864* (1908).

In 1893, Ware moved to Topeka, where he practiced law. Then, in 1909, he moved to Kansas City, Kansas, where he practiced law in partnership with his son until the spring of 1911. He then retired to the Ware farm in Cherokee County. Eugene Fitch Ware—"Ironquill"—died on July 1, 1911, while on vacation in Cascade, Colorado. He was seventy years old. His body was returned to Kansas and buried in the National Cemetery at Fort Scott, where his grave can be seen today.

# Theodore R. Davis's
# First Journey across Kansas

It was about the middle of November, 1865, when Theodore R. Davis arrived in Atchison, Kansas. Davis was a special artist-correspondent for *Harper's Weekly,* the prominent eastern magazine. Davis had been sent west to report and to illustrate what was happening in Kansas and in Colorado, to the west. This was long before magazines and newspapers could reproduce photographs in their publications.

The journey was Davis's first one to the West. A native of Boston, Davis became a traveling artist-correspondent for *Harper's* in 1861. He witnessed the battle between the *Monitor* and the *Merrimac,* the battles at Shiloh and Antietam, the Atlanta Campaign, and the Union's grand march to the sea. During the Civil War he was wounded twice, and once he held off, at gunpoint, surgeons who wanted to amputate his leg.

Davis's western assignment after the Civil War must have seemed rather dull, especially as he climbed aboard a stagecoach belonging to the Butterfield Overland Despatch on the morning of November 17. It was a cool and crisp morning in Atchison, the stage line's eastern terminal, when three other passengers also climbed aboard. As Davis wrote, the passengers, including himself, were "entirely innocent of any knowledge of the plains." The three other people with Davis were Lawrence Hasbrouk, of Kingston, New York; William M. Calhoun, probably a resident of Atchison; and Gen. W. R. Brewster, vice-president of the Butterfield Company.

154

"Departure from Atchison" is the title given to this illustration by Theodore R. Davis, which appeared in the July, 1867, issue of *Harper's Monthly Magazine*.

The stage made good time the first day. Davis rode much of the day on top of the coach, next to the driver, who said that stock stations were located about every twelve miles. On the first day the coach passed many freight wagons that were being pulled by eight to ten yoke of oxen. And when the sun set on the western horizon, the coach continued on. As Davis later wrote, "passengers evince a desire to make a noise. Conversation quickly gives place to song. This night our songs were of home, and our wandering thoughts annihilated the long miles between our rumbling coach and the bright firesides on the Atlantic coast." By nightfall, Davis was riding inside the coach, joining the others in song. But when the riders tired and began to get sleepy, Davis climbed to the top of the coach, where he went to sleep. "The rest of the party disposed themselves as best they could inside, and complained of cramps," wrote Davis.

By dawn on the second day, the coach had moved well beyond the woodlands of eastern Kansas. The day passed uneventfully, and at suppertime the coach passed Fort Ellsworth, on the north bank of the Smoky Hill River. About a year after Davis passed the post, which was located southeast of modern Ellsworth, Kansas, it was renamed Fort Harker.

After another night of trying to sleep aboard the moving coach, the travelers entered what Davis described as "Buffalo Country" on the morning of the third day. It was there that Davis saw buffalo chips being used as fuel because of the scarcity of wood. Davis and the other passengers cooked breakfast at a makeshift stage station — a cave that had been dug in the side of a hill — while fresh horses were brought to the coach. "The air of the plains is a wonderful appetizer. A cup of good coffee, steaming hot, is a good foundation. Venison steak, baked potatoes, and a hot corn-dodger composed the bill of fare," wrote Davis. On the third day of the journey, the driver reminded his passengers that they were now in Indian country, but the passengers saw only buffalo, thousands of the shaggies. Davis wrote: "To estimate their number would be impossible. It is said that they are rapidly decreasing in number but that would seem impossible. The herds move in regular order, the cows and calves occupying the center, and the bulls ranging themselves on the outside. In this way the wolves are kept off."

On the afternoon of the third day the coach reached Fort Fletcher, a post that had been established about a month earlier. In truth, it was a fort in name only. About three hundred soldiers, under the command of a Colonel Tamblyn, had established a camp in a grove of cottonwood trees on Big Creek, about fourteen miles southeast of modern Hays, Kansas. The actual construction of the fort had not yet begun. Several months later, after a flood, the military moved the fort to a spot a mile west of present-day Hays, and the fort came to be called Fort Hays.

After a brief stop at Fort Fletcher, the coach continued on its journey, stopping about sunset at Ruthden Station, which was located about twenty-two miles west of Fort Fletcher. There Davis saw stage-company employees washing their clothes with the root of the soapweed. He declared that it was an excellent substitute for soap. After supper the passengers climbed aboard the coach and continued their westward journey.

It was about midnight when the driver suddenly reined his horses to a stop and shouted to his passengers, "Turn out! Indians."

Theodore Davis's drawing of Fort Fletcher, in what is now Ellis County, Kansas. Fort Fletcher was located about fourteen miles southeast of modern Hays, Kansas. This illustration appeared in *Harper's Monthly Magazine* in July, 1867.

Davis and the others, with their revolvers drawn, quickly jumped from the coach. In the distance they could see a small body of men advancing toward the coach. Davis and his party soon discovered that the strangers were white men, who had been attacked by Indians.

As Davis pieced the story together, three of the men had been aboard another Butterfield coach, traveling west ahead of Davis's coach. When they had arrived at Downer's Station, which was located about fifty miles west of Fort Fletcher, Indians had charged and surrounded the station. The coach's driver, a company messenger, one passenger, two stock tenders, perhaps two carpenters, and a blacksmith had rushed for the safety of the adobe building that served as the stage station. They prepared to fight for their lives. What happened next is told by Davis:

> A half-breed son of Bill Bent, the old mountain man, was one of the leaders of the Indians; being able to speak English,

"On the Plains—Indians Attacking Butterfield's Overland Dispatch Coach,"
by Theodore Davis, which appeared in *Harper's Monthly Magazine,* July,
1867.

he managed to call to the occupants of the adobe that he
wanted to talk. This was assented to. He came up and inquired
whether the treaty had been signed. He was informed that it
had, to which he replied, "All right!" They would have peace
if the occupants of the adobe would come out and shake hands,
leaving their arms behind, and the Indians would do likewise.
The men came out, and a general hand shaking followed. The
Indian is great at this; he will shake your hand all day and
at night-fall will take your scalp. It is simply a way he has of
expressing his brotherly sentiments toward the white man.

The Indians still further deceived the party by driving up
the mules that had been stampeded by them, telling the
messenger that the coach should proceed without molestation.
Such evidence of friendship disarmed the party of any suspicion of hostility, though the Indians were in full paint and
without squaws. In a moment all was changed. The Indians
turned upon the party—bows, arrows, and revolvers were produced, and a desperate attack at once inaugurated. The
messenger, Fred Merwin, a very gallant young man, was killed
instantly; others of the party were wounded, and the two stock-
tenders captured. Mr. Perine, the passenger, the driver, car-

penters, and blacksmith ran for the neighboring bluffs, which they succeeded in reaching. Taking possession of a buffalo wallow, they fought
until nightfall, when the Indians withdrew, and they made good their
escape.

It was decided that Davis and his party would take the other
men back to Ruthden Station and send a message to Colonel
Tamblyn at Fort Fletcher, telling about the raid and requesting
a military escort. This was done, and the next night, soldiers arrived at Ruthden Station. On the morning of November 21, Davis
and his party left Ruthden and started west again, this time with
a military escort. But the coach had to travel slowly to enable the
troops to keep pace.

On the afternoon of November 21 the coach and military escort
reached Downer's Station. Davis recalled that

> the devastation here had been complete. The coach, and
> everything about the station that would burn, had been
> destroyed. The ground was everywhere tracked over by the un-
> shod hoofs of the Indian ponies. We could not find a trace of
> the bodies of Merwin or the stock-tenders; neither could we
> account for their disappearance. Mr. Perine, who had now
> become one of our party, was at a loss to know the reason as
> he was confident that Merwin was killed at the first fire.

The party, including the soldiers, camped at Downer's Station, and at dawn they broke camp and started west again. A few
miles from the stage station they found the remains of a man, but
wolves had stripped all flesh from the bones. The party continued
on, seeing no sign of Indians, only wolves and many buffalo.

At noon on the following day, however, the party found a corraled wagon train that was carrying governmental supplies. The party
was a welcome sight for the freighters, who had been attacked by
Indians. One soldier with the wagon train had been killed, and
another had been shot through the neck with an arrow and had been
scalped. He had played dead while the Indians were scalping him.
Davis recalled that "his wounds were not considered serious, but the
doctor says that he will have a bald spot on the top of his head."

The party met an eastbound Butterfield coach at this spot,
and it was here that Colonel Tamblyn left Davis and his party and

escorted the eastbound coach back to Fort Fletcher. The colonel did, however, leave five cavalrymen to travel with Davis's coach, which then continued west, reaching what Davis called the Monuments that evening. There they camped for the night.

At dawn on November 25 the party continued its journey westward, along with an ambulance — a military wagon — which carried a surgeon and four men plus the five cavalrymen whom Colonel Tamblyn had assigned as an escort. All went well until the group reached Smoky Hill Springs. Within about two hundred yards of the adobe stage station, someone glanced to the rear and saw a hundred Indians on their ponies, charging toward the coach. Davis wrote:

> The sight, frightful as it was, seemed grand. "Here they come!" and the crack of a rifle was responded to by a yell, followed by the singing whiz of arrows and the whistle of revolver bullets. The first shot dropped an Indian. Next a pony stopped, trembled, and fell. The driver crouched as the arrows passed over him, and drove his mules steadily toward the station. The deadly fire poured from the coach windows kept a majority of the Indians behind the coach. Some, however, braver than the rest, rushed past on their ponies, sending a perfect stream of arrows into the coach as they sped along. We were by this time in front of the station. The cavalrymen opened with their revolvers, and the Indians changed their tactics from close fighting to a circle. One, more daring than the rest, was intent on securing the scalp of a stock-herder whom he had wounded. He lost his own in so doing.

Davis and those in the coach, including the driver, made it safely to the adobe station; but the doctor's ambulance, with its passengers, was still being chased by the Indians. The five troopers on horseback started to the doctor's rescue. Seeing the troopers coming, the doctor and the others in the ambulance jumped from the moving vehicle and ran toward the troopers. While the Indians sought to bring the ambulance and its mules to a stop, the troopers and those men who had been riding on the ambulance made their way to the adobe stage station.

Inside, Davis's party was waiting. Altogether there were twenty-one men in the station; they were armed with seven rifles and thirteen revolvers. Davis learned that the station had been furnished with a garrison of ten soldiers, but five of these had taken the best arms and most of the ammunition and had gone buffalo hunting that morning. There was, therefore, only enough ammunition for four of the rifles and for five of the revolvers.

As those inside the adobe building were surveying their situation, the Indians set fire to the tall dry grass around the adobe structure. The men inside grabbed blankets and went outside to beat down the flames near the building. As they were doing so, the Indians attacked. For a few moments it was a doubtful contest, but then the Indians were driven back, and the fire was extinguished. A few men had been wounded by arrows before the Indians withdrew at nightfall.

About three hours after dark, a rustling whiz cut the air over the adobe. Flights of arrows came in, but the men did not fire back. A shot from a pistol or a rifle would have exposed the person who was firing, as the flash would reveal his location. It was then that the white men decided that something should be done. An old hunter volunteered to stampede the Indians. He stripped down to his underclothing and crawled out into the darkness toward the spot from which the twang of bow strings was coming most frequently. According to Davis: "In five minutes the repeated crack of the revolvers and the yells of the Indians told of the successful issue of the bold effort. The bows were still and in another moment our Indian fighter returned to the adobe to receive the heartfelt thanks of the garrison."

The rest of the night was uneventful, but at dawn, everyone waited for the Indians to attack. Some Indians did crawl close to the adobe building, but each time one was seen, one of the white men would fire a single shot at the Indian. The Indians withdrew each time. At about noon a body of men was seen, approaching from the east. When the Indians saw the approaching men, the Indians suddenly retreated. The men were a company of infantry and a small cavalry command, plus wagons. Davis and the others had been saved. Later that day, the Butterfield coach that was carrying Davis left Smoky Hill Springs with a strong military escort. And a few days later, on December 2, 1865, it reached Denver, after a trip of fifteen days across the plains from Atchison and the Missouri River.

"Pond Creek" is the title of this drawing by Theodore Davis, which appeared in *Harper's Monthly Magazine*, July, 1867.

Davis produced several illustrations as a result of his first journey across the plains. He remained in Denver for several months, taking side trips as far south as Santa Fe and into the mining districts near Central City, Colorado. On February 18, 1866, he left Denver for the East, again following the Butterfield route to Atchison. His journey eastward, which lasted only five days and four hours, was uneventful.

During the ensuing years, Davis visited the South and then traveled to Texas. He returned to Kansas in the spring of 1867 to accompany Gen. W. S. Hancock, the commander of the Department of the Missouri, and a large military force, which was designed to put an end to the Indian wars in Kansas and on the plains. Davis returned east in the fall of 1867, never again to return to Kansas. He continued to draw illustrations for *Harper's Weekly* until about 1884, when he became a free-lance artist. On November 10, 1894, at the age of fifty-four, Davis died at his home in Asbury Park, New Jersey.

# Part V

## TORNADOES, FLOODS, GRASSHOPPERS, BLIZZARDS, AND PRAIRIE FIRES

*Oh, what a blamed uncertain thing*
*This pesky weather is;*
*It blew and snew and then it thew,*
*And now, by jing, it's friz.*

—Philander Johnson

# When Tornadoes
# Were Called Cyclones

During the late nineteenth century, many old-timers referred to Kansas as the Cyclone State. And by 1900 the term "Kansas cyclone" had become something of an idiomatic expression in the American language. The use of the word *cyclone,* however, was improper. In tornadoes a funnel-shaped cloud reaches to the ground, but a cyclone does not contain such a cloud. Then too, a cyclone is composed of masses of air that may be five hundred to a thousand miles or more in diameter and may last for several days. A tornado usually develops from a much-smaller cloud mass that lasts for only a few hours at most.

Perhaps the first account of a Kansas tornado is contained in the recollections of Ely Moore of Lawrence. In the summer of 1854, soon after Kansas Territory was established, Moore went buffalo hunting with a large party of Indians. One morning in August, Moore awoke to find the weather sultry and warm. He joined a hunting party, which went out from camp to locate a herd of buffalo, but about noon, the hunting party received a signal to return to camp. As Moore started toward camp, he noticed that the Indians were rushing to reach it. Moore also hurried to camp and asked an Indian chief why the hunters had been told to return. In answer, the chief pointed toward the sun. Moore recalled that he had "noticed millions of insects, grasshoppers, winging their way east. So dense were they that the sun was obscured for minutes at a time. The chief, with gestures of foreboding evil, further ex-

165

plained: 'They [grasshoppers] know. Devil wind come, kill all, maybe. Great Spirit knows best!' "

Moore then related how the hunting party was put to work with axes and spades to dig trenches about three feet in length, six inches wide, and two feet deep. The hunting party's wagons were then moved so that their wheels fit into the trenches, in order to hold them against a heavy wind. The trenches had been dug in a circle, so that once the wagons were in place, they also formed a circle. The covers of the wagons were tied down with ropes made of buffalo hides that had been cut in narrow strips and tied together. The Indian ponies were corraled inside the ring of wagons. Moore recalled that

> it was after five o'clock when all this was accomplished. At that time could be seen in the southwest a dark, greenish-purple cloud hanging close to the horizon, revolving and bounding as it approached. This baloon-shaped lowering monster had many laterals that were licking up the beasts, earth, water and air to satiate the ponderous maw of this fiend of might. Respiration was a struggle, the utter stillness most enervating, and the darkness impenetrable.

Moore told how the "fear-shaken ponies stood huddled together, as if for mutual protection, with the head of one thrown over the neck of another, or with their heads close to the ground." The Indian hunters stood with their arms around their horses' necks, then waited.

From Moore's description, there may have been more than one funnel in the approaching tornado. As the storm neared, Moore said it sounded like muffled drums. It was more than a mile in width. He wrote that "as it neared us, it seemed to bound into the air some hundreds of feet." When the cloud had reached the hunters' camp, a strike of lightning shot from the dark cloud to the ground, some distance outside the circle of wagons. When it did this, sand, earth, grass, weeds, and limbs of trees fell from the sky onto the camp. Moore recalled that the debris weighed "many hundred tons." And as the debris fell, the tornado funnel lifted and passed over Moore and the Indians, though the strong winds turned over some wagons and "flicked" some bales of robes.

After the storm had moved on, everyone gave thanks and then enjoyed a jolly supper. Later, Moore inspected the area northeast of the hunters' camp. The tornado funnel had come down again, beyond the camp, and had stripped acres of sod and soil from the prairies. Moore wrote that he found "two dead buffalo completely denuded of hair, and every bone in their bodies crushed. These animals must have been picked up . . . carried to a great height, and then dashed to the earth."

The recollections of other old-timers in Kansas also contain accounts of tornadoes during the years that followed. So do old newspapers, one of which tells about a tornado that struck just west of Olathe in Johnson County in late May, 1864, and destroyed several buildings. In July, 1871, another tornado ripped through the new settlement of Wakefield in Clay County, leveling a church and other buildings. Apparently no one was killed in either tornado.

As more and more settlers moved into Kansas during the 1870s, there were more reports of tornadoes. And on May 31, 1879, five tornadoes moved across northern Kansas, hitting the towns of Delphos, Centralia, Frankfort, and Irving. Most authorities believe that the two tornadoes that struck Irving on that day were the most violent in the recorded history of nineteenth-century Kansas.

The first tornado at Irving moved in from the southwest at about 5:30 P.M., with its funnel-shaped cloud clearly visible. Its force was so great that a large iron bridge across the Blue River was lifted bodily from its piers and abutments and was twisted into a shapeless ruin. As the vortex, or funnel, passed over the river, water from the channel was sucked up into the cloud, thus exposing the bed of the river for a considerable distance. The violent upward rush of air in the whirling cloud carried the water in spray above the tops of the tallest trees along the river.

The people of Irving had barely emerged from their dugouts and other places of shelter when there appeared in the west another cloud of inky blackness and enormous dimensions. It was at least two miles wide. Some residents of Irving actually believed that the Judgment Day had arrived; they offered prayers and then ran for shelters.

According to several accounts, the huge funnel cloud covered the small town with a roar "like that of a thousand cannons." In an instant the cloud swept away everything in its path. Irving residents who lived through the tornado said that the air was filled with fumes, like sulfurous smoke; the sky had a reddish tinge, bordering on purple; and the ground was rocked, as if by an earthquake. What seemed to them to be vast waterspouts reached the ground in several places, swinging to and fro in the gale like elephants' trunks, seizing and sucking up everything in their paths. These waterspouts apparently were additional funnels, one on each side of the main funnel cloud.

Twelve people were killed in Irving, and many were injured. On that day a total of forty persons died throughout the state when the tornadoes hit. The U.S. Army Signal Bureau, then the governmental agency that was responsible for weather reporting, sent Sgt. John P. Finley to retrace the routes that the tornadoes had followed. In his report, which was published in 1882 in Washington, D.C., Finley noted that Kansans called the storms *twisters* and *cyclones*. Finley's report was in part responsible for dubbing Kansas the Cyclone State in the early 1880s.

Even before his report was published, other tornadoes had struck in Kansas. On June 12, 1881, tornadoes struck portions of Osage, Cowley, Ottawa, and other counties in Kansas. Later that month, three persons were killed in Osage County in another tornado, and in the following year, 1882, tornadoes struck on April 6 and 7. The most serious damage was reported at Fort Riley, Kansas. Later that month, Henry Inman, a retired army officer who had become a Kansas writer, told a Topeka newspaper reporter that he believed tornadoes were "magnetic, and have their origin in the sun."

By the early 1880s, many Kansans were constructing what they called "cyclone cellars," which were actually small caves dug into the ground near their homes. These were designed for shelter in the event of a tornado. Most cyclone cellars were constructed by scooping out a small area of earth about six feet deep, constructing a frame support about five to six feet high, and placing the support in the hole. Dirt was then piled over the top of the support. Each cellar had a door that opened outward and had stairs just inside that led down into the cellar. The cellars also served as places in which to store fruits and vegetables.

Although many tornadoes destroyed property and caused deaths in nineteenth-century Kansas, the two that struck Irving in 1879 were the most violent and destructive until the twentieth century arrived. Since 1900, many more-serious tornadoes have occurred in Kansas. On May 21, 1903, a series of tornadoes swept across portions of Clark, Clay, Ford, Hodgeman, Saline, Dickinson, Marshall, Riley, Pottawatomie, Norton, Morton, and Wallace counties, causing much damage. Then, on April 11, 1911, more than $200,000 worth of damage occurred when a tornado that was moving northeastward swept across Lawrence, beginning about 8:20 P.M. Lifting and dipping several times, the twister destroyed and damaged many homes and businesses, but no one was killed. A few years later, eleven people died, many were injured, and damage amounted to more than $1 million when Great Bend, Kansas, was struck by a tornado on November 10, 1915.

The Great Bend tornado in 1915 occurred unusually late in the year for tornadoes. The storm, which first appeared sixteen miles southwest of Great Bend, was moving to the northeast. It skipped a few rural places, but it struck the Moses and Clayton south ranch and killed a thousand sheep. It then demolished everything in its path as it swept across the southeastern part of Great Bend, its path being two or three city blocks in width. Residents of Great Bend said the roar "sounded like a hundred locomotives." The tornado destroyed the electric power and water plant, several large flour mills and grain elevators, and the Santa Fe passenger and freight depots, plus a hundred and twenty-five homes. Debris from the storm was strewn for a distance of sixty miles to the northeast, the path that the storm followed. According to one account, an unmailed letter and a check from Great Bend were found near Glasco, Kansas, which is about eighty-five miles to the northeast. And a cancelled check from a Great Bend bank was picked up in Nebraska, where it apparently had been carried by the wind.

Such stories are commonplace. Early in the twentieth century a small tornado near Topeka picked up a farm hand, carried him a hundred feet, and let him down in as good shape as when he had been taken off, except that he was covered with mud. And on June 5, 1917, according to weather-service records, the sash of

Photograph of a tornado near Hardtner, Kansas, in 1929.

the ticket window from the demolished railway station at Elmont, Kansas, was blown into a nearby field, where it was found under a heavy scale weight that was resting on the glass pane. The glass was not even cracked. And near Cottonwood Falls, Kansas, a tornado that was moving southeastward pulled up a north-south barbed wire fence that was nearly a mile long. All of the posts and the wire were rolled up as neatly as if the job had been done by a gang of men.

The year 1917 was especially bad for deadly tornadoes in Kansas. A twister on May 25 destroyed practically everything in its sixty-five-mile path across Sedgwick and Harvey counties in south-central Kansas. Twenty-six people were killed, and property damage totaled $.5 million. Then, on June 1, twelve people died when tornadoes struck Coffeyville, Morse, and McCune, Kansas. Four days later, eleven people died and nearly fifty were injured when tor-

This photo shows a 1930 tornado near McLouth, Kansas, in Jefferson County.

nadoes skipped across northeastern Kansas between Topeka and the Missouri River.

More than half of the tornadoes that have been recorded in Kansas have occurred during the months of May and June, causing them to be called the tornado season. The hours of greatest frequency have been between 4 and 7 P.M., but tornadoes have been known to occur at all hours of the day and night. Most tornadoes also seem to move from the southwest to the northeast, but there have been exceptions. Since the federal government established a weather-bureau office in Topeka on June 1, 1887, its records indicate that more tornadoes have occurred in eastern than in western Kansas.

By 1887, many Kansans were beginning to drop the label *cyclone* from such storms and were beginning to call them by their correct name—*tornado*. By the early part of the twentieth century, Kansas began to lose the label the Cyclone State. But the state's violent weather heritage was revived after Lyman Frank Baum's

An unidentified photographer took this picture of a tornado crossing Kansas highway 73W north of Oskaloosa, Kansas, on May 1, 1930.

book *The Wizard of Oz* was made into a movie. A young Kansas farm girl, Dorothy, is whisked away by a tornado to the land of Oz in the story. In more recent years the state of Kansas officially sought to capitalize on its notoriety in the story, and especially the film, seeking to attract tourists to Kansas by calling the state the Land of Ahhhhhhhhhhs.

# Before the Dams Were Built

If you believe the stories that have been told by old Indians, trappers, and traders, the worst flood in what is now Kansas occurred in 1844, ten years before Kansas Territory was established. Every stream in Kansas overflowed its banks that year, after days of nearly continuous rain. Sarcoxie, an old Delaware Indian chief, recalled many years later how the valley of the Kansas River was flooded from west of modern Manhattan, Kansas, east to where the river flows into the Missouri at present-day Kansas City. Near what is now Lawrence, Sarcoxie told how the river had stretched from the bluffs in southern Jefferson County south to what is called Blue Mound, which is southeast of modern Lawrence in Douglas County. At that point, the Kansas River was nearly ten miles wide until the flood waters receded.

At what is now Topeka, the flooding washed away all of the houses and boats that belonged to the Papan brothers, who operated a ferry across the Kansas River. According to one account, a United States Army paymaster, who wanted to cross the swollen stream from the south to the north, stepped into a canoe at about what is now the corner of Topeka Avenue and Second Street in Topeka. An Indian rowed him north to the bluffs in what is now Soldier Township. The water was twenty feet deep where North Topeka now stands.

To the west, on what we now call the Solomon River, the flooding was just as severe. Although no eyewitness accounts have

173

been located, old-timers told how, a few months after the flood, they had found driftwood and animal carcasses lodged high up in trees. They observed that even the highest bottomlands of the Solomon River valley must have had several feet of water when the flooding was at its peak. On the Smoky Hill River, where modern Salina, Kansas, now stands, the water level on the downtown streets would have been at least four feet, had the city existed in 1844.

Even on the Arkansas River in far southwestern Kansas, the flooding was severe. William Bent, who operated the trading post called Bent's Fort on the Arkansas in what is now southeastern Colorado, reported that every river in the region was full from bluff to bluff. In taking a wagon train of perhaps fifty wagons east toward Westport, which is now Kansas City, Bent had to follow the high divides in order to avoid the flooding. And his wagon train had to wait almost thirty days to cross Pawnee Fork—called Otter Creek by the Indians—in present-day Pawnee County simply because the stream was impassable.

Rev. Jotham Meeker, who was living among the Ottawa Indians near what is now Ottawa, Kansas, witnessed the 1844 flooding. His diary provides a vivid account of human hardships on the Marais des Cygnes River. His entry for May 30, 1844, notes: "Never saw such a time of rain. It has fallen almost every day in the last three weeks. The river has overflown its banks, and the bottoms in many places have been inundated more or less for three weeks, and continues all of to-day within our dooryard."

For a few days in early June the sky had cleared and no rain had fallen, but on June 10 it had rained all day. And two days later, Meeker and his family fled their home and Indian mission for higher ground. The Meekers lost most of their property and belongings, as did many of the Indians. Meeker's losses were so great that he had to take his family to Shawnee Mission, in present-day Johnson County.

The "great flood of 1844," as old-timers called it, was not the first recorded flood in what is now Kansas. One of the earliest occurred in 1826, when nearly all streams in the eastern half of modern Kansas overflowed their banks, first in March, because of early spring rains, and again in September, after a very wet summer. Rev. William F. Vail, who was then living among the Indians on the lower Neosho River, close to what is now the southern border of Kansas, recalled that the "product of the toil and sweat of the poor Indians—their summer's work and winter's dependence already gathered into the granaries—was swept away." He recalled how the log buildings, cultivated fields, and fences had been swept away in one night.

The 1826 flood was undoubtedly severe, but few white men were then living in Kansas, and property damage was not extensive. The same is true of the 1844 flood. It was not until white settlers began to move into Kansas Territory in 1854 that more complete accounts of Kansas floods were recorded, along with larger figures for property damage. The Saline River overflowed and covered much of its river valley in 1858 and again in 1867. Emily Haines Harrison, who came to Kansas in 1866 and homesteaded in Ottawa County with her son, later recalled that in June, 1867, she and her son had noticed the Saline River rising rapidly near their log-cabin home, which was located at the junction of the Saline and Table Rock Creek:

> By evening the water had raised from between fifteen to twenty feet, and was on a level with our cabin floor. It kept raising in the night and we took refuge on the roof, where I lay awake gazing at the stars until morning. At daybreak Waldo [her son] took the horse, which had been lariated to the corner of the house, and reconnoitered. Our place . . . was covered to a depth of nearly two feet. For miles, it seemed to me, was an expanse of water. Waldo returned, I climbed onto the horse, astride, my arms clasping the horse's neck, my skirts wrapped as closely about me as possible, and my feet held up to avoid the water. Waldo led the horse perhaps a half-mile north to the former crossing of the Saline. There we could see people on the further bank. Near the crossing was an enormous cottonwood tree. This was now partially washed out, had fallen into the stream, and, clinging by some of the roots, was tossed slowly backward and forward by the current. This was the only landing visible, and I climbed from my horse to this foothold. Then I stood up and called to the people on the further bank. They were soon attracted by our cries, and called repeatedly to me to "hold on." . . . The men were soon at my side with a skiff, and I was safe on the north side of the Saline. My son came across in the same manner, and the horse, turned loose,

swam over. We stayed a couple of days with our rescuers, and then returned to our cabin, the floor ankle deep in mud.

Charles Raber, a wagon freighter, also witnessed the 1867 flood. He later recalled: "It kept on raining until the entire Smoky Hill valley was under water, carrying away about half of the new town of Ellsworth situated two miles from Fort Harker. Later, what was left of the town was moved two miles farther up the river and rebuilt on higher ground."

Between 1867 and 1900, other floods occurred in Kansas, the worst years being 1876, 1881, 1888, and 1892. This flooding was caused by heavy rains in Kansas. In contrast, the flooding that occurred on the Missouri River, along the state's northeastern border, was and still is due to heavy winter snows in the Rocky Mountains and the annual spring melting. In Kansas, aside from the Missouri River in the northeast, only the Arkansas River is born in the Rockies.

Soon after the twentieth century began, another major flood occurred. In early May, 1903, heavy rains fell in western Kansas, where rainfall amounts totaled three to four inches in many places. In central and eastern Kansas, however, rainfall amounts were even greater. This excessive amount of water, which fell within ten days, came down, not in occasional showers, but in regular and continuous downpours, all of which had to be carried off by rivers that were already bank full. Nearly all streams in the eastern half of Kansas rapidly overflowed their banks. Train service came to a standstill, and people who lived along most of the streams fled for higher ground. In Topeka, Edward Grafstrom, a native of Sweden who had come to America and was employed as chief mechanical engineer by the Santa Fe railroad, hurriedly designed and built a small side-wheel steamboat. With a volunteer crew of six men, Grafstrom rescued hundreds of people who had been stranded by the flooding Kansas River in the Topeka area. But on the night of June 2, 1903, while making his last trip, the little steamboat capsized, and Grafstrom drowned. He was called a hero by Topeka citizens, and a bronze tablet was dedicated to his honor.

About twenty miles east of Topeka, in Lawrence, G. A. ("Dolly") Graeber put his gasoline-powered launch into service during

Lawrence residents view the ferry boat that was placed into service in 1903 after the northern section of the Kansas River bridge had collapsed during the flood. The ferry was used until the bridge was repaired.

the flood after the northern section of the Kansas River bridge had collapsed. Graeber is credited with having transported more than twenty-three thousand passengers and about a hundred tons of provisions from Lawrence to North Lawrence and back during a six-week period. Graeber docked his launch only after a ferry boat was placed into service, which was used until the bridge was repaired.

Another serious flood occurred on the Kansas River and several other streams in the state in 1904. There was still another in 1908, when heavy rains occurred over much of Kansas during May. The high water first occurred on the Blue River, where, at Blue Rapids, Kansas, the river level reached 31.9 feet on June 4. On the following day the Vermilion River in Marshall County was a mile wide, and the water was three feet deep in the streets of Frankfort. On that same day a cloudburst in Wilson, Woodson, and Greenwood counties, many miles to the south, caused the Verdigris River to overflow its banks. And a day or so later a cloudburst in the Cottonwood and Neosho valleys caused both of those streams to flood. Emporia, Kansas, came within a few inches of recording flood waters as high as in 1903.

The rains did not end. From three to five inches of rain fell in Gove County on June 17, and by June 20 the water in the Solomon River at Beloit stood at 33.24 feet above the low-water mark, or twenty inches higher than in 1903. In Sumner County, ten inches of rain fell in about six hours on June 28, drowning five people and causing thousands of dollars worth of property damage. The 1908 flooding broke all previous records for duration, and because most of the water found its way to the Kansas River and east into the Missouri River at Kansas City, the latter naturally flooded. The Missouri was out of its banks from June 8 until July 6, 1908.

Not until May and June of 1935 did Kansans experience another major flood, but it never reached the levels of 1903 and 1908. That did not happen until 1951, when record-breaking rains fell in the Kansas River basin, beginning in mid June. Business in much of eastern Kansas came to a halt. National Guardsmen were called into service, as thousands of Kansans had to evacuate their homes and businesses near the flooding streams. Whether the flood-waters were as high as those of the great flood in 1844 is not known, but damage was certainly far greater, amounting to millions of dollars in 1951.

Since that time the construction of large dams and reservoirs on the Big Blue, Smoky Hill, and several other major streams by the U.S. Army Corps of Engineers has greatly reduced the likelihood of another major flood like those of 1951, 1908, 1903, or even 1844.

# When Grasshoppers Ruled the Day

Today, grasshoppers are simply pests in the eyes of many Kansans, especially farmers, who can usually eliminate or control them with pesticides. More than a century ago, however, grasshoppers were more than just pests. And in that fact lies a story.

Grasshoppers — any of a large group of leaping, plant-eating orthopterous insects — were undoubtedly in what is now Kansas long before the white man arrived, but what may be the earliest recorded account of their presence is dated July 19, 1820. On that day, French trappers reported that grasshoppers had invaded much of what is now Kansas and Missouri.

The earliest report of grasshoppers in Kansas Territory occurred in late August, 1854. Father John Schoenmakers, who resided at the Osage Mission in what is now Neosho County, reported that grasshoppers had arrived: they "came down like a fall of snow." He reported serious damage to crops and asked for help. Help came, but so did more grasshoppers the following year. The hoppers that had come in 1854 had laid eggs, and these had hatched in the late spring of 1855, destroying all the crops and "all the grass on the prairies" in the vicinity of the mission.

The year 1860 was another bad year for grasshoppers. The *Emporia* (Kans.) *News* reported in September that the grasshoppers had arrived and were destroying

what the drought has left. Late corn, buckwheat, potatoes and
turnips are fast being destroyed. Many of our farmers are cutting their corn now for the purpose of saving the fodder. Misfor-
tunes never come singly, and Kansas has had enough of them
this year to last for several years to come. If it is true that this
is a world of compensations, we shall look for rousing crops
and unchecked prosperity in Kansas for the next five years,
at least, as compensation for the disasters of the last twelve
months.

The drought continued, however, and the grasshoppers returned in 1861. On May 21, 1861, the *Topeka Conservative* reported:

Judge Lambdin, who is just from Butler County, states that
the reports of damage done by grasshoppers are not exaggerated. The insects have traversed a belt of country about six
miles wide, devouring every green thing. Young fields of wheat
have been completely destroyed by their ravages, not one blade
remaining; early corn and vegetables and the foliage of trees
have suffered with equal severity; and the evil seems to be on
the increase, with no means of prevention.

During the years of the Civil War, more rain fell, and conditions improved across the state. Grasshoppers were reported in Colorado in 1864 and again in 1865, but none invaded Kansas. They
did return in 1866, however, especially in eastern Kansas. They arrived in Lawrence on September 14 and appeared in Leavenworth
County the following day.

When the Kansas Legislature met in Topeka early in 1867,
the lawmakers considered a bill giving a bounty for "all scalps of
grasshoppers furnished with their ears." The lawmakers were having their fun. Although a few grasshoppers were reported in Kansas in 1867, the spring was wet, and the destruction by grasshoppers was not great. Large swarms of 'hoppers were reported in the
Cottonwood River valley and were seen flying over Leavenworth
in September, 1867, and again in 1868, but there was no major
damage in Kansas until 1874.

In July, 1874, a grasshopper invasion was first reported in Jewell
County in western Kansas, and soon other reports reached Topeka,

telling that the 'hoppers were moving east. Mrs. Olive A. Clark, an early settler in the Solomon valley, recalled that the 'hoppers came "by the millions." She later recalled that

> the sky was darkened as though a terrific storm was coming, and in fact it was a storm, not of the elements but a storm of invading insects. They swooped down upon the land, and of course being vegetable feeders, and, as in all orthopterous insects, have an incomplete metamorphosis, so that the destructive powers are continuous from the moment of emergence from the egg until death, they ate every spear or twig of all green vegetation. Nothing was spared by them, not even the leaves of the trees.

At about the same time as Mrs. Clark witnessed the invasion, E. D. Haney, a homesteader in north-central Kansas, saw 'hoppers arriving in his area:

> Shortly after harvest we heard rumors of a grasshopper invasion. Strike us it did—good and plenty. The day before they arrived in our neighborhood I was down at the city of White Rock to do some trading and there was a man there from up creek over in Jewell County. He said that the hoppers were just cleaning the country of every green thing, and so many of them gathered on the cornstalks that they were breaking them down, and he could shovel up a peck at a scoop between rows.

On the next day the grasshoppers arrived in Haney's neighborhood, and he recalled that

> they began to drop down and went to work. They damaged grain in the shock soon by shelling it out. . . . Corn was completely ruined, all garden truck consumed. We had some good sweet corn and I cut it and hauled it, covered with hay, and saved some of it. We had a fine patch of onions. My wife told me I had best go and pull them. When I got to the patch there was nothing left but little round holes where the onions had been. The grasshoppers invaded the house and ate holes in the window curtains. They stayed late and laid eggs in all sheltered places.

Gradually the grasshoppers moved eastward. They arrived in Pottawatomie County, east of Manhattan, at about ten o'clock many days later. William Darnell, who had settled in Pottawatomie County in 1855, recalled that by noon "not a leaf was left on our trees. One tree that had lost its leaves and fruit put out fresh leaves and bloomed again and brought forth a small crop of small fruit late in the season."

When the 'hoppers reached Shawnee County and other areas of eastern Kansas, the destruction continued. One Topeka man, W. P. Popenoe, observed:

> They seem to cover the face of the earth. This visitation . . . was the most serious of any in the history of the state. They reached from the Platte River [in Nebraska], on the north, to northern Texas, and penetrated as far east as Sedalia, Missouri. Their eggs were deposited in favorable localities over this vast territory. The young hatched the next spring (1875), did great damage to early crops, but in June, having passed into the winged state, they rose into the air, and flew back to the northwest, whence their progenitors had come the year before.

In early February, 1876, grasshoppers from eggs that had been laid the summer before began to hatch in various areas of Kansas. By March, Alfred Grey, a Kansan, had written, published, and was selling copies of a pamphlet describing how to kill grasshoppers. One could use

> ditches and pits, rolling, nets and seines, various devices for burning, Chinese plan, guard in form of letter V, with a pit at point of intersection, constant stirring of soil, burning prairie at intervals, dragging ropes over fields of grain where lodgment had been had, etc. A constant annoyance of this kind will often cause them to abandon the field in disgust. Protection of fruit and shade trees [can be provided] by encircling the trunk with bright tin or bands of raw cotton; concussion theory.

Whether any of these methods worked is not known, but Grey did sell many copies of his pamphlet, and many people probably tried his methods.

In late April, 1877, newspapers across Kansas reported that many recently hatched grasshoppers in eastern portions of the state had been killed by other insects or, for some unknown reason, had simply died. But the grasshoppers in western Kansas did not die; they invaded the unsettled counties in early July, 1877. Since settlers had not yet moved into much of western Kansas, damage was limited to a few trees and to the short grass on the virgin plains.

By the 1880s, Kansas had gained something of a reputation as "the grasshopper state." When Kansans went to the Cincinnati Centennial Exposition in 1888, they constructed a seven-foot-high model of a grasshopper to guard the entrance to the four-story pagoda called the Wichita Building, which housed the Kansas displays. Inside there were no grasshoppers, but the building did contain samples of Kansas corn, wheat, rye, oats, cotton, and grasses that had been raised in spite of the grasshoppers.

The last decade of the nineteenth century was relatively free of grasshopper invasions in Kansas, although some damage was reported in scattered parts of the state during the summer of 1893. It was not until 1911 that another major invasion of grasshoppers occurred. The year was very dry, and by July the 'hopper invasion was causing much damage. Officials of the Santa Fe railroad even complained about the millions of grasshoppers along their line's right of way, and they asked farmers to help stop the 'hoppers.

Grasshoppers were again a problem in western Kansas in July, 1913. In fact, one Barton County farmer who lived near Great Bend said, with a twinkle in his eyes and a smile on his face, that the 'hoppers were so big that his chickens were running for shelter, thinking the grasshoppers were hawks. And a Ness County farmer said that it was nothing to see one or two grasshoppers tugging against a steer for a stalk of corn. Joking about the 'hoppers seemed to ease the pain of the destruction that they were causing.

The summer of 1919 was also a bad year for grasshoppers. The Kansas weather was hot and dry. In twenty-seven counties, farmers cooperated with scientists at Kansas State Agricultural College in Manhattan by feeding the grasshoppers with 5,500 tons of mash that contained 2,000 tons of bran, 100,000 gallons of syrup, 60,000 lemons, and a hundred tons of arsenic. The farmers reported some success in killing 'hoppers. But in the intervening years, grasshoppers have often returned, and in some years they have been cussed, swatted, sprayed, and stepped on. To many Kansans, the grasshopper has become as commonplace as the sunflower.

# Some Kansas Blizzards

Most Kansans seem to agree that fall is usually the nicest season of the year, but the pleasant falls are often forgotten when very cold winters follow. In December, 1855, temperatures dropped well below freezing, and at least two blizzards swept across much of Kansas Territory. It was so cold that between December 20, 1855, and early March, 1856, the Kansas River was "bridged with ice." Many other streams were also frozen solid.

In the following December (1856) another vicious winter storm pushed across much of the territory. A. B. Whiting had just completed the construction of a cabin northwest of Fort Riley when the storm hit. He later recalled:

> The morning was cold and raw, the wind from the north, and an hour later it began to snow. The wind came harder, the snow fell faster, and in two hours a furious blizzard was raging. The air was so full of snow that it seemed like a dense, swirling fog. I busied myself trying to make my cattle as comfortable as possible in their insufficient shelter, and then hugged my little stove in the cabin, listening to the roar of the storm outside.
>
> Night came on, and the wolves added their howling to the music of the gale. By morning the snow had stopped falling, but the north wind blew furiously for two days longer, and the cold was intense. On the morning of the third day I started for my neighbor's camp. The high wind had swept the snow from the burned prairie and piled it in immense drifts in the

ravines and sheltered spots, and I made slow progress. . . . Along
the leeward crest of a ridge, where the grass was burned, a great
flock of prairie chickens had taken refuge from the storm and
had been covered by the snow. For fifty rods the wolves had bur-
rowed after them, and the blood and feathers bore evidence of
the great slaughter and the feast they had enjoyed.

Many miles northwest of Whiting's cabin, near what is now Clay
Center, Kansas, a United States surveying party was caught in the
blizzard, and two of its members froze to death. Rivers, including
the Kansas, were again frozen solid.

Other blizzards struck parts of Kansas in the years 1863, 1866,
1870, and 1871, causing much suffering and killing much wildlife
and livestock. During the blizzard of 1871, George W. Brown, a buffalo hunter who was working near the Saline River in central Kansas, reported that his thermometer registered twenty degrees below
zero, and he added that the wind blew sixty miles an hour during
the peak of the storm. Brown told about an outfit with four ox teams,
which was carrying wood to Fort Hays and was caught in the storm:

Every man in the outfit froze to death that night; and there
was also a big Newfoundland dog froze to death. . . . There
were quite a number of other people froze to death that night,
but their names escape my memory.

Then there are the experiences of Robert W. Wright, another
Kansas pioneer who helped to found Dodge City. During the summer and fall of 1872, Wright had been freighting supplies from
Fort Dodge to Camp Supply in Indian Territory. The fall had been
mild; in fact, the weather was mild in December, and there was
plenty of grass along the route for the mules that pulled the freight
wagons. About December 20, Wright loaded some twenty mule
wagons with corn for Fort Supply. Wright remained in Fort Dodge,
and the outfit crossed the Arkansas River and went into camp that
night at Five-mile Hollow, about five miles from the post. What
happened next is told in Wright's own words, written in 1901:

It had been a warm, pleasant day, and the sun disappeared in a clear sky. Along in the night the wind whipped

around in the north, and a blizzard set in. By morning the draw that they were camped in was full of snow, and the air so full that one could not see from one wagon to the other. The men with the outfit were all old, experienced plainsmen, but the suddenness and severity of the storm rendered them almost helpless. They had brought along only wood enough for breakfast, and that was soon exhausted. They then tried burning corn, but with poor success. As a last resort they began burning the wagons. They used economy in their fire, but the second day saw no prospect of the storm letting up. In fact, it was getting worse hourly.

It was then that P. G. Cook . . . and another whose name escapes men, volunteered to make an effort to reach Fort Dodge, only five miles distant, for succor. They bundled up in a way that it seemed impossible for them to suffer, and each mounting a mule, started for the fort. The first few hours, Cook told me, they guided the mules, and then recognizing that they were lost, they gave the animals a loose rein and trusted to their instinct. This was very hard for them to do, as they were almost convinced that they were going wrong all the time, but they soon got so numbed with the cold that they lost all sense of being.

They reached the fort in this condition, after being out eight hours. They each had to be thawed out of their saddles. Cook, being a very strong, vigorous man, had suffered the least, and soon was in a condition to tell of the trouble of his comrades. Major E. B. Kirk, the quartermaster at the fort, immediately detailed a relief party, and, with Cook at their head, started for the camp. The storm by this time had spent itself, and the relief party, with an ample supply of wood, reached them without great hardship, and the entire outfit, minus the three wagons which had been burned for fuel, were brought back to the fort. Cook's companion was so badly frost-bitten that amputation of one of his limbs was necessary to save his life

Still another violent winter storm swept across much of Kansas on April 12, 1873, and lasted for three days. One homesteader, E. D. Haney, who lived in north-central Kansas, remembered that

the day had been rather mild with a rather strong south wind. Sometime in the night it shifted to the north and became very strong. It commenced to rain, then hail, sleet and snow. Such a wind! It made the shack groan and tremble. Sometime during the night it blew in the north window and the shack was filled with swirling snow. I had plenty of bedding, so I pulled the covers up over my head. In the morning I found myself completely covered with snow. I pulled my bedding out from under the snow and hung it over the joists. The shack was filled with corn up to the windows, and that kept it from blowing away.

When Haney was able to dig his way out, about three days later, he bundled up and headed for a friend's dugout, which was perhaps half a mile away. Haney found the dugout completely covered by snow. He called down through the chimney to make sure that his friend was alive, which he was. Then Haney began to dig through the snow until he had reached the door to the dugout. Haney remained with his friend until the next day, when both of them went outside and checked the homestead. Presently they heard a rooster crow. There was a ravine nearby, and Haney's friend had built a chicken coop in the ravine, but the snow had covered it. His friend believed that his chickens had died during the storm, but the two men began to dig through the snow. Eventually they uncovered all of the chickens — alive.

Of all the nineteenth-century blizzards in Kansas, perhaps the worst occurred at the beginning of 1886. The morning of December 31, 1885, dawned clear and mild across the state. The weather for Christmas had been good, better than in most years, and as Kansans prepared to welcome the new year, spring did not seem far off. But that morning a yellowish-purple tint appeared along the northern horizon. And when fleecy white clouds began to move into northwestern Kansas and the barometer began to drop, old-timers, who were wise to Kansas weather, predicted that there would be a storm.

Kansans awoke on New Year's Day to find winter on their doorsteps. Temperatures were ten to twenty degrees below zero, and the north wind was whipping fine, dry snow. By the fourth morning of the new year, everyone knew that the weather had to change, but it did not. The freezing temperatures remained, and the wind continued to blow. Drifting snow blocked all railroads in Kansas. Several eastbound cattle trains that had been caught in southwestern Kansas made it to Dodge City, a feeding station. There the animals were unloaded, but by the following morning, less than a fourth of the cattle were alive. The rest of the animals had frozen to death.

Thousands of cattle on the open range south of the Platte River in Nebraska had drifted south into Kansas with the storm. When they had reached the railroad right-of-way fence, they had stopped. They froze to death in their tracks. Years later it was a common remark in western Kansas that a person could walk along the Kansas Pacific tracks from Ellsworth to Denver—more than four hundred miles—on the carcasses of cattle that had died in January, 1886.

Those terribly cold temperatures killed countless jack rabbits, prairie chickens, deer, antelope, and birds of every description. One homesteader reported that he "counted a dozen antelope within twenty rods of my house, and . . . three came into my dooryard, within fifteen feet of my front door." They were seeking shelter. It was so cold that some western Kansas farmers who had livestock in barn stalls kept reversing the animals' positions to prevent the north side of the animals from freezing. Yet the animals' eyes, noses, ears, and hooves froze.

A few stage lines were still in operation in 1886, and they had as much trouble as the railroads did. Stages, when they became trapped in storms, often wandered miles off their routes. One Kansas stagecoach that was going from southwestern Kansas to Camp Supply, Indian Territory, arrived with its driver sitting on the box, frozen to death. The passengers had no idea that he was dead until the stage was stopped.

Residents of many towns, especially in western Kansas, used up what fuel they had. Corn was then burned. Business was suspended in most communities across the state, and schools were dismissed for nearly all of January. Finally, as the weather began to warm up, a systematic search of dugouts, shanties, and other prairie homes was made. Many people—some newspaper accounts say nearly a hundred—were found frozen to death in their homes. Thomas County, in northwestern Kansas, recorded thirty-five deaths due to the storm; most of these people had frozen to death after they had run out of fuel.

Some homesteaders survived by staying in bed for days after they had used up all of their fuel. But one Ness County family of

A train stranded somewhere in western Kansas following the great blizzard of 1886.

seven — a father, a mother, and five children — failed to survive in this manner. When searchers reached their home, they found that the family had not only used up all of its fuel, but it had also burned all of its furniture, except for one large bed, in an effort to survive. All seven had climbed into the bed to keep warm, and there they slowly had frozen to death. In northwestern Kansas, one homesteader and his team of horses were found frozen within a hundred and fifty feet of his dugout. His family, in front of the dugout's warm fire, knew nothing of his presence outside for two days. And other people — hunters, cowboys, and travelers — froze on the prairie as they searched for shelter.

One settler, in an effort to save two prize horses, took them inside his house with his family. Another man found one of his horses under a snowdrift, close to his house, so he dug a hole through the snow, then cleared a small area for the animal in the drift. The man fed and watered the horse for three days, but the animal died.

Just how many storms swept across Kansas during that January of 1886 is not known. No one really kept an accurate count. Most Kansans were too busy trying to keep warm. And the government's weather bureau was not established in Kansas at Topeka until the following year. Not lost in time, however, is the fact that the terrible winter storms of early 1886 claimed more lives and caused more damage in Kansas than have those of any other Kansas winter up to the present.

# Prairie Fires

For many Kansas pioneers, it was not Indian raids, blizzards, floods, or invasions of grasshoppers that they feared the most; it was prairie fires. The recollections and reminiscences of many pioneers, including Mrs. Clara M. Fengel Shields, attest to this. Clara Shields lived at Lost Springs, once a crossing on the Santa Fe Trail, in what is now Marion County, Kansas. In 1918 she recalled that to the southwest of her home there had been a broad sweep of unsettled prairie, with no large streams and no settlements of any size. She wrote that

> a light low down on the horizon in that direction might mean danger, and always brought anxiety. Naturally it was in the evening that it would be noticed first, and the light would seem but a few rods long. By the second evening the reflection had mounted higher in the sky and the light was brighter and longer; and as night closed in, what appeared to be a string of gold beads would lie flashing on the rim of the horizon. It was watched apprehensively, and no one slept soundly, for if the wind shifted to the direction of the light it meant a swift drawing in of the string of beads until they became shooting tongues of flame.

She recalled that the whole community would turn out to fight the prairie fires:

> They drove in wagons, taking with them barrels of water, buckets and sacks. A back fire was started usually, and the work

192

This illustration, which appeared in *Scribner's* magazine in June, 1892, shows a herd of Texas longhorns stampeding ahead of a prairie fire that had been started by lightning during a thunderstorm. Such stampedes were commonplace on the plains during the period from the late 1860s into the middle 1880s.

of beating out the flames began—a long and wearisome business; many a man had dropped exhausted from it. A fire pushed forward by a favorable wind advanced as rapidly as a horse could gallop, the flames leaping high in the air; so men, women and children worked with tremendous energy, driven by fear. They were fighting to save their homes, and sometimes even life itself, for more than one person lost his life in these demoniacal fires

Many prairie fires were started by lightning during thunderstorms, especially in dry weather, but others were started by man. In the early days it was not uncommon for Indians to start prairie fires in order to trap and to confuse their enemies. But there were also fires that were started by men who did not understand that they could not control most such fires once they had started.

Thomas F. Doran, who was born to pioneer parents in a two-room log cabin near Council Grove, grew up fully aware of the

This illustration, by Paul Frenzeny and Jules Tavernier, depicts pioneers fighting a prairie fire in Kansas. It appeared in *Harper's Weekly* in early 1874, but the illustration probably was made near Emporia, Kansas, in the autumn of 1873, when many prairie fires occurred there.

destruction of a prairie fire. In 1922 he recalled the story that had been told to him by a university professor from Virginia who had settled in Kansas to regain his health. The professor's name was William Pilcher, and he had bought a farm that had been neglected. The land was overgrown with tall sunflowers. One day Pilcher was plowing them under with a four-horse riding plow, but he found that the rough, dry stalks of the sunflowers were chafing the breasts of his horses as they pushed their way through the dense growth. Doran recalled that Pilcher

> was wholly inexperienced in the control of fire, but decided to set fire to the troublesome weeds and burn them off. He had forgotten that he had a large quantity of hay stacked on the adjoining prairie. He lighted a match in the weeds, the flames mounted high, the wind caught them, and they bounded away through the field and over the prairie. His stacks were soon black, smouldering mounds. He ran out to one of them and with a stick raked off the outer covering of black ashes. He saw the packed mass of bright, green hay beneath,

and at once dispatched his brother to the house, half a mile distant, to bring a rake to remove the ashes and fire. The rake came and he hurriedly raked the side of the stack, but as soon as the air reached the fire it burst into flames, and he saw that his effort was useless. He then looked around, and to his amazement saw that the fire had jumped the firebreak and was rapidly burning down the hedge row toward my father's stack yards, a quarter of a mile away.

I was plowing in an adjoining field and saw the danger. I unhitched the horses, procured an ax and hand rake from a near-by house, went to the hedge some distance ahead of the fire, cut an opening in the fence, raked the ground clean and started a back-fire, the flames from which were soon burning the other way, and my father's grain stacks and buildings were safe. I could not see Pilcher, so I walked past the back-fire, up the fence row, and found him in the hedge madly trying to tear away the grass and thorny brush with his naked hands. His clothes were almost torn off; his face, arms, hands and body were badly cut, lacerated and bleeding and full of broken thorns. I had difficulty in pulling the poor, crazed fellow away from his foolish and useless task and convincing him that the danger was over.

Thomas Doran, who had witnessed many prairie fires and had fought most of them, explained that they were particularly dangerous in the tall-grass region of Kansas, especially where the pioneers had constructed rail fences. These fences always led to the stack yards, where hay was kept, and to barns and buildings. Doran wrote: "The grass when killed by the frost and dried by the wind became a constant menace through fire. Fire guards were made around each farm by plowing a furrow on either side of a strip of land fifty feet wide, and mowing between while the grass was green, then burning off the hay when dried by the sun. This afforded ample protection except when the fire was driven by a gale of wind."

Doran recalled that new settlers, who were not familiar with the tall-grass country, often set fire to the grass to burn off a camping ground or to clean land for breaking, believing they could put it out when desired. Sometimes, he added, "they negligently allowed it to catch from camp fires or discarded matches and torches. They did not know, but soon learned that a prairie fire

This illustration, dated 1868, depicts a farmer plowing a fire guard in hopes of stopping the prairie fire that can be seen in the distance.

started in the wind is uncontrollable. Only a back-fire started from a road, furrow or firebreak by one of experience can turn it aside."

Doran then related some of his experiences as guidelines. He noted that the heat from a prairie fire that starts on a perfectly still day can create air currents which drive it forward toward the burning grass:

> If a strong wind is blowing it becomes a gale, and the fire a thing of terror unimaginable. The tall grass seeds out into a feathery top which burns like gasoline. The approach of a fire miles in length, driven by a gale, fills the air with suffocating clouds of smoke, ashes and burning cinders, through which leaps tongues of flame often ten to fifty feet high, making the whole heavens a fiery cauldron through which no living thing can pass. The flames jump and roll forward with terrific force and speed, driving birds, rabbits, wolves, cattle, horses, and all living things before it to safety beyond the streams or death in its seething furnaces.

Doran observed that the tops of the grass burn first and that the flame is often a hundred yards in width before the grass has burned to the ground. He wrote: "A horse of fastest speed has difficulty in keeping ahead of such a fire. Cattle caught out on the prairies run ahead of the fire until exhausted and then perish in the flames. I once saw sixty head of fine cattle that had thus burned to death. I have seen a whole community devastated by such a fire; all feed, grain and stables went up in smoke, though no houses were destroyed."

This is a list of some of the more serious prairie fires in Kansas history:

April 10, 1887: A prairie fire near Nicodemus in Graham County caused nine deaths and large property damage. The fire also swept through parts of Rooks and Phillips counties, pushed by a forty-mile-per-hour wind.

March 24, 1890: Prairie fires in southern and western Kansas destroyed thousands of dollars worth of grain, livestock, and other property. The loss in Sedgwick County alone was estimated at $150,000.

March 12, 1893: Prairie fires in Graham, Rooks, and Ellis counties caused great damage to crops and livestock. Seven persons died, and many suffered burns.

April 1, 1893: Prairie fires had been burning for two days in Rawlins and Thomas counties. Smoke and dust from fires twenty miles away blotted out the sun at Colby.

April 24, 1893: Ford County farmers around Dodge City put in claims against the Santa Fe railroad for more than $10,000 for damages that had been caused by prairie fires that sparks from locomotives had started.

March 27, 1896: One person was burned to death and great damage was done to livestock, crops, and buildings by prairie fires in Ford and Edwards counties.

November 17, 1903: Prairie fires, caused by sparks from trains, swept across portions of Wallace and adjoining counties, burning twenty thousand acres of range land between the Smoky Hill River and the Union Pacific tracks.

March 3, 1904: Many families lost their homes in prairie fires that swept across Lincoln, Russell, and Ellsworth counties.

March 27, 1905: Improvements on a dozen ranches located in Wallace County were destroyed by prairie fires.

March 1, 1906: A prairie fire swept over two thousand acres of the Fort Riley military reservation. Adjoining farms were saved by backfires.

March 23, 1910: A prairie fire near Abilene burned nine farm homes for a loss of $50,000.

March 26, 1910: Prairie fires swept through five townships in Rawlins County, causing $50,000 damages.

March 23, 1913: Prairie fires swept over Kearny, Lane, Gray, Scott, and Finney counties. Crops and farm homes were damaged, but most of the livestock were saved.

March 5, 1916: Prairie fires along the Ford-Hodgeman county line caused one death and heavy property damage. Similar fires struck parts of Clark and Grant counties, causing losses to homes, livestock, and feed. During the month of March, other prairie fires swept through areas of western and central Kansas. Thousands of acres were burned near Hutchinson, killing two people and destroying many buildings in rural areas. Near Dodge City, Miss Eva Carrier, a school teacher, piloted her fifty students to safety in a newly planted wheat field when a prairie fire swept toward and destroyed her schoolhouse.

There were many other prairie fires in Kansas during the nineteenth and early twentieth centuries. Fortunately, however, prairie fires are not the threat today that they once were in Kansas. In fact, many ranchers in the Kansas Flint Hills burn their pastures each spring to destroy weeds, buckbrush, and other woody vegetation. The grass can then grow without competition and be sufficient for their cattle. Most authorities who favor burning say that it must be done at the proper time each spring, usually during the last two weeks of April into early May. The burning of pasture land is now a cooperative effort, with ranchers helping each other.

Before they burn, they check the weather service's forecast, and they check conditions, including wind speed. The ranchers usually start burning in the morning, after the dew is off the grass. And all cattle and other livestock are removed from the pastures before the first fire is set. The ranchers then set backfires, and they move either trucks that have tanks of water or tanks that are pulled behind tractors into the area. Rural fire departments, should they be needed, can be called upon—something that the early pioneers could not do.

# Part VI

## PEOPLE, PLACES, AND THINGS

*History fades into fable.*

—Washington Irving

# The Real Birthday of Kansas

For more than a hundred and twenty-five years, Kansans have adhered to the belief that January 29 is the birthday of their state. After all, it was on January 29, 1861, that President James Buchanan signed the act that admitted Kansas to the Union as the thirty-fourth state. Nevertheless, the evidence is overwhelmingly clear—Kansas, as a state, did not officially exist until February 9, 1861.

The people of Kansas Territory were taken by surprise when Kansas was granted authority to join the Union. Their state government was not yet ready to assume control. Three months before the president signed the act, the House of Representatives had passed a bill to admit Kansas as a Free State; but the Senate, which was controlled by proslavery elements, had rejected it. Kansans apparently believed that statehood was not possible in the foreseeable future. Three weeks later, however, Abraham Lincoln had been elected president, which generated new optimism in Kansas about statehood. Many people believed that it would come after Lincoln had taken office in March, 1861.

After Lincoln's election, the political battle between Territorial Governor Samuel Medary, who leaned toward slavery, and the Free State territorial legislature became heated. Medary resigned, and George M. Beebe, the territorial secretary, was appointed as acting territorial governor by President Buchanan. Beebe, a Democrat, then proposed a scheme to smooth over the factional dif-

203

George M. Beebe, acting territorial governor of Kansas, who early in 1861 proposed that Kansas should become a republic, an independent nation.

ferences in Kansas. Beebe proposed that Kansas become a republic, an independent nation.

In his message to the territorial legislature on January 10, 1861, Beebe said: "If God in his wrath shall tolerate the worst portent of this tempest of passion, now so fiercely raging, Kansas ought, and I trust will, declining identification with either branch of a contending family, tendering to each alike the olive offering of good-neighborship, establish, under a Constitution of her own creation, a government to be separate and independent among the Nations." Most Kansans seem to have ignored Beebe's proposal, as have most historians since then. Kansans had fought too long to join the Union, so they were not about to cease their efforts to join the Union and start a nation of their own. The thought, however, is interesting, and one may imagine what might have happened if Kansans had followed that course.

Regardless, eleven days after Beebe had made his proposal, Jefferson Davis and other southern senators withdrew from the Senate, thus giving that body a Free State majority. It was then

President James
Buchanan, who
signed the bill
admitting Kansas
as the thirty-
fourth state.

that the bill to admit Kansas to the Union as a Free State was rein-
troduced. It was passed on January 21, but because of a Senate
amendment concerning the judiciary, it had to go back to the House
of Representatives, where it was passed on January 28, and on the
following day, President Buchanan signed it.

Kansans were surprised, and they were not yet ready to take
the reins of state government. In Lawrence, members of the territorial legislature, after learning that the House had passed the
measure on January 28, held three sessions per day, and they rushed
through many bills, mostly of a private nature, including incor-
porations and divorces. When they received word that the president had signed the act that admitted Kansas to the Union,
members of the territorial legislature generally maintained that
their body was legal and that Kansas was still a territory until such
time as the official notification reached Kansas.

The territorial legislature finished its business and adjourned
*sine die* on February 2, 1861. Although the measure to admit Kansas
was signed by President Buchanan on January 29, Kansans did not
receive the official notification from the federal government until
February 8, when Marcus Parrott, a Kansas territorial delegate in
Congress, arrived in Lawrence from Washington. Parrott carried

Charles Robinson of Lawrence, first governor of the state of Kansas.

with him the official notification. On the following day, February 9, 1861, in Lawrence, Caleb S. Pratt, the county clerk of Douglas County, administered the oath of office to Charles Robinson, governor-elect. It was then that George Beebe, the acting territorial governor, turned over the sovereignty of Kansas to Robinson.

Thus, Kansas was officially born on February 9, 1861.

# The Kansas River in History

On a map of modern Kansas the river that bears the same name does not appear to be very long. At first glance it seems to flow only through the eastern quarter of the state, from Junction City eastward to Kansas City, Kansas, where it joins the Missouri River. The distance is about a hundred and thirty miles as the crow flies, or about a hundred and eight-five miles as the river flows.

If one looks more closely at the map, however, the river's beginnings can be traced as far west as modern Colorado. Actually, five major rivers—the Solomon, the Saline, the Smoky Hill, the Republican, and the Big Blue—as well as many smaller streams, feed the Kansas River, or the Kaw, as Kansans sometimes call their wide and generally shallow stream.

The Solomon River and its South Fork originate in northwestern Kansas, southwest of Colby. The two forks flow eastward across the rolling plains to west of Beloit, in Mitchell County, where they join together as one—the Solomon River. That river then flows southeastward, to near Abilene, where it empties into the Smoky Hill River.

Several miles west of Abilene, another stream empties into the Smoky Hill. It is the Saline River, which, like the Solomon, has its beginnings southwest of Colby. The Smoky Hill, unlike the Solomon and Saline rivers, begins farther west, on the eastern plains of Colorado. As it flows eastward, the Smoky Hill carries the waters from the Solomon and the Saline eastward to Junction City. There

207

the Republican River, which begins in south-central Nebraska, perhaps two hundred miles to the northwest, flows into the Smoky Hill. At that spot close to Junction City, the Kansas River is formed.

The Big Blue River, which, like the Republican, originates in southern Nebraska, is the next major stream to empty into the Kansas as it flows eastward. This happens just east of Manhattan; and between Manhattan and Kansas City, two other smaller rivers—the Delaware and the Wakarusa—also empty into the Kansas River before it flows into the Missouri River at Kansas City. In all, the Kansas River is about seven hundred miles long from the source of its farthermost tributary to its mouth at Kansas City—a city that, like the river, was named for Indians who once lived in what is today eastern Kansas.

Just when the Kansa Indians first arrived in the area is not known, but scholars believe they were descended from Indians who spoke a Siouan dialect. In the 1600s, these Siouan Indians moved from east of the Mississippi and followed the Missouri River west. In time they broke up into smaller groups, one of which moved westward to the point where the Kansas River joins the Missouri. They became known as the Kansa Indians.

The spelling of their name, and in turn the spelling of the river, state, and town names, has gone through perhaps more changes than any other name in American history. Between 1650 and 1854, when Kansas Territory was established, more than eighty variations of the name appeared on maps, in books, and in the pages of journals and diaries kept by early pioneers. These variations include

| | | | |
|---|---|---|---|
| Acansis | Cansa | Cauzes | Excausaquex |
| Akansa | Canses | Caw | Kah |
| Akansea | Cansez | Chanzes | Kamse |
| Canceas | Canzan | Ercansaques | Kancas |
| Cancez | Canzas | Escanjaques | Kances |
| Canceze | Canze | Escansaques | Kanees |
| Cancezs | Canzes | Escanxaques | Kans |
| Canchez | Canzez | Estansaques | Kansa |
| Canips | Canzon | Estanxaques | Kansae |
| Cans | Caugh | Excanjaque | Kansas |

| | | | |
|---|---|---|---|
| Kansaws | Kanzau | Kausau | Konzo |
| Kanse | Kanze | Kauzau | Kunza |
| Kansea | Kanzeis | Kaw | Okames |
| Kanses | Kanzes | Kaws | Okams |
| Kansez | Kanzon | Kawsa | Okanis |
| Kansies | Karsa | Kawse | Quans |
| Kansus | Karsea | Kawza | Quaus |
| Kantha | Kasas | Konaz | Ukasa |
| Kants | Kathagi | Konsa | Ukasak |
| Kanzan | Kau | Konses | |
| Kanzans | Kaus | Konza | |
| Kanzas | Kausas | Konzas | |

Most historians and those who study languages agree that the state derived its name from the Kansas River, which in turn received its name from the tribe of Indians who lived along its banks. Yet an unsolved mystery remains. Is the present-day spelling of Kansas the correct spelling? One of the earliest spellings of the word — Cansa — is neither of Indian nor of French origin. It is Spanish, perhaps dating back to the visit of Oñate, a Spanish explorer, who visited the Indians early in the seventeenth century. Oñate called them *Escansaques,* meaning "the disturbers, the troublesome."

From *Escansaques* came the spelling Cansa or Kansa. The sound of the letter *c* being hard, like *k,* it may be assumed that early writers spelled it by ear. Spelling the word by sound is no doubt one reason for so many recorded spellings of the word. The seventeenth-century journals of Père Marquette, Robert Cavelier, La Salle, and other early explorers mention the Indians, but the spelling of the tribe's name varies in each account. Isaac McCoy, the early-day Baptist missionary, spelled the word Kanzau (Kauzaus for the plural) in a series of letters to the government in which he described the conditions of various Indian tribes in 1828.

George Catlin, the artist and naturalist, and Maj. Stephen H. Long, who crossed the plains early in the nineteenth century, both spelled the word Konza. Meriwether Lewis and William Clark, in their journals, seem to have been the first to spell the word Kansas. They were not consistent, however; they also spelled it in five other ways.

Edward Everett Hale,
author of *Kanzas and
Nebraska* (1854), the first
book written about Kansas.
In his book, Hale insisted
that the people of "Kanzas"
would eventually adopt
that spelling.

Kansas City, when it began in 1838, was called simply Kansas. It officially became the "Town of Kansas" in 1850 and the "City of Kansas" in 1853. It was not named Kansas City (Missouri) until 1889. As late as 1854, however, the year in which Kansas Territory was organized, Edward Everett Hale, a writer and minister from Roxbury, Massachusetts, wrote a book about the new territory, in which he spelled its name Kanzas. He believed that the people of Kanzas would finally adopt that spelling, but of course they didn't.

Long before the arrival of the white man, the Kansa Indians probably navigated the Kansas River in boats made of buffalo skins stretched over a light framework of wood. The seams on the boats were sewn with sinews. These watertight boats were very buoyant and were capable of carrying much weight in items such as pelts and furs.

At the junction of the Kansas and Missouri rivers, perhaps late in the 1600s, the Kansa Indians first met the "Big Knives," as their legends call the white man. These first white men probably were French. Kansa legends say that the French brought gifts and convinced the Kansa to establish trade.

Just who was the first white man to navigate the Kansas River is not known, although in 1724, members of Etienne de Bourgmont's exploring expedition may have traveled as far west as Saline or Ellsworth County in modern Kansas to make contact with the Comanche Indians. Whether Bourgmont's men navigated the Kansas River during their journey is not recorded, but they may have done so.

After the Louisiana Territory was purchased by the United States from France in 1803, President Thomas Jefferson sent Lewis and Clark to explore the new area. Their party arrived at the mouth of the Kansas River on June 26, 1804. They camped in several locations while they spent several days gathering data for maps and gaining information on French trade with the Kansa Indians.

Government records tell how keelboats were being used in 1827 to carry supplies from the mouth of the Kansas River westward to the mouth of what later became known as Stonehouse Creek, which is located about ten miles northwest of modern Lawrence. There, Daniel Morgan Boone, Daniel Boone's son, worked as a government farmer among the Kansa Indians.

In the following year, 1828, Frederick Chouteau used a keelboat to take goods up the river to a point about fifteen miles west of modern Topeka, where a trading post had been established. In 1880, Chouteau, then an old man, recalled:

> We would take a boat up with goods in August, and keep it there til the next spring, when we would bring it down loaded with peltries. At the mouth of the Kaw we shipped on a steam boat to St. Louis. . . .
>
> The keel-boats were made in St. Louis. They were rib-made boats, shaped like the hull of a steamboat, and decked over. They were about eight or ten feet across the deck and five or six feet deep below deck. They were rigged with one mast, and had a rudder, though we generally took the rudder off and used a long oar for steering. There were four rowlocks on each side.

By Chouteau's time the Kansas River was shown on maps of the region that Zebulon M. Pike and Stephen H. Long had crossed and had labeled the Great American Desert. Compared to the rich woodlands of the East, the Kansas River valley and all of what is today eastern Kansas was different. It was prairie land, but it was not a desert. The missionary Isaac McCoy wrote to the secretary of war in 1831 that what is today eastern Kansas was anything but "poor land." McCoy described the soil as "almost invariably rich."

In that same year, "Peck's Guide to Emigrants," which was published in Boston, described the Kansas River as a "large, bold, navigable river, although its fickle channel and numerous snags must forever endanger commerce." Many steamboat captains found the "fickle channel" when, in 1854, Kansas Territory was organized and the vast area from the Missouri River westward to the summit of the Rocky Mountains was up for grabs. It was then the center of the Free State versus slavery controversy. The Kansas River became interwoven with the events that followed, as steamboats flocked to the Missouri River from all the rivers of the Mississippi Valley, "like white winged-gulls to their banquet on the generous table of the sea." The steamboats were bringing settlers to Kansas Territory.

The first steamboat to ascend the Kansas River any distance was the *Excel,* in the spring of 1854. A newspaper story in the Worcester (Mass.) *Spy* in March, 1854, reported: "The steamer *Excel* has been bought for a packet in the Kansas river trade, which will be the pioneer steamer of the territory, to ply between Kansas City at the mouth and 'as high as she can get.' " The seventy-nine-ton sternwheeler, which had a draft of two feet, started upstream in April, 1854, loaded with 1,100 barrels of flour. One passenger, H. D. Meekin, later recalled, "We were two days on the trip . . . and found no more difficulty in navigating the Kansas than we did the Missouri."

In October, 1854, the *Excel* made a short exploratory trip up the Smoky Hill River with little difficulty. Word of the successful navigation spread like a prairie fire, and more and more steamboats began to ply the Kansas River. It soon became obvious, however, that only boats that had a very shallow draft could do so successfully. The distance, by river, from Kansas City to Fort Riley was about 178 miles. The successful navigation convinced some New Mexican traders that freight could be carried up the Kansas River

This late 1850s poster advertised steamboat travel on the Kansas River.

to Fort Riley, where it could be transferred to wagons bound for Santa Fe. These traders saw a savings in the cost of land transport, as well as a shorter journey over the Santa Fe Trail, by perhaps two hundred miles.

Between 1854 and 1864 at least thirty-three steamboats, with such names as *Bee, New Lucy, Lizzie, Hartford, Perry, Morning Star, Far West, Jacob Sass,* and *Kate Swinney,* plied the Kansas River at one time or another. Most of the early settlements in Kansas were along the river—cities such as Lawrence, Lecompton, Topeka, Manhattan, and Junction City; and many settlers arrived by steamboat. In 1859 the *Silver Lake* took the first load of Kansas corn down the river to Kansas City, and other steamboats carried the first wheat to eastern markets.

When gold was discovered in 1859 in far-western Kansas Territory—now Colorado—a Pittsburgh, Pennsylvania, newspaper reported that the steamboat *Col. Gus Linn* would go up the Kaw within a hundred and fifty miles of Pike's Peak. Obviously, this report was false; it was more than five hundred miles from Kansas City to Cherry Creek, now Denver, and steamboat travel was pretty much limited to about two hundred miles west of Kansas City at best.

Steamboating on the Kansas River came to an abrupt end soon after February, 1864, when the Kansas Legislature, swayed by powerful railroad interests, declared that the Kansas, Republican, Smoky Hill, Solomon, and Big Blue rivers were not navigable and authorized the railroads to build bridges across these streams. Albert R. Greene, who became Kansas railroad commissioner in 1887, later wrote that the railroads wanted the Kansas River "lawfully obstructed by bridges and destroyed as a competitor." Ironically, in the spring of 1866 a flood carried away the Union Pacific Railway, Eastern Division, bridge at the mouth of the Kansas River. The railroad chartered the *Alexander Majors,* a big side-wheeler, to carry passengers as far as Lawrence until the bridge could be rebuilt. The *Alexander Majors* was the last steamboat to ply the Kansas River.

In 1879 the U.S. Army Engineers undertook a survey to determine whether the Kansas River could be made navigable. To make it so, they reported, "would probably be of much benefit to the people living along the stream." Their report said that if dams or dykes were built, if bridges were provided with draws, if a short canal with a lock were built around the dam at Lawrence, and if the snags in the river were removed, small steamers could navigate the stream at all the lowest stages of water. The cost, aside from remodeling bridges and building the canal, was estimated in 1879 dollars at $450,000. The railroads, however, which did not want

The *Lightfoot* was the first steamboat to ply the Kansas River in the spring of 1857 after the proslavery blockade of the Missouri River had been lifted. Built in Pittsburgh, Pennsylvania, the *Lightfoot* made only one trip up and back on the Kansas River. Because of low water during the ensuing months, the steamboat entered the Missouri River trade and never again attempted to traverse the Kansas River. Drawing by Albert Reid.

to remodel their bridges or encourage competition, appear to have influenced the final decision against improving the Kansas River for navigation.

While the railroads were largely responsible for the politics of prohibiting steamboating on the Kaw, the early pioneers also had a hand in reducing its navigability, provided you believe what a veteran riverman wrote in 1908. G. A. ("Dolly") Graeber, who had been a resident of Lawrence for thirty-five years, did not claim to be a river engineer, but he spent many years watching the erosion along the Kansas River. He wrote:

> All swiftly moving rivers in their natural state, which overflow their banks, deposit more silt or soil near their shores, while little or none is deposited on the balance of the overflow. The reason for this is that the force of the current is broken near the shores, but still the water moves with some motion

which always brings in a new supply of silt which the slowly
moving water allows to settle, and of course adds to the height
of land on which it does settle; therefore the river banks were
in most cases higher than the adjoining land behind them.

In the early days of our state, before the land was taken
up and cultivated, the undisturbed processes of nature had contracted our river into its narrowest limits. Nature had jettizoned
its banks with undisturbed forests and dense thickets which
grew along its shores. This gave the stream a definite direction under high banks. The water confined in this manner had
to go somewhere, therefore it was compelled to scour out its
own channel. There was then a much narrower but deeper
river, which is proven by the navigation of the river with steamboats which ascended the river as far as Ft. Riley in the early
days, which would be an impossibility now (1908). . . .

In the last thirty-five years cultivation of the soil on the
river bottoms has gone to its very edge. The land owner in order
to do this has in the majority of cases cut away the timber on
the adjoining land, leaving a small fringe of trees along its
shores. These trees, not intended by nature to stand alone
without the support of a heavy growth of trees back of them
for a wind break, soon toppled over into the river, usually taking with them a large part of the bank also. The river here
finding a place of least resistance soon cut its way into the
cultivated field, changing its course and directing its powers
against some new point. This process has been repeated so often
without any intelligent hindrance of the land owner himself,
that at last the banks which confined it are eroded away, and
this most valuable support is taken to fill up the bed of the
stream where it does the most harm possible. The result of it
all is that we now have a river with the bottom brought near
the top and the top nearer the bottom, and a great many of
those who brought about these disasterous results are crying
most loudly for help, and blaming everything and everybody
for their injury but themselves, while the river now runs through
an alluvial valley wherever its erratic course may direct.

Graeber recalled how he had come down the Kansas River
in a skiff in 1876 from Junction City to Lawrence. "The river was
at that time well within its banks as they were still in their natural
state," he wrote. But when Graeber had traveled the same course
eighteen years later, he noted that he found the conditions much
changed, "the banks being cut on one side and long stretches of

mud flats on the other side." In 1904, Graeber again made the journey from Junction City to Lawrence on the river. He wrote that he was impressed with the "immense damage that had been done since his last trip, especially so at St. Mary's, where he found barely enough water to float a skiff in the widely distributed channel where steamboats navigated it years before, and still with this great width subject to overflow at ordinary rises in the river. This merely shows what a great mistake has been made when its depth has been sacrificed for its additional width."

While the Kansas River has contributed little to commerce in Kansas since the state's earliest days, it still remains attractive. Many trees still line its banks along its gently winding route through eastern Kansas. Fishermen still find many catfish and other varieties of fish in its muddy waters. But gone are those magic days when a whistle blast signaled a steamboat around the bend.

# Theodore Weichselbaum,
# Trader and Beer Maker

Theodore Weichselbaum was not unique as Kansas pioneers go. In many ways he was typical: he was determined to succeed, and he was one of many immigrants from Europe who found a home and made good in Kansas. While his experiences seem, in retrospect, romantic and filled with adventure, he is remembered more for a brewery that he built and for the fine German beer that he produced.

The story of Weichselbaum began when he was born in Furth, near Nuremburg, Bavaria, on June 10, 1834. At the age of twenty-two he came to the United States, landing in New York City during the summer of 1856. There he found a job in a jewelry store, where he hoped to learn English; but the store's owner spoke only German. Discouraged, Weichselbaum quit his job and became a peddler. In his daily contact with New Yorkers, he soon learned English.

One day he ran into some friends from the old country. After having arrived in America a few years earlier, they had built a small business into a large wholesale firm that manufactured clothing, which was located in Cincinnati. While they were visiting New York City on business, they offered Weichselbaum a job. Being single and anxious to make good, he accepted. He returned with them to Cincinnati, where they gave him goods and money and told him he should go west, open a store, and sell their clothing in the new territory called Kansas.

Weichselbaum arrived in Leavenworth, Kansas Territory, in 1857. But he did not like the town, so he went south to Kansas City and decided to open a store on Main Street. He stocked the small store, opened its doors, and waited for customers; but few came. He soon realized that conditions along the border were unsettled because of the Free State and proslavery troubles in Kansas. His business was so poor that he decided to go farther west, away from the troubles. After talking to several people, Weichselbaum decided to locate his store on the frontier near Fort Riley, one of a handful of military posts then scattered across the West.

Loading his goods into three wagons, Weichselbaum, with the help of a few hired hands, followed the old military road south to near Gardner in what is today Johnson County, Kansas. There he turned west and followed the Santa Fe Trail until he reached a point 110 miles southwest of Kansas City. There he turned north and followed the Mormon Trail. Mormons followed this trail north to present-day Nebraska, where they joined the Oregon Trail and traveled westward to the Great Salt Lake.

Weichselbaum and his wagons traveled north on the Mormon Trail until they reached Whiskey Point, near Fort Riley. In 1857, Whiskey Point was a small settlement that had many saloons and a few stores. "The soldiers bought whiskey there," wrote Weichselbaum, who did not stay long. He turned northeastward and followed the river for about five miles, to what was then the settlement of Ogden, the county seat of Riley County and the location of a government land office. There he located an empty log cabin, made arrangements to use it, and opened his store.

"I slept on my counter," he later recalled, and business was good. It was so good that within a few months he moved into a larger log cabin, which had a loft. There Weichselbaum slept on a bed. "In 1859 I put up my first stone building, the one in which the post office is now (1908) kept," he recalled.

In the same year that Weichselbaum built his first stone store, he was appointed postmaster. He later recalled: "My commission is dated October 26, 1859. It was signed by the President [Buchanan]. . . . I also had the post office under Lincoln and until Grant's administration, when the Republican party put me out. I was postmaster twice under Cleveland's administration."

The interior of the sutler's store at Fort Dodge, Kansas, early in 1867, when Theodore Weichselbaum had a financial interest in it. This illustration appeared in *Harper's Weekly*, May 25, 1867.

During the late 1850s Weichselbaum expanded his business interests, becoming a partner in the sutler's store at Camp Alert (later Fort Larned); and during the 1860s he became financially involved with the sutler stores at Forts Dodge, Harker, and Wallace in Kansas and Camp Supply in Indian Territory. He wrote:

> I think it was in 1868 that I opened the sutler's store at Camp Supply. . . . When Major Inman (chief quartermaster for the Western Department) and I went down to Camp Supply, soon after it was opened, we had an escort of ten Cheyenne Indians. They would always have fresh buffalo meat ready for us in camp. I traded with the Cheyennes, Arapahoes and Kiowas between the Arkansas River and Camp Supply.

He also remembered that when George Armstrong Custer was stationed at Fort Riley, Weichselbaum, at his home in Ogden, had entertained Custer and his wife.

About 1860, Weichselbaum received a governmental contract to go to Camp Alert to produce hay for the military. He recalled:

"The government allowed me sixty-five dollars per day from the time I left Fort Riley until I returned. I had about ten wagons and about ten extra hands. The men did the mowing with scythes, a half-dozen great big Dutchmen, all in a row. I cleared twenty dollars a day for my own services. I was gone thirty days."

During the early 1860s, Weichselbaum dealt with Capt. Nathaniel Lyon, who was in command at Fort Riley. Weichselbaum remembered that Lyon "would punish soldiers by making them carry two or three sticks of cordwood on their shoulders. There would always be some of these men marching up and down there. Lyon was a little fellow. He was a terrible growler. He was smart. He was a hard nut. He was an honorable man, and a good friend to me."

When the Civil War broke out early in 1861, Weichselbaum carried the first news from Fort Riley to Fort Wise, located in present-day eastern Colorado. As he remembered, it was in April of that year, and he drove an ox team.

> I took a soldier's wife out there to her husband. He was a bugler in the company. She begged me to take her out. I asked her $20 for the trip, 500 miles out and the same back, but I took some Indian goods out and sold them, so made something. In those days there was only one mail from Independence, Mo., to Fort Union, N.M. The same animals they started with had to go through the whole trip to Fort Wise.

During the 1860s, while Weichselbaum was involved in the sutler stores, he hauled thousands of buffalo robes to Leavenworth with his teams. He later wrote: "I sold them there mostly to W. C. Lobenstine, for from five to six dollars apiece cash. He made so much money from his trade there that he went to Milan, Italy, and was still there when I last heard of him enjoying the fruits of his Kansas trade."

In June, 1862, when he was twenty-eight years old, Weichselbaum married. There was little romance involved, however, for his wife came directly from Germany. As he wrote: "I had never known her nor seen her. My parents picked her out for me and sent her out. They made a good selection—the best woman that ever lived." She presented Weichselbaum with eight children, four of whom lived.

Theodore Weichselbaum as a young man.

Weichselbaum obtained merchandise in the East. He would go to St. Louis, New York, and Chicago about once a year to buy his goods, which were then shipped by steamboat down the Missouri to Leavenworth and then freighted by Weichselbaum's own wagons to Ogden. "Once," he recalled, "I think it was in the spring of 1859, I brought several barrels of whiskey and salt, heavy goods, from a steamboat that came up to Ogden [on the Kansas River] and landed the goods on the bank for me. The river was high. I think this was the only time a steamboat reached Ogden."

In his travels across the prairies and plains, Weichselbaum never had much of a problem with Indians. For one reason, he never took chances. "Whenever the Indians became hostile," he wrote, "we made our trips after dark. The Indians were afraid to tackle anything they could not see. I have driven many a night between Larned and Dodge, fifty-six miles, by myself."

In May, 1869, Weichselbaum sold his interests in the sutler's stores and turned his full attention to operating his Ogden store.

Theodore Weichselbaum, second from left, sitting in front of his Ogden, Kansas, store. This 1910 photo was taken by my grandfather, A. W. Long, a long-time friend of Weichselbaum. The woman to Weichselbaum's right is my grandmother, Laura Engel Long; the young girl to the right is my mother at the age of six. The man to the left is not identified.

Not quite two years later, in 1871, he decided to build a brewery in Ogden:

> I built a large brewery, with cellars underground, and employed four or five men, who were originally brewers in Germany and had come directly from the old country, and knew all about the making of malt. We made beer from barley and hops. The grain was raised in our neighborhood. I bought lots of barley right in the county and made malt of it. The hops I bought from St. Louis dealers.

Weichselbaum did well as a brewer; his income from beer sales grew to about a thousand dollars a month. Even though he had to pay his men and buy materials with the money, the profit was good. And he not only hauled his beer to saloons in Riley County but to other neighboring counties as well. Some of it was shipped by rail to Hays, Kansas.

On May 1, 1881, however, the prohibition law went into effect in Kansas. After ten years as a brewer, Weichselbaum was forced to close his brewery. He lost $15,000, for which he received no compensation from the state. Another brewer named Walruff in Lawrence planned to take legal action. He asked if Weichselbaum wanted to join him. Weichselbaum said: "No, I have lost enough already. I will stop where I am." And he did.

About thirty years ago there were still a few old-timers around Ogden who remembered Weichselbaum's beer. Most of them considered it very good, but they are gone now. As for Theodore Weichselbaum, he was forty-seven years old when he was forced to close his brewery. He returned to his store, which he had continued to operate.

In 1896, Weichselbaum's wife died. Four years later, in June, 1900, when Weichselbaum was sixty-six, he married Bertha Koch. For many years he took pride in the fact that he was the oldest merchant still in business in Kansas: he had operated his store in Ogden for more than half a century. On the evening of March 11, 1914, at the age of eighty, Theodore Weichselbaum died peacefully in his Ogden home.

# The Lost Kansas Cattle Town

Abilene, Dodge City, Wichita, Newton, Caldwell, and Ellsworth are well known in Kansas history as cattle towns. Between 1867 and 1886, Texas drovers trailed thousands of longhorns north to railhead towns in Kansas. There the cattle were loaded into railroad cars and shipped to eastern markets. Until recent years, however, few Kansans were aware that Waterville, in Marshall County, also was a cattle town.

This fact was uncovered a few years ago in a letter found among the files of the Missouri Historical Society in St. Louis. The letter has helped to substantiate old-timers' claims that Waterville was, at least for a time, a real cattle town, competing against Abilene. The letter was written by Mrs. R. A. Parks on June 26, 1868. On that day, Mrs. Parks was among thirty people who left Atchison on an excursion trip to Waterville, a hundred miles to the west. Only six months earlier the tracks of the Central Branch of the Union Pacific had reached the site of Waterville, which was named in honor of Waterville, New York. Mrs. Parks had followed the construction of the railroad very closely because her husband, R. A. Parks, was superintendent of the Central Branch and her father, William Osborn, was chief contractor of the line.

The Central Branch had been organized in 1859 as the Atchison and Pike's Peak Railroad Co., but the Kansas Legislature had changed the name to Central Branch in 1867. The CB, as everyone called the line, had been provided for in the acts that

225

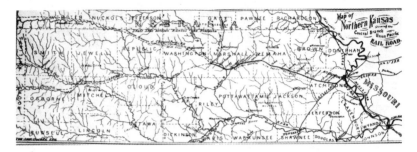

This map of northern Kansas was published in 1871. Whoever drew the map played down the importance of Kansas City and the Kansas Pacific Railroad and emphasized Atchison and the Central Branch line. Although by the summer of 1871 the St. Joseph and Denver City Railroad had pushed west from St. Joseph, Missouri, past Marysville, Kansas, the map maker omits mention of that railroad.

provided for the incorporation of the Union Pacific. And the line had received 187,608 acres of land from the government, plus bonds at the rate of $16,000 for each of the 100 miles along the line west of Atchison.

As Mrs. Parks rode west from Atchison on that June day in 1868, she was moved by what she saw. She began to record her impressions of the journey in a two-page letter that she sent to the Waterville, New York, newspaper:

> How can I describe to you the beauty, the grandeur, the freedom of these Kansas prairies? Undulating to the right and left on either side, a sea of verdure — unfenced, unbroken — unadorned, yet beautiful in their sunny repose of light and shade in their hills and hollows. They call to mind the primeval world and are a type of land given to Adam which God himself pronounced "good."

Three hours after leaving Atchison, Mrs. Parks's train arrived at Waterville. She noted that "when the railroad first reached this point, there was no settlement . . . but now there are a number of houses beside those belonging to the company, a telegraph office and a two-story stone hotel. The little Blue River with its wooded banks adds to the beauty of the site, and the never ending prairies stretch away on every side."

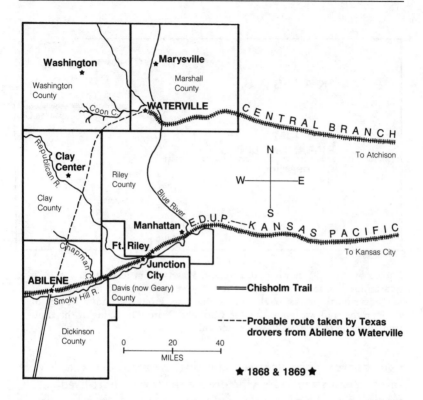

Washington
Washington
County

Marysville
Marshall
County

WATERVILLE

Coon C.

CENTRAL BRANCH

To Atchison

N
W——————E
S

Clay
Center

Clay
County

Republican R.

Riley
County

Blue River

Chapman C.

Manhattan

E.D.U.P.—— KANSAS PACIFIC

To Kansas City

Ft. Riley

Junction
City

ABILENE

Smoky Hill R.

Davis (now Geary)
County

Dickinson
County

====Chisholm Trail

-----Probable route taken by Texas
drovers from Abilene to Waterville

0        20        40
├────────┼────────┤
MILES

★ 1868 & 1869 ★

Mrs. Parks was impressed by the potential of the new town as a cattle-trading center. This was unusual, because in the late 1860s the subject of cattle was one thing that most women ignored. For some unexplained reason, however, Mrs. Parks was fascinated by it. In what is the earliest-known account of plans to make Waterville a Kansas cattle town, Mrs. Parks wrote:

> The company is now engaged in building large stockyards at Waterville for the accommodation of droves of Texas cattle which are to be driven to this point and shipped hence by rail to Chicago. During the last week the managers of the road made a contract with a large cattle drover to carry from 10,000 to 50,000 head of cattle over their line this season—which will make Waterville quite a business point at once.

How many cattle were actually shipped out of Waterville during that summer and fall of 1868 is not known; unfortunately, no

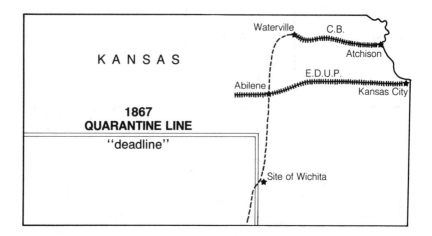

Kansas map (1868) showing Abilene and Waterville in relation to the 1867 quarantine line for Texas cattle. Drovers were not supposed to trail longhorns north or east of the quarantine line. From the Kansas border to Abilene the trail was known as the Chisholm Trail. The name of the trail from Abilene to Waterville is not known.

figures have yet been located indicating how many Texas cattle were shipped east from Waterville during the town's short-lived cattle-trading days. There is little doubt, however, that several thousand longhorns were shipped out.

Why Mrs. Parks made no mention in her letter of the quarantine, or "deadline," as the pioneers and drovers called it, is not known. The "deadline" had been established by the Kansas Legislature in February, 1867, to protect livestock from Texas fever, sometimes called Spanish fever. This was really a splenic fever caused by ticks and was spread by the immune, but tick-infested, Texas cattle. Waterville was north and east of the "deadline" and was well inside the area where the trailing of Texas cattle was prohibited.

In 1868, however, the quarantine law was of concern to few people, including officials of the Central Branch. Many Kansans thought the law was unconstitutional, "an infringement of interstate commerce," as one writer put it. Even Kansas' Governor Samuel J. Crawford did not really enforce the law in 1868. What enforcement there was came from grangers, as the Texas drovers called the Kansas farmers. The farmers resented the Texans, whose cattle trampled crops and spread Texas Fever. Sometimes the settlers would band together to enforce the law, but in the spring of 1868, Central Branch people were not concerned about having settlers interfere with Texas cattle being trailed to Waterville. The area southwest of Waterville, toward Abilene, was still free from heavy settlement. Drovers who were trailing their longhorns north from Abilene to Waterville passed mostly through country that was not settled. Then too, Joseph McCoy and the officials of the Union Pacific Eastern Division (the line became the Kansas Pacific on March 3, 1869) ignored the law at Abilene. They encouraged drovers to cross the "deadline," which was some forty miles south by southwest of Abilene, to bring the Texas cattle to market. And the drovers did cross the line. During 1868, according to McCoy, "about 75,000 head from Texas were marketed at Abilene." And many others were sold elsewhere in Kansas, including Waterville.

On July 18, 1868, only twenty-two days after Mrs. Parks had visited Waterville, the *Atchison Weekly Free Press* reported: "The 7,000 head of Texas cattle to come in over the Central Branch road are still at Chapman's Creek getting another bite of Kansas grass before starting to Chicago." Now, in 1868, the area along Chapman's Creek—the stream cuts across northeastern Dickinson County near Abilene—was considered good for cattle grazing. Waterville was only a three-days' journey to the northeast for Texas drovers who were trailing their cattle.

Why should drovers take their cattle to Waterville? Abilene was a larger market. Recalling the stories that he had heard from his father and others, D. Linn Livers of Barnes, Kansas, recalled that there were frequently shipping problems at Abilene: "Not only car shortages but also feed. The cattle grazed off all the grass for miles around." Early accounts from Abilene confirm this.

While no evidence has been found, it seems likely that the Central Branch may have had a representative at Abilene to drum up business for Waterville and the CB. One selling point undoubtedly was freight rates, which were less from Waterville to the Missouri River than from Abilene. Another plus for Waterville was the availability of feed. The area around Waterville had excellent grass. It was blue-stem country. One pioneer in the Waterville area, Peter Nelson, recalled that in 1869, "the blue stem grass was so tall

The track of the Central Branch of the Union Pacific just east of Waterville, Kansas. Cattle loading pens and two or three freight cars can barely be seen right of center in this nineteenth-century photo, which was probably made after Waterville's days as a cattle town.

that if you walked across the prairie you had to take your hands and part the grass so as to walk through it."

When they arrived at Waterville, the Texas drovers sometimes grazed their animals in the valley of Coon Creek, west of town. It was a popular holding area. Livers recalled that "it took a week or two for the railroad to get a herd shipped out, so the tired and thirsty cowboys visited Waterville, where it is reported that half the business places were saloons." While the early histories of Waterville claim only one saloon for the town, there probably were more. The first saloon in Waterville, a one-story building on Railroad Avenue, was owned by Mike Niggley. "A keg of beer, a hoop of cheese, a sack of dried apples, and a gallon of whiskey composed the first stock," according to one early history of Waterville.

Old-timers around Waterville recalled few problems with the Texans. Unlike Abilene and the other Kansas cattle towns of the nineteenth century, Waterville seems to have been rather quiet. But Livers noted that when the Texans left town, "some of the cowboys were so drunk they had to be helped from the saloon to their horses, but once in the saddle they stuck like glue."

When the longhorns were shipped east from Waterville on the Central Branch, usually on special trains, they arrived in Atchison on the same day. There they were unloaded and ferried across the Missouri River, because there was no bridge at Atchison until 1875.

Once across the river, the animals continued their journey aboard freight cars belonging to the Atchison and St. Joseph Railroad.

If any officials of the Central Branch had fears during the summer of 1868 that the quarantine, or "deadline," law might get them into trouble, those fears were alleviated by the end of July. On July 30, 1868, the Kansas Supreme Court ruled that the 1867 quarantine law was unconstitutional. This news was undoubtedly cheered by officials of the Central Branch. It meant that the "deadline" no longer existed under law and that Texas cattle could be trailed to Waterville without any fears of the law. A new problem was beginning to take shape, however: the railroad that carried the cattle east was also bringing settlers west. Settlement of the area west of Waterville in Washington County was increasing. The county's limits included at least 400,000 acres of land that was subject to homestead entries. As the settlers built their homes and planted their crops, they began to demand that Texas drovers stop trailing their longhorns across their homesteads.

It was not uncommon for settlers to take matters into their own hands with the assistance of the local "law." One such incident was reported in the *Atchison Champion and Press* in September, 1868:

> We learn from the Marysville *Enterprise* of yesterday that five men, who were driving 1,500 head of Texas cattle through Washington County, were arrested last Tuesday and taken to Washington, the county seat of Washington County, for trial. The sheriff announced a posse and went after the fellows, but did not overtake them until they reached a considerable ways into Marshall County, where he got additional help. The people along the line where those cattle have passed are very indignant, and threaten vengeance if this business is not stopped.

With more and more settlers in the area between Waterville and Abilene, the Texas drovers found it more difficult to trail their herds to Waterville and the Central Branch line. Hopeful of changing this, officials of the Central Branch sought legislation that would establish a trail over which Texas cattle could be driven without interference to Waterville.

A view of Atchison, Kansas, in the early 1870s, looking toward town from St. Benedict's College. Atchison was 100 miles east of Waterville at the eastern end of the Central Branch line, the point to which Texas cattle were shipped and then ferried across the Missouri River to Missouri and shipped east on another line.

When the Kansas Legislature convened in Topeka in January, 1869, John Fletcher Broadbent, a state senator from Mound City, introduced a bill titled "An Act to Protect Stock From Spanish Fever," a copy of which is in the files of the Kansas State Historical Society in Topeka. The bill proposed measures to protect grangers' livestock from Texas cattle; it also proposed to open a trail to Waterville, so that the Central Branch could enjoy more of the cattle business. That was the main thrust behind the proposed bill.

When its third reading came up on March 1, 1869, the House spent most of the afternoon debating the bill. But it had been so amended that by nightfall its passage was doubtful. A state representative named Tiernan then made a motion to postpone consideration of the bill indefinitely. The motion carried, and the bill died, along with any future hopes on the part of the Central Branch line for a bigger share of the Texas cattle trade at Waterville. After the defeat of the bill, the Central Branch line made little effort to entice Texas drovers to Waterville. Abilene dominated the trade, and Waterville, as a cattle town, was soon forgotten.

# Tellers and Portrayers of
# Tall Tales about Kansas

Not many years ago it was easy to find storytellers wherever you traveled in Kansas. Nearly every community had at least one good storyteller whose tall tales were enjoyed by many but were rarely believed. Today, however, it appears that tall-tale telling, or hyperbolizing, has become something of a lost art, except among politicians. No longer do you hear stories about catfish in the Kansas River that grow sacks under their chins in which to carry water should the Kaw go dry. Nor is there a farmer in Kansas who bragged last summer that he had a corn stalk so high that when he climbed to the top he could see the Rocky Mountains.

Times have changed. But residents of the Sunflower State can still be proud of the inventive skills of old-time Kansans, many of whom lived before radio, television, and other forms of canned entertainment replaced story-telling.

There was F. J. Cloud of Kingman, Kansas, who claimed that he had the most intelligent toad ever born. Cloud told how the toad knew every member of the Cloud family on sight and would follow them around like a pet dog. At night, when the toad had had his fill of insects, it would pester some member of the family until that person would turn off the light that was attracting the insects. And when the toad was happy about something, it would perform acrobatic stunts, including handsprings. Cloud said he never learned where the toad hibernated during the winter months, but it turned up regularly every spring for many years.

There was the tale told by Grant Constable of Bennington, who was a professional fisherman along the Solomon River many years ago. Constable described how he hypnotized catfish. After locating a catfish napping in the shade along the riverbank, Constable would tickle the fish. He said: "If your ears are good you can hear him purr. Just keep on tickling him until you can slip your hands into his gills, and the fish is yours."

Such fish tales were plentiful in old-time Kansas. One of the best stories was told by a fisherman along the Neosho River in eastern Kansas. He liked to recall the time when he had caught two large catfish in a net. The fisherman said he treated the fish so well that they became friendly. He rigged a harness on them, which attached to the bottom of his boat, and the catfish happily pulled his boat along the river as he checked his trotlines and fish nets.

Back in the 1880s, when blizzards were frequent in western Kansas, residents of some areas that were cut off from the outside world claimed that they waited until Ground-hog Day for help. When the ground-hogs came out of their holes to gaze skyward, they were put to work digging tunnels through the snowdrifts. Residents then used the tunnels to go for help.

The weather was often the subject for tall tales in early-day Kansas. "Give-a-dam" Jones, who lived in central Kansas during the 1890s, liked to tell how a tornado took his plow one day and "spun it 'round, 'til the hull give-a-dam land I'd laid out was plowed up slick as if I'd done it myself."

Late in the nineteenth century, a newspaper at Lakin, Kansas, reported: "Some states have high winds, but not Kansas. We have zephyrs (gentle breezes). But a two-gallon funnel flaring end windward and gimlet end downward will collect enough of a Kansas zephyr in seven hours to drill a hole in solid rock 108 feet deep. We never dig wells in Kansas. Condensed wind does it for us."

During the dust-bowl days of the early 1930s, firemen in one Kansas community told housewives with fishbowls to move the bowls out of south or west windows. The firemen warned that bubbles in the glass were likely to become magnifying glasses and would boil the water and the fish and possibly set the houses on fire.

In 1912, Abe Peters, a western-Kansas storyteller, observed:

I have seen some hard winters out in western Kansas. There are some things that an old resident learns out there from observation and experience. One is that when you are facing a hard wind to keep your mouth shut.

One day I was traveling with a tenderfoot from the East. He was a long, slender man about 6 feet 3 inches long and about 6 inches wide. He had no more meat on his bones than a fork handle and was about the most emaciated looking person I ever saw.

As I was saying, one day we started to ride across the prairie when the wind came up in our faces, blowing at the rate of a hundred miles an hour or so. The tenderfoot opened his mouth to say something to me. I heard him make a curious noise and looked around to see what was the matter and saw that he had inadvertently swallowed about six or seven barrels of wind.

He looked like an inflated air cushion and seemed to be about four times the size he was naturally. It seemed to set him sort of crazy and he jumped out of the buggy. When he lit on the ground he bounced into the air like a rubber ball and then went bounding across the prairie like a tumblewood before the wind. At the end of three miles he fell into a canyon where the wind couldn't hit him and stopped, but it was a week before he was back to his normal size.

Then there was George Evans of McFarland, Kansas, who recalled the time when, on a very hot day, a farmer decided to get a bucket of water for a yoke of oxen that he was driving. The farmer rushed to a well to get the water, but by the time he returned to the wagon, his oxen had died from the heat. When he looked at his bucket a moment later, the weather had changed. The wind had changed to the north, a cold front had moved through, and the water in the bucket was frozen solid.

When the motorcar came to Kansas around the turn of the century, Leslie Wallace reported from Larned, Kansas, that "tire" turtles were causing a great deal of trouble—they were eating tires on autos. The trouble ended when tire manufacturers put carbon black into the tires and hardened the rubber. Wallace said one man lost the heels off both shoes to a tire turtle while he was changing a tire. Kansas storytellers in the past have also told about cinder beetles, which ruined many a railroad track by eating the cinder ballast and damaging the ties and rails.

"Peach Canning Time—on the Farm" is the caption on this trick photograph, made by an unknown photographer early in the twentieth century.

A trick photograph by an unknown photographer.

"A Potato Harvest" is the caption on this fictitious photo by an unknown photographer in 1909. It was distributed by the North America Post Card Company of Kansas City.

This 1908 photo by William H. Martin depicts the size of ears of corn raised in Kansas.

Adventures on the plains of Western Kansas are depicted in this 1909 photo by William H. Martin.

"Harvesting a Profitable Crop of Onions in Kansas" is the caption on this photo by Martin, produced in 1909.

Kansas cabbage, as depicted by William H. Martin in this 1908 photo.

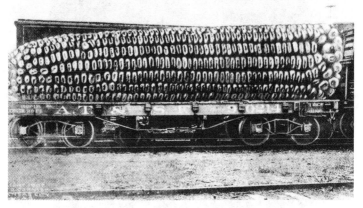

George B. Cornish of Kansas City, Kansas, produced this photograph in 1907.

"May the Best Man Win" is the
caption on this photo by F. D.
Conrad.

"Gathering Corn in Our Country"
is the caption on William H.
Martin's 1909 photo.

"I'm On My Way—I'll Be Seein' Yeh" is the caption on this photograph by
Conrad.

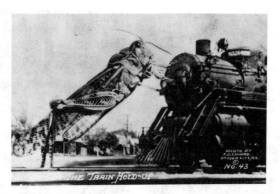

"The Train Hold-Up" is the caption on this photo by F. D. Conrad of Garden City, Kansas.

An example of a Kansas potato harvest.

"Only a Fair Sample of What Kansas Can Do When She Tries" is the caption on this fictitious photo that appeared in *Facts about Kansas*, published in 1899 by the Missouri Pacific Railway.

Perhaps the tallest of tall tales about Kansas — the teller is not identified — involved sunflowers. During the late 1860s, when the Union Pacific Railway, Eastern Division (later the Kansas Pacific) started across Kansas, sunflowers grew so high and thick that they were cut up and used as firewood. It was reported that one farmer, whose entire corn crop was shaded out by sunflowers, made a small fortune sawing up sunflower stalks for railroad ties. He also built a long barn out of sunflower stalks and kept his cow in it. The cow would wander away from time to time, so one night he tied her to a sunflower stalk. The next morning the cow was gone. The farmer looked, but he could not find her. Then he heard her bawl from up in the sky. The sunflower stalk had grown during the night, and the cow was hanging by her halter, forty feet in the air. The farmer had to chop the stalk down before he could milk that morning.

Can anyone top that story?

Tall tales have not been the only form of hyperbolizing in Kansas. During the late nineteenth and early twentieth centuries, photographers joined the storytellers and produced exaggerated illustrations that depicted everything from giant ears of corn to wagonloads of giant farm produce. These illustrations were sold as postcards. The illustrations in this chapter are a sampling of some of the better photographs of this type produced by William H. Martin, F. D. Conrad, and George B. Cornish.

# Some Kansas Fish Stories

"The Kaw River is said to be unsafe for the navigation of large-class catfish this season"—thus read a Topeka newspaper in September, 1859, as the editor commented on the lack of water in the river after a dry summer.

More than a century ago, when lakes were few and far between in Kansas, fishermen concentrated their efforts in the numerous rivers and creeks. Fishing was then not only a sport; for many pioneers it was essential. Many Kansans who lived near rivers and creeks often survived on fish, especially in hard times. Fish, especially catfish, were plentiful in the early days. They also were big. In the summer of 1859, two giant catfish were caught early one morning in the Kansas River near Topeka. The larger weighed 160 pounds and the smaller, 110 pounds. One bystander reported: "The mouth of the larger one measured, on the inside, eight by twelve inches. That fellow could carry a pretty good lunch in his head."

Not many days later, a 106-pound catfish was caught near the same spot. It was just one of many weighing slightly more than a hundred pounds that were caught in the Kansas River that summer. And the catching of the really big ones was not limited to the Topeka area. In 1865, a group of soldiers from Fort Riley were fishing with a seine — then there was no law against this — in the Republican River near Junction City. On one sweep they pulled in seven fish, each of which weighed between 40 and 105 pounds. A reporter for a Junction City newspaper saw two of the fish. One

242

weighed 68 pounds; the other one, 73. Each one measured about four feet long. The reporter observed: "These finny gunboats ply the Smoky Hill Republican, Saline, Solomon and their tributaries."

Then there is the fish story from Bachelder, Kansas. In October, 1866, a 125-pound catfish was taken from the Republican River near the town. The settler who caught the giant took it to Junction City, where he sold it to Watson and Record's butcher shop. The fish was five feet long and about fifteen or eighteen inches across at the head. Not quite a year later, another giant was pulled in from the Smoky Hill River near Junction City. It weighed 120 pounds, and it also ended up in a Junction City butcher shop.

Rocky Ford Dam, just north of Manhattan on the Big Blue River, was an especially good fishing spot. In 1870, one Manhattan newspaper editor wrote: "People from all the country gather there for the sport. Some very large ones have been taken lately. Mr. Thomas Hair, from Wild Cat, took about 400 pounds a few days ago. On Thursday, Messrs. Jenkins, Horton Elder and A. M. Tyler made a visit to the dam, and returned with about 100 pounds of fish. The largest cat weighed 48 pounds. They left a 20-pounder at "our hourse." . . . baked catfish is good."

For some fishermen, pulling in a giant catfish could be dangerous. In April, 1871, Harry Pipher of Manhattan went fishing in the Kansas River. After quite a struggle he pulled in a 40-pound catfish, which almost pulled him into the water. Harry himself weighed only 56 pounds.

Well into the early twentieth century, some Kansans fished for a living. Meat markets offered catfish along with beef, pork, lamb, and, in the very early days, buffalo meat. When a hundred-pound catfish was taken from the Kansas River at Lawrence in the late 1870s, the fisherman sold it to Kretsinger and Timmons's grocery store. The fish's head was on display for several days. A bragging newspaper editor said the fish was so big "you have to go in at the back door of the store to get out at the front, the thing's snute sticks a good ways across the street."

The King brothers found river fishing so good near Manhattan in 1869 that they formed the Manhattan Fishing Company. During the several years that they seem to have remained in business, their giant catches included a 131.5-pound catfish, another that

Doug Smith used a hoop net to pull this 120-pound catfish from the Kansas River between Lawrence and Eudora, Kansas, in 1915.

weighed 89 pounds, several in the 60-pound range, and countless other "cats" of lesser weight.

During the late nineteenth century, fishermen often used grab hooks to catch the really big catfish; but like seines and nets, grab hooks are illegal today. Several years ago the late Phil Ernst, Sr., who owned a hardware store in Lawrence, told the story about Abe Burns, a Lawrence fisherman during the 1890s. Burns, said Ernst, liked to strap a grab hook to his wrist, dive into the water near the Bowersock Mill at the dam on the Kansas River in Lawrence, and try to hook the big catfish that lived under the dam and the mill. Ernst recalled that

> old timers around Lawrence said the big catfish under the mill and the dam were like hogs in a hog lot. Burns would dive into the muddy water and go under the wooden dam or back under the mill. He had to feel around for the big catfish. When he found one he would try to hook it. If he did, Burns would tug on a line. A man on shore would help Burns pull the fish in.

Abe Burns, left, and Jacob Washington display two blue catfish, sometimes called Mississippi channel catfish, caught in the Kansas River at Lawrence early in the twentieth century. The fish at left weighed 90 pounds, the other, 110 pounds.

An early Lawrence newspaper story leaves little doubt that other men, long before Abe Burns, had used grab hooks to catch the big catfish. The *Lawrence Journal* for June 13, 1884, reported that on the day before, a Lawrence man named George Potts had drowned in the Kansas River while fishing with a grab hook. According to the newspaper account, Potts had made several attempts to catch a big fish by diving underwater with a grab hook attached to his wrist. When, five minutes after making his last dive, Potts had not come to the surface, a young boy on shore, who was holding Potts's line, called for help. Several men were trying to pull Potts to the surface, but before they could get Potts to shore, the line broke. Potts sank again, and it was an hour before the body could be recovered.

Whether the early-day catches with grab hooks were channel catfish, flatheads, or blue catfish is not recorded. Old-timers simply called them catfish. Professor Frank Cross, curator of fishes at the Museum of Natural History at the University of Kansas, believes that most of the catfish that were caught with grab hooks were flatheads: "They are usually found under such dams as on the Kansas River in Lawrence, at Rocky Ford on the Big Blue and elsewhere. Then too, it's hard to wrestle blue catfish. They're too quick. Flatheads are more docile."

It seems quite possible that many years ago, blue catfish may have run up the Kansas River to the Big Blue and the Republican rivers. Cross said that frequent floods would have enabled them to swim over the low mill dams then. With flood-control dams today, however, the fish do not have a chance to swim very far upstream in the Kansas River. They are stopped by the dam in Lawrence, he said.

Cross pointed out that the largest catfish is the blue species, sometimes called the Mississippi channel catfish. Early in the twentieth century, blue catfish were found mostly in the lower Kansas River below Lawrence and along the lower Marais des Cygnes River. These fish probably came to Kansas by way of the Missouri River. Their home is on the lower Mississippi River and its tributaries. Tradition has it that they arrived each summer, about June, probably to spawn, according to Cross; but he added: "The giant blue catfish are now rarely found in the Kansas River. Most of them were depleted from Kansas streams by 1920, probably because of commercial fishing."

The blue catfish may be gone from Kansas, but the fish stories remain, including the one about what is believed to be the largest fish ever taken from the Kansas River. It was a "shovel-nosed cat"— which is actually a paddlefish but is often referred to colloquially as a catfish—that was caught at Lawrence on April 11, 1877. A Lawrence newspaper reported that the fish had a "guessed-at-weight" of 250 pounds.

# "Bear" Facts about Kansas

In the summer of 1809 the St. Louis Missouri Fur Company sent an expedition of 150 men up the Missouri River from St. Louis to trade with Indians. When the expedition's ten flatboats, which were loaded with trading goods, reached the point where the Kansas River flows into the Missouri, the expedition moved up the Kansas River. Near what is now Manhattan, Kansas, members of the expedition traded with the Kansa Indians. One member of the expedition, a physician named Thomas, kept a journal of the trip, and in it he wrote that the country abounded with game, including black bears. His account is one of the earliest to mention the presence of bears in what is now Kansas.

As more and more white men ventured west during the first half of the nineteenth century, they left accounts of other sightings of bears. In 1812, members of a trading expedition killed three black bears in one day just north of where Leavenworth, Kansas, stands today. And in 1818, the year when the first U.S. military post was established on what is now Kansas soil, a post that was located north of modern Fort Leavenworth, the handful of soldiers who were stationed at the post survived by killing wild game, including many black bears.

Black bears, however, never roamed over all of what is now Kansas. They pretty much limited their range to the wooded areas of the eastern two-thirds of the state. Black bears stayed away from the treeless prairies and plains where the buffalo roamed. It was

247

there, in open country, that the grizzly bear survived by following the buffalo herds and preying on the weaker shaggies.

In 1824, one trapper, O. J. Pattie, killed a rare albino grizzly a few miles northwest of where present-day Salina, Kansas, is located. Pattie wrote in his journal: "He [the grizzly] had killed a buffalo bull, eaten part of it, and buried the remainder. When we came upon him he was watching the spot where he had buried it to keep off the wolves, which literally surrounded him. His claws were four inches long and very sharp."

Although Cheyenne Indians would occasionally organize a grizzly-bear hunt, more often than not they left bears alone. The Cheyenne, along with other plains Indians, knew that grizzlies were powerful animals, afraid of no living creature, and few Indians wanted to tangle with one.

Col. Richard I. Dodge, who spent many years on the frontier, recalled much later that a "grizzly will always run away if he can, and never attacks except when wounded, or when he thinks himself cornered. The female will occasionally attack in defense of her young, but more generally runs away and leaves it to its fate." Dodge remembered having seen only one grizzly on the plains of what is now western Kansas: "He ran like a deer. I pursued on horseback; but, after an exciting chase, he escaped into a beaver dam thicket, from which it was impossible to dislodge him."

By the early 1870s, however, few grizzlies remained in western Kansas. Those that had not been killed retreated to the Rocky Mountains or northward onto the rugged plains of western Nebraska or Dakota Territory. Black bears, however, have survived much longer in Kansas, in spite of the fact that many early settlers in eastern Kansas became fond of smoked bear hams, and bear hunting became a popular sport.

Black bears sometimes wandered into the new frontier towns. In late June, 1859, a large black bear slowly walked into Atchison during a thunderstorm. The *Atchison Union* reported that the bear "was attacked by some fifty dogs near the corner of 5th and Commercial street, and finally succeeded in making his escape through the western part of the city. Probably bruin saw the elephant, and returned to the rural districts satisfied."

In July, 1861, John J. Greenhalgh of Madison Center, which is located on the Verdigris River about twenty miles south of Emporia, Kansas, saw two young bears while he was on his way to Emporia with the mail. The *Emporia News* reported that Greenhalgh

> pursued the animals for some distance, but being entirely unarmed he was unable to capture either of them. Several times he came within five or six feet of the bears, when they would stop, turn on him, and throwing themselves upon their hind feet, evincing a desire to give him a "hug" which he would not soon forget. He drove them half a mile or more in this direction, but they finally made their escape through the tall grass.

Between 1864 and about 1866, J. R. Meade, an old-time hunter, trapper, and plainsman, found many black bears in the broken canyons of Comanche County in south-central Kansas, near Coldwater. The bears, which perhaps had been forced westward by white settlement, were rearing their young in dens located in the gypsum caves. Meade would smoke the bears out of the caves to kill them for meat.

Although a few black bears reportedly reached five hundred pounds in weight, most of them weighed three hundred pounds or less. The *Manhattan Standard* reported in November, 1868, that a black bear weighing about two hundred pounds had been killed by Orlando Legore in the vicinity of Timber City, which was in Pottawatomie County.

Black bears seem to have survived in large numbers in eastern Kansas as late as 1880, but after that date their number dwindled. Kansas is still bear country, however. In 1970, at least one black bear was sighted in heavily wooded country in southern Douglas County, and there have been reports of others having been sighted in woodlands close to major streams in eastern and, especially, southeastern Kansas.

Most authorities believe that the animals move north from northeastern Oklahoma or northwestern Arkansas by following major waterways, especially the Grand River, which becomes the Neosho River in Kansas. The black bears follow the rivers, sticking close to the woodlands that, in most instances, line the river banks. In this manner they usually avoid detection by man, although occasionally a hunter or outdoors man or farmer will spot one and report it. Unfortunately, by the time that officials of the Kansas Fish and Game Commission arrive on the scene, the bear has usually disappeared, so the report cannot be confirmed.

As of 1987, there were no laws in Kansas against hunting bears. Perhaps because of this, some game protectors choose not to discuss how many bears there may be in eastern Kansas. In 1986, Bob Nease, a Kansas Fish and Game protector who lives at Hugoton, in far southwestern Kansas, talked freely about a black bear that wandered into that area from Colorado:

> The bear was first sighted (early May 1983) about nine miles north and fifteen miles west of Elkhart. Later it was again sighted about eleven miles north and seven miles west of Elkhart. . . . The final sighting and capture was made just northeast of Elkhart, along U.S. highway 56, the capture being made about one-half mile south of the highway.

The bear, an adult male, weighed about two hundred and fifty pounds, and he led the lawmen and others on a merry chase through several fields until Joe Dougherty and Gary Grice mounted their horses, gave chase, and roped the animal. A wire-cage trash trailer that belonged to Panhandle Eastern was brought to the scene, and the bear was transported to the Morton County Fairgrounds for all to see. Later the bear was turned over to Colorado Fish and Game people, who released it in rugged country near La Junta, Colorado.

# When Every Town
# Had a Band

On the night of August 20, 1863, a group of musicians that called itself the Lawrence Band serenaded the citizens of Lawrence. Its members included Joseph Savage from Vermont, his brother, two cousins, and a handful of musicians who had settled in Lawrence. This was to be their last concert together. On the next morning, Quantrill's Raiders laid waste to Lawrence. By the time Quantrill and his men left, three members of the band had been wounded. One of them, the band's director, later died.

The Lawrence Band, like others that later developed in Kansas, was a symbol of culture. The pioneers loved band music. And during the nineteenth century, nearly every Kansas town, large or small, had a band. A band represented civilization.

The Lawrence Band is considered to have been the first truly Kansas band, although the U.S. Army reportedly had had a band at Fort Leavenworth before Kansas Territory was established. The Lawrence group reorganized after Quantrill's raid and continued to play concerts until 1879. In September of that year the band played its last concert at the old settlers' meeting at Bismarck Grove, north of Lawrence.

During the 1870s and 1880s, as the settlement of central and western Kansas increased, bands were organized in nearly every community as soon as enough musicians had arrived. Brass bands, most of which had eight to fifteen members, became as common as a town well on Main Street or the hitching posts in front of the

The Dodge City Cowboy Band in about 1886. A few members were actually cowboys, but most of them were businessmen and residents of Dodge City.

Fifteen Kansas bands posed for this photo on the steps of the Statehouse in Topeka in 1882. They had participated in a band contest held during a soldiers' reunion. The Dodge City Cowboy Band is at the upper right.

The Chetopa, Kansas, town band in the early 1890s. The thirteen members are posing in front of a local eating house.

The ten-member La Crosse, Kansas, band in about 1886.

The Cheney, Kansas, cornet band in 1884.

post office and the blacksmith's shop. And it did not take much to get a bandsman to don his uniform, get his cornet or bass drum, and march down Main Street.

Of all the brass bands in early-day Kansas, the most unusual was the Dodge City Cowboy Band. Chalkley M. ("Chalk") Beeson organized it in about 1881. Within a few months it had twenty-five members and was described by one Dodge City newspaper as being "the band of the land, of which Dodge may justly be proud." During the summer of 1882 the Cowboy Band performed in the evenings in front of the Long Branch Saloon or on the balcony of the Opera House. Late that summer the group was invited to enter a music contest at a soldiers' reunion in Topeka. The townspeople raised money for the trip, and the band went to Topeka, where it made a good showing. One newspaper reported that "their rigging presented a peculiar appearance, dark shirt with leather breeches full of stitches, together with revolvers buckled on making up the uniforms."

During the ensuing years the Dodge City Cowboy Band became well known from Texas to the Dakotas and from Denver to Kansas City. In 1884 the band went to the cattlemen's convention in St. Louis, where it was a great success. A reporter for one St. Louis newspaper observed:

> The appearance of the band was gorgeous. It was wild; it was ne plus ultra, sui generis, and superb. The inseparable gray slouch hat with a band inscribed "Cowboy Band of Dodge City, Kansas" and bearing also the picture of a steer, each hat having a different brand. . . . A flannel shirt, leather leggings of a conventional type, bandana handkerchief around throat, belt with a 6-chambered ivory-handled revolver and fierce spurs completed the genuine cowboy outfit.

A newspaper reporter for another paper noticed the band's leader swinging his gun as he directed the group.

> "What do you swing that gun for?" asked the reporter.
> "That's my baton," was the answer.
> "Is it loaded?" asked the reporter.
> "Yes," replied the leader with a smile.

"What for?"

"To kill the first man who strikes a false note."

During the years that followed, the Dodge City Cowboy Band appeared at every cattlemen's convention, plus the Kansas City Exposition in 1887. Then, in 1889, the band went to Denver and presented a concert in the Tabor Opera House. Profit from the band's performances was used to pay the group's way to Washington, D.C., where the band performed at the inauguration of Benjamin Harrison. For more than fifteen years the band continued to perform in Kansas and across the nation. But times were changing, and in 1905 the Cowboy Band disbanded.

Although the Dodge City Cowboy Band was the best known, it was not the only cowboy band in Kansas. G. C. Gillett of Woodbine, a Dickinson County rancher, organized a band among his cowboys in early 1895. Gillett bought the instruments and the uniforms. The band accompanied him on cattle-buying trips.

The period between 1890 and 1920 might be described as the era of cornet bands in Kansas, for such groups were very common. The Kansas Band Association was formed, and the size of the bands began to grow in such cities as Topeka, Lawrence, Manhattan, Emporia, and Wichita. It was also the period of Sousa marches, which were very popular. John Philip Sousa made several trips to Kansas with his band.

Kansas produced many excellent bandsmen during the period. By the early twentieth century, there were four Kansans in Sousa's band—V. R. Eychner of Jewel City, K. J. Henney of Hanover, E. W. Nelson of Courtland, and E. L. Miller of Randall.

By the middle 1920s, however, most of the pioneer bandsmen in early-day Kansas were gone. Still, the traditions that they had established have not been forgotten. In many Kansas communities, local bands still exist. And during the summer months the music of John Philip Sousa and others breaks the stillness of a warm summer evening in many a city park or around a town square. Kansans continue to enjoy a tradition that was established by their forefathers.

# NOTES AND CREDITS

# PART I

### William Becknell, Father of the Santa Fe Trail

Becknell's newspaper notice that announced his planned trading journey appears in the *Missouri Intelligencer,* Franklin, Mo., June 25, 1821. Nearly two years later, the April 22, 1823, edition of the Franklin newspaper published a firsthand account of Becknell's journey. This is the basis for "The Journals of Capt. Thomas Becknell from Boone's Lick to Santa Fe, and from Santa Cruz to Green River," which was edited by F. A. Sampson and was published in the *Missouri Historical Review* 4 (1910): 65–84. The closest thing to a biography of Becknell is Larry Beachum's *William Becknell, Father of the Santa Fe Trade,* a monograph published by Texas Western Press, El Paso, in 1982. It is especially valuable concerning Becknell's life after his days on the Santa Fe Trail. A longer account of Becknell's role in opening the Santa Fe Trail appears in my book *Entrepreneurs of the Old West,* published by Alfred A. Knopf, Inc., New York City, in 1986.

### Indian Trails and Isaac McCoy

This story is based on an article in the *Lawrence Republican Daily Journal* for March 28, 1869, which was written by an unidentified white man at the request of J. C. Trask, an early Lawrence newspaperman. The author may have been either Marston G. Clark or John Campbell, government sub-agents with the Indians during the early 1830s. Both men accompanied Rev. Isaac McCoy on his journey. In the introduction to the 1869 article, the editor of the paper noted: "We have heard it stated that some excavations made upon Mt. Oread, by our earliest settlers, revealed human remains that had evidently been exposed to fire." Those excavations were made about

256

1859 on or near the spot where Old North College stood, the first university building in Lawrence. I included this story in my book *Lawrence, Douglas County, Kansas: An Informal History* (Lawrence: Allen Books, 1982).

## Martias Dias's Escape across Kansas

The principal source, as mentioned in the story, is the article that appeared in the *New Orleans Weekly Picayune* for June 13, 1842, page 1. By-lines were not used by newspapers in that period; therefore the author of the article is not known. Reference to a Martias or Matias Dias with the Texas Santa Fe expedition may be found in Thomas Falconer's *Letters and Notes on the Texan Santa Fe Expedition* . . . (New York: Dauber & Pine Bookshops, 1930), page 40. And material concerning the spring caravan of traders bound from Independence, Missouri, for Santa Fe may be found in the *Daily Missouri Republican* for May 9 and 11, 1842.

## Seth M. Hays and Council Grove

Bits and pieces about Seth Hays's early years can be found in Louise Barry's *The Beginning of the West: Annals of the Kansas Gateway to the American West, 1540–1854*, published by the Kansas State Historical Society, Topeka, in 1972, pages 383, 537, 570, 671–72, 740, 1059, 1138, 1153, and 1206. Additional information may be found in Lalla Maloy Brigham's *The Story of Council Grove on the Santa Fe Trail* (Council Grove, Kans.: n.p., 1921). Brigham drew from a history of Council Grove that had been written by her father, John Maloy, a newspaperman. His history appeared in newspaper form in 1876, in 1886, and again in 1891. I used the 1886 edition, which appeared in the *Cosmos,* published in Council Grove. George Ruxton's account may be found in his book *Adventures in Mexico and the Rocky Mountains,* published in New York City in 1848 (see page 292). Seth Hays's freighting figures may be found in the *Kansas Historical Collections,* volume 11, page 533; and the quote from Wilson Hobbs appears in volume 8 of the *Collections,* pages 258–59.

## When Horace Greeley Followed Kansas Trails

Horace Greeley's own letters were the source for most of this story. First published in the New York *Tribune,* his letters were later reprinted in book form under the title *An Overland Journey, from New York to San Francisco, in the Summer of 1859* (New York: C. M. Saxton, Barker & Co., 1860). In addition, Martha B. Caldwell, a member of the staff of the Kansas State Historical Society, wrote an informative article on Greeley's visit to Kansas. Her article appears in the *Kansas Historical Quarterly* 9 (1940): 115–40. Her article provided the modern locations of the various stage stations that Greeley visited.

### Lizzie Johnson Williams,
### the First Cow Woman to Come up the Trail

Much material can be found in volume 50 of the *Southwestern Historical Quarterly* (1947), pages 349–66, in Emily Jones Shelton's article "Lizzie E. Johnson: A Cattle Queen of Texas." I have emphasized the Kansas aspects. Lizzie's story is also sketched in Evelyn King's *Women on the Cattle Trail* and in the *Roundup*, which was published in 1983 by the Brazos Valley Corral of the Westerners, College Station, Texas. Lizzie's contribution to early Kansas history apparently has been ignored by most Kansas historians.

## PART II

### Outlaw's Treasure in Cowley County

Background on Bill Doolin's life may be found in Bailey C. Hanes's fine biography titled *Bill Doolin Outlaw O. T.*, first published by the University of Oklahoma Press, Norman, in 1968. A few bits and pieces relating to Doolin and his alleged treasure may be found in the *Burden* (Kans.) *Times* for December 11, 1947. From all indications this treasure legend is based more on speculation than on any factual documentation. Like so many tales about treasure, this one seems to have been born through someone's wishful thinking.

### Entangled Legends about Treasure in Ellis County

A modern account of the two tales, told as one, is Jack Chegwidden's article that was published in August, 1961, by the *Hays* (Kans.) *Daily News*. The story was picked up by the Associated Press and was carried across Kansas. The article appeared under the headline "Gulches Hold Secret of Missing Cash" in the *Topeka Capital-Journal* for August 27, 1961. Chegwidden based his story on historical notes owned by Mrs. Vic Martin Roth of Hays and compiled by C. J. Bascom of Ellis. Kittie Dale sought to correct the error in an article titled "Glitter Gulch Has Vanished," published by the *Hays Daily News* for December 19, 1965. Dale cites as her main source C. J. ("Cal") Bascomb, whose notes were used earlier by Chegwidden but with different results. Details concerning the Big Springs, Nebraska, train robbery and the outlaws who were involved may be found in Wayne Gard's fine biography titled *Sam Bass* (Boston and New York: Houghton Mifflin Co., 1936).

### The Treasure Legend That Wasn't

As related in the story, this tale appears in Matt Thomson's *The Early History of Wabaunsee County, Kansas . . .* , published at Alma, Kansas, in 1901. The chapter containing the tale is titled "The First Log House" and appears on pages 141–45. Samuel B. Harvey's letter was written on February 10, 1903, to Stephen Jackson Spear. Spear's subsequent account was written later in 1903. Both documents are in the manuscript section of the Kansas State Historical Society in Topeka. Additional background concerning the early settlement of the area may be found in Spear's "Reminiscences of the Early Settlement of Dragoon Creek, Wabaunsee County," which appears in volume 13 of the *Kansas Historical Collections*, pages 345–63, published in Topeka in 1915. Spear was born in Connecticut in 1838 and died in Burlingame, Kansas, in 1904. He first settled in Wabaunsee County in 1858. In 1865 and 1866 he served in the Kansas Legislature.

### The Missing Indianola Treasure

The primary source for this tale is the undated newspaper story headlined "Like Capt. Kidd: Buried Treasure Said to Have Been Dug up Near Ancient Indianola, on the Old Military Road . . . ," published by the *Topeka State Journal* in 1893. The otherwise undated story may be found in the library of the Kansas State Historical Society, Topeka, in a newspaper clippings book. Background information on Indianola may be found in volume 12 of the *Kansas Historical Collections*, page 427.

### Legends of Treasure in Morton County

I first ran across the story of the Illinois traders in an article published by the *Kansas City Times* on March 9, 1953. It is the only source for the tale that I have located thus far. The other story concerning the robbery is contained in an old undated newspaper clipping in my collection. Good background information on the Point of Rocks Ranch may be found in a brief history of Morton County published by the *Morton County Record*, June 3 and 10, 1949, and in Rev. R. L. Wells's article titled "Point of Rocks Ranch," in the *Elkhart Tri-State News* for February 16, 1961.

### Abram B. Burnett's Treasure

Reference to the legend about Abram B. Burnett's treasure may be found in an article written by Clara Francis, librarian at the Kansas State Historical Society in Topeka. Her article, including a biographical sketch of Burnett, was written in about 1914. It appears in volume 13 of the *Kansas Historical Collections*, pages 371–73, published in Topeka in 1915. Additional information on Burnett may be found in Louis C. Laurent's article titled "Reminiscences by the Son of a French Pioneer," ibid., pages 364–70.

### Legends about Treasure in Lincoln County

The story about the Meyer brothers was carried statewide by the Associated Press on November 22, 1930, and appeared in many Kansas daily newspapers that day. The tale about the buried military payroll was published in the *Kansas City Times* on March 9, 1953. The payroll story was simply reported as a traditional tale that was told in Lincoln County, yet it does not appear in the late Dorothe Tarrence Homan's fine and very complete history of the county titled *Lincoln—That County in Kansas,* published in 1979. The author wonders if the incident has any basis in fact. If true, the incident may have occurred in a different Kansas county to the west or southwest of Lincoln County, where several streams are also named Cow Creek on early maps.

### The Devil's Den Treasure

The Chicago newspaper account appears in the *Blade* for Saturday, February 24, 1923. An interesting summary of the history of Devil's Den was compiled by June Van Dyke and was published under the title "Coyotes Only Inhabitants of Famed Natoma Caves," in the *Wichita Eagle-Beacon* for February 9, 1964. Rich Meyer, a native of Natoma, read my account. He observed: "I have heard these stories. I don't know of anyone who places much credibility on them."

### The Mysterious Iron Box in Sedgwick County

Brady DeVore of North Platte, Nebraska, is the source for this story. We exchanged several letters during 1985 and 1986. A review of early Wichita newspapers failed to produce any information relating to a robbery involving an iron box, as described in the tale, or of anyone's having reported the loss of such an iron box in the vicinity of Wichita during the early 1880s.

## PART III

### Bloody Bill Anderson

Perhaps the best source for information relating to Anderson's early days in Kansas is O. F. O'Dell's recollections, which are tucked away in volume 1 of Charles R. Green's book titled *Early Days in Kansas along the Santa Fe Trail.* Green's book, one of a series, was published in Olathe, Kansas, in 1912. Perhaps only a hundred copies were printed. O'Dell's recollections were written in March, 1888, and may be found on pages 48–51 in Green's book. They were sent to Green by O'Dell, who then was living in Allerdice, Montana. The *Eighteenth Biennial Report,* published by the Kansas State

Historical Society in 1913, contains a description of Agnes City and some background on the community (see page 111). Additional information on Agnes City may be found in the *Kansas Historical Collections,* volume 4, page 716, published in Topeka in 1890. A. T. Andreas's *History of the State of Kansas,* published in Chicago in 1883, contains a version of Anderson's Kansas adventures that is slightly different from the one told by O'Dell. And there also are differences in Matt Thomson's telling of the story in his chapter "A Raid by Bill Anderson," in Thomson's book *The Early History of Wabaunsee County, Kansas,* published in Alma, Kansas, in 1901.

### Dutch Henry, Horse Thief

The story of Dutch Henry Born was pieced together from many sources, including the *Topeka Daily Commonwealth,* June 15 and September 5, 1876; *Hays* (Kans.) *Sentinel,* June 21, July 6, September 6, 20, 27, October 4, and November 29, 1876; the *Ellis County* (Kans.) *Star,* June 22, 1876; *Rocky Mountain News* (Denver, Colo.), January 3, 1879; *Dodge City* (Kans.) *Times,* January 4, 7, 11 and 14, 1879; and Frank M. Lockard's *The History of Early Settlement of Norton County, Kansas,* which was published by the *Norton Champion* in 1894. Lockard's account provides a detailed summary of Born's background and his activities in 1878. Material on Born's involvement in the Battle of Adobe Walls came from T. Lindsay Baker of the Panhandle-Plains Historical Museum in Canyon, Texas. Baker uncovered much material on Henry Born while doing research on the Battle of Adobe Walls. His material is on file at the museum in Canyon and can be found in *Adobe Walls: The History and Archeology of the 1874 Trading Post,* written by Baker and Billy R. Harrison and published in 1986 by Texas A & M Press. The material includes two letters that were written to Baker by Born's surviving daughter, Mrs. Mabel L. Bennett of Pagosa Springs, Colorado, and Born's letter to Charles Siringo, dated July 6, 1920. Copies of these letters are in my files. There is something of a mystery surrounding Henry Born. While the evidence is very strong that he fought in the Battle of Adobe Walls in June, 1874, the *Ellsworth* (Kans.) *Reporter* for June 18, 1874, tells about a man who was identified as Henry Born being wounded by lawmen near Ellsworth, taken to Hays City, and later turned over to federal marshals in Topeka. It is possible that the man who was arrested near Ellsworth in June, 1874, was not the really Henry Born but was an impostor. At the top of Henry Born's 1920 letter to Charles Siringo, Siringo added a note: "This is the Dutch Henry who was at the head of about 300 horse thieves." It is possible that some members of his gang claimed to be Dutch Henry. The life of Henry Born deserves more study.

### The Rescue of John Doy

The source for this story is Doy's own little book titled *The Narrative of John Doy of Lawrence, Kansas*, published in New York City in 1860. I included John Doy's story in my book *Lawrence, Douglas County, Kansas: An Informal History*, which was published in Lawrence by Allen Books in 1982.

### The Most Violent Town in Kansas

Much of what is known about Phil Sheridan, Kansas, is contained in the recollections of old-timers and in contemporary Kansas newspaper accounts, which include stories in the *Kansas Weekly Tribune* (Lawrence), July 30, 1868; the *Western Home Journal* (Ottawa), October 22, 1868; the *Leavenworth Times and Conservative*, June 25, 1869; the *Daily Kansas State Record* (Topeka), December 11, 1869; and the *Kansas Commonwealth* (Topeka), August 1 and 4, 1869. In addition, the *New York Tribune* for December 11, 1869, carried Nathan Meeker's account, and *Harper's Magazine* (1968) carried W. E. Webb's account. Col. Homer W. Wheeler's recollections may be found in his book *Buffalo Days*, published in Indianapolis in 1925, pages 272–75, and in his *The Frontier Trail: A Personal Narrative*, published in Los Angeles in 1923, pages 49–51. The tale of the gambler's lost winnings was told to me by Leslie Linville, a long-time resident of northwestern Kansas, in a letter dated May 25, 1986.

### James M. Daugherty's Kansas Journey

Perhaps the earliest published account of Daugherty's experiences appears in Joseph McCoy's classic book *Historic Sketches of the Cattle Trade of the West and Southwest* (Kansas City, Mo.: Ramsey, Millett & Hudson, 1874), pages 24–28. McCoy's account, however, varies from Daugherty's own recollections, which he recorded in 1923. They may be found in volume 2 of *The Trail Drivers of Texas*, edited by J. Marvin Hunter (San Antonio, Texas: Jackson Printing Co., 1923), pages 137–40. Daugherty makes no mention of having been whipped by the Jayhawkers. I have followed Daugherty's version in my story.

### Gunfights and Gunfighters

Perhaps the best source for material on Kansas gunfighters is Nyle Miller and Joe Snell's fine book *Why the West Was Wild*, published by the Kansas State Historical Society in 1963. Their informative and accurate narrative, which is supported by contemporary newspaper stories, many of which they reprint in full, provides a valuable source for information on fifty-seven frontier lawmen and gunfighters in early Kansas. I have relied heavily on their source material, plus Joseph G. Rosa's *They Called Him Wild Bill*, which was first published in 1964 and then reprinted, with additional material, in 1974. Rosa's book is the definitive study of "Wild Bill" Hickok. Both volumes are indispensable for students of early Kansas gunfighters.

**PART IV**

**The Saga of Lew Cassel, Trapper**

I first ran across Lew Cassel in Jeff Jenkins's rare little book titled *The Northern Tier: or, Life among the Homestead Settlers*, published in Topeka in 1880. In his book, Jenkins, who then lived in Concordia, Kansas, included a chapter on Cassel's life and death. But Jenkins spells Cassel's name with an *i* (Cassil). As I searched for more information on Cassel, I found that Adolph Roenigk had included Jeff Jenkins's version in the book *Pioneer History of Kansas*, which was privately printed by Roenigk in 1933. This was of little help, but more pieces of information were found in A. T. Andreas's *The History of the State of Kansas*, published in Chicago in 1883, page 1015. Andreas spelled Cassel's name Castle. The spelling Cassel was found in Franklin G. Adams's book *Homestead Guide*, published at Waterville, Kansas, in 1873, and in Mrs. E. F. Hollibaugh's *Biographical History of Cloud County, Kansas*, published in Logansport, Indiana, in 1903. Cassel is the correct spelling. Mrs. Hollibaugh's book also provided information about Cassel that was provided by the Collins brothers' sister, who in 1903 was still living in Concordia. My version of Cassel's life and death on the Kansas frontier is a careful composite of the more accurate of the accounts mentioned above.

**The Jordan Massacre**

An early newspaper account of the Jordan massacre may be found in the *Topeka Weekly Commonwealth* for October 17, 1872, which was written by John H. Edwards. The massacre is also mentioned in James H. Beach's article titled "Mother Smith, of Ellis," in volume 12 of the *Kansas Historical Collections*, pages 347–58; and in "Life and Adventures of George W. Brown," edited by William E. Connelley, in volume 17 of the *Collections*, pages 98–134. Efforts to locate Mary Jordan are contained in Governor's Correspondence, Impression Book, 1870–1873, pages 101, 111, 121–25, which is on file in the archives of the Kansas State Historical Society, Topeka. The most moving account may be found in Jennie Martin's *A Brief History of the Early Days of Ellis, Kansas*, a small undated pamphlet that was printed about 1900.

### John O'Loughlin, Trader and Town Builder

O'Loughlin's obituary may be found in the December 11, 1915, issue of the *Topeka Capital*. Leola Howard Blanchard touches on O'Loughlin's life in her book *Conquest of Southwest Kansas*, published in Wichita in 1931. Additional background may be found in *The History of Kearny County Kansas*, volume 1, published by the Kearny County Historical Society in 1964. Background material on Lakin, Kansas, may be found in volume 6 of the *Kansas Historical Quarterly*, pages 90–91.

### Hugh Cameron, the Kansas Hermit

Early Lawrence newspapers contain many references to Hugh Cameron, as do documents of the proslavery territorial legislature. Many of the early newspaper clippings may be found in scrapbooks on file in the Kansas Collection, Spencer Research Library, University of Kansas, Lawrence. The biographical sketch in A. T. Andreas's *History of the State of Kansas* (Chicago: A. T. Andreas, 1883) may be found on page 348. Cameron's obituary appeared in the *Lawrence Daily Journal* for December 10, 1908, and in the *Lawrence Daily World* for December 11, 1908. The December 11 issue of the *World* also includes an editorial that is critical of Cameron's life style. Much on Cameron's military career may be found in the records of the Kansas adjutant general and in *Official Military History of Kansas Regiments*, which was published by W. S. Burke in Leavenworth in 1870. I included this story in my book *Lawrence, Douglas County, Kansas: An Informal History* (Lawrence: Allen Books, 1982).

### John Baxter and the Town That Was Named for Him

Much of the material on John Baxter was found in a small booklet titled *John Baxter of Baxter Springs*, written by Dolph Shaner and published in Baxter Springs by Shaner in about 1943. The booklet contains a revised reprint of Shaner's article on Baxter, which first appeared in the *Joplin* (Mo.) *Globe*, January 17 and February 7, 1943. Additional information was provided in correspondence that Shaner received, after the booklet was written, from C. C. Baxter of Dublin, Texas, a grandson of John Baxter's.

### Eugene Fitch Ware, "Ironquill"

Ware's first published collection of verse, titled *Rhymes of Ironquill*, was published in Topeka by T. J. Kellam in 1885. It provides a cross section of Ware's poetry to that time. Later verses were included in later editions. Biographical material came from several sources, including volume 3 of William E. Connelley's *A Standard History of Kansas and Kansans* (Chicago and New York: Lewis Publishing Co., 1918), page 1297; *History of*

*Kansas Newspapers* (Topeka: State Printing Plant, 1916), pages 23–24; and a series of scholarly articles by James Malin that appeared in the *Kansas Historical Quarterly,* volumes 25, 26, 32, and 33. They contain a wealth of information on Ware, his life, and his work. In addition, of some value is Ware's own narrative relating to his early days in Kansas, which was published as an article titled "History of Sun-Gold Section," in volume 6 of the *Kansas Historical Quarterly,* pages 295–314, in 1937.

### Theodore R. Davis's First Journey across Kansas

The basis for this story is Davis's own article, which was written and illustrated by him and was titled "A Stage Ride to Colorado." It was published in *Harper's New Monthly Magazine,* July, 1867, pages 137–50. The illustrations are taken from the original article. Background material on Davis's career can be found in Robert Taft's *Artists and Illustrators of the Old West, 1850–1900* (New York: Charles Scribner's Sons, 1953) and in Peggy and Harold Samuels's book *The Illustrated Biographical Encyclopedia of Artists of the American West* (Garden City, N.Y.: Doubleday & Co., 1976). Both are fine reference works.

### PART V

### When Tornadoes Were Called Cyclones

This story was pieced together from contemporary newspaper stories found in the files of the Kansas State Historical Society, Topeka, plus the recollections of old-timers in the *Kansas Historical Collections.* Ely Moore's account is contained in "A Buffalo Hunt with the Miamis in 1854," in volume 10, pages 402–9. Additional information was gleaned from D. W. Wilder's *The Annuals of Kansas, 1541–1885* (Topeka: T. Dwight Thacher, Kansas Publishing House, 1886), and from Snowden D. Flora's book *Tornadoes of the United States* (Norman: University of Oklahoma Press, 1953). When the book was written, Flora was in charge of the U.S. Weather Bureau office in Topeka, Kansas.

### Before the Dams Were Built

The numerous sources for this look at early floods in Kansas include old newspaper accounts and old-timers' recollections. The material on Sarcoxie, the Delaware Indian chief, may be found in the *Lawrence Daily Gazette* for September 4, 1903. Helpful was Phil E. Chappell's article titled "Floods in the Missouri River," in volume 10 of the *Kansas Historical Collections,* pages 533–63, published in 1908. Although concentrating on the Missouri River, Chappell provides much information on those Kansas streams that feed the Missouri River. "High Waters in Kansas," in volume 8 of the *Collections,* includes excerpts from Rev. Jotham Meeker's diary, plus Rev. William F. Vail's account. Other bits and pieces came from D. W. Wilder's *The Annals of Kansas, 1541–1885* (1886) and from the newspaper-clipping scrapbooks in the library of the Kansas State Historical Society. Mrs. Emily Haines Harrison's account of the 1867 flood on the Saline River may be found on pages 626–27 of her "Reminiscences of Early Days in Ottawa County," in volume 10 of the *Collections.*

### When Grasshoppers Ruled the Day

Old newspaper clippings provided much information on grasshoppers in early Kansas. William Darnell's account appears in volume 17 of the *Collections,* page 513. In the same volume, Mrs. Olive A. Clark's recollections are on page 729, and E. D. Haney's account is on page 317. D. W. Wilder's *The Annals of Kansas, 1541–1885* provided some information.

### Some Kansas Blizzards

Material relating to the blizzards of 1855 may be found in Ely Moore's account in volume 12 of the *Collections,* pages 432–43; A. B. Whiting's account may be found in volume 12, pages 118–20; and George W. Brown's material appears on page 114 in volume 17. Information on the 1873 blizzard came from volumes 12 (p. 101) and 17 (p. 314) of the *Collections.* My story of the 1886 blizzard first appeared under my by-line in the *Kansas City Star* for Sunday, January 2, 1972, under the title "Life Came to a Standstill in the Blizzard of 1885–86." Additional material on the major blizzards during the nineteenth century came from contemporary newspaper accounts and from Robert Wright's recollections in volume 7 of the *Collections,* pages 80–81.

### Prairie Fires

Thomas F. Doran's recollections may be found in volume 15 of the *Kansas Historical Collections,* pages 492–94; and Mrs. Clara M. Fengel Shields's recollections are in volume 14, pages 168–69. Other bits and pieces came from D. W. Wilder's two volumes *The Annals of Kansas, 1541–1885* and *The Annals of Kansas, 1886–1925,* published by the Kansas State Historical Society.

## PART VI

### The Real Birthday of Kansas

The facts for this story were gleaned from the files of the Kansas State Historical Society. Why the official birthday of Kansas has been ignored for so long is not known, but it seems possible that Kansans were so thrilled at learning that the president had signed the bill admitting Kansas to the Union that they paid no attention to technicalities. Then too, most Kansans were not concerned about such formalities of government in 1861. The result was the adoption of January 29 as the state's birthday. In 1935, however, David D. Leahy, who was then the dean of Wichita newspapermen, sought to have Kansans acknowledge the fact that the state's real birthday is February 9, not January 29, but he got caught up in the political ramifications of Republicans, who had used January 29 as a day to gather in Topeka, and Democrats, who thought another date, such as February 9, would be a good day on which to celebrate the state's birthday. Leahy's efforts to get the state's birthday changed failed, especially after Kirke Mechem, secretary of the Kansas State Historical Society and a Republican, wrote an article pointing out that many, but not all states, accept as their birthdays the dates upon which the president of the United States signs the bill making a territory a state. Mechem added that he could not find any law governing the selection of the birthday of a state. After so many years, it is unlikely that anyone will seek to change the day on which Kansans each year celebrate the birth of their state.

### The Kansas River in History

The sources for this story include numerous articles in the *Kansas Historical Collections,* a total of seventeen volumes published between 1881 and 1928. They contain a wealth of primary source material relating to people and events in Kansas history. G. A. ("Dolly") Graeber's observations are contained in a letter to the editor of the *Jeffersonian Gazette* (Lawrence), published on December 30, 1908. Other information came from Louise Barry's *The Beginning of the West: Annals of the Kansas Gateway to the American West, 1540–1854,* published by the Kansas State Historical Society in 1972. A much-shorter version of my story appears in *Rolling Rivers: An Encyclopedia of America's Rivers,* edited by Richard A. Bartlett and published in 1984 by McGraw-Hill Book Co., New York City.

### Theodore Weichselbaum, Trader and Beer Maker

As a child, I first learned about Theodore Weichselbaum from my grandmother. She and my grandfather had been close friends with Weichselbaum and his second wife. They frequently visited the Weichselbaums in their home on the hill overlooking Ogden early in this century. When my grandmother died, I was given Weichselbaum's personal copy of volume 11 of the *Kansas Historical Collections,* which contains his published recollections, written in 1908. Shortly before his death, Weichselbaum had given his copy to my grandfather. I have relied heavily on these recollections in writing this sketch. A brief biographical sketch of Weichselbaum appears in the *Nineteenth Biennial Report of the Board of Directors of the Kansas State Historical Society* (1915), page 95.

### The Lost Kansas Cattle Town

Mrs. R. A. Parks's letter is cited in the story. So are several newspaper sources. The files of Atchison's *Weekly Free Press, Champion and Press,* and *The Patriot* were reviewed, along with Junction City's *Weekly Union,* the *Leavenworth Times and Conservative,* and Marysville's *Enterprise* (all in Kansas) for 1868. Material relating to the Central Branch line can be found in George Anderson's fine article titled "Atchison and the Central Branch Country, 1865–1874," published in the *Kansas Historical Quarterly* 27 (Spring, 1954): 153–65. In addition, other background material was located in J. Marvin Hunter, editor, *The Trail Drivers of Texas,* two volumes, published in San Antonio, Texas, in 1920 and 1923. These volumes contain the recollections of drovers who trailed Texas longhorns to Kansas. Another valuable book for background on the early Kansas cattle trade is Joseph McCoy's *Historic Sketches of the Cattle Trade of the West and Southwest* (1874).

### Tellers and Portrayers of Tall Tales about Kansas

These tall tales came from the pages of old newspapers in the files of the Kansas State Historical Society. A couple were borrowed from S. J. Sackett and William E. Koch's fine book *Kansas Folklore.* A portion of this story first appeared in print in late December, 1974, when the Associated Press transmitted the piece to newspapers across Kansas. The trick, or fictitious, photographs came from the files of the Kansas State Historical Society.

### Some Kansas Fish Stories

Much of the material in this sketch first appeared in my article titled "When Fish Grew Big in Kansas," published in *Star Magazine,* the *Kansas City Star,* February 4, 1973. The article was later reprinted in *Kansas Fish and Game* magazine, May/June, 1973, published by the Kansas Forestry, Fish and Game Commission in Pratt.

## "Bear" Facts about Kansas

A slightly shorter version of this story first appeared in the *Topeka Capital-Journal* for June 14, 1970. Then, as now, my sources include the *Manhattan* (Kans.) *Standard*, November 21, 1968; the *Atchison* (Kans.) *Union*, June 25, 1859; and the *Emporia* (Kans.) *News*, 1861, an undated clipping in the "Animal Clippings" scrapbook in the library of the Kansas State Historical Society. The late E. Raymond Hall provided much information on very early sightings of grizzlies and black bears in what is now Kansas, and a few bits and pieces came from Louise Barry's *The Beginning of the West, 1540–1854*. Col. Richard I. Dodge's account may be found in his book *The Plains of the Great West*, published in New York City in 1877. Material on the 1983 sighting and capture of a black bear in southwestern Kansas was provided by Bob Nease in a letter to me dated May 12, 1986.

## When Every Town Had a Band

Robert Wright includes some material on the Dodge City Cowboy Band in his classic book *Dodge City, Cowboy Capital*, published in Wichita in 1913. Other facts were found in early issues of the *Dodge City Globe*, June 25, 1878, May 27, 1879, December 26, 1880, June 27, July 18 and 25, August 8, September 5 and 12, and December 12 and 19, 1882, and April 3, 1883. Additional bits and pieces came from D. W. Wilder's *The Annals of Kansas, 1541–1885*, and *The Annals of Kansas, 1886–1925*, published by the Kansas State Historical Society.

# INDEX

This index is intended primarily as a reference guide to place names and leading characters. It is not an index to subject matter, nor does it cover the notes and credits.

Abbott, James B., 91, 92
Abilene (Kans.), 85, 104ff., 110, 198, 207, 225ff.
Adobe Walls (Tex.), 82
Agnes City (Kans.), 73ff.
Alamo (saloon), 105–106
Alamo, The (Tex.), 15
Albany (Mo.), 79
Albany (N.Y.), 134
Alexander, _____, 60
*Alexander Majors* (steamboat), 214
Allen, H. C., 84
Alton (Ill.), 51, 52
Anderson, Jim, 74ff.
Anderson, William T. ("Bloody Bill"), 23, 73–79
Andreas, A. T., 135
Angus (Nebr.), 70
Applejack (saloon), 105
Arapahoe Indians, 31–32, 82, 220
Arkansas (state), 39, 41, 88, 137, 249
Arkansas City (Kans.), 42
Arkansas River, 6, 15, 82, 83, 100, 127, 174, 176, 186, 220
Armijo, Gov. Manuel, 14
Army Corps of Engineers, 178, 214
Army Signal Bureau, 168
Arrow Rock (Mo.), 4–5

Asbury Park (N.J.), 162
Associated Press, 64
Atchison (Kans.), 25, 26, 154, 161, 225, 226, 230, 248
Atchison and Pike's Peak Railroad Company, 225
Atchison and St. Joseph Railroad, 231
*Atchison* (Kans.) *Champion and Press,* 231
Atchison, Topeka and Santa Fe Railroad, 39, 130, 183, 197
*Atchison* (Kans.) *Union,* 248
*Atchison* (Kans.) *Weekly Free Press,* 229
Aunt Sallie, 19, 23
Auer, David, Jr., 83–84
Auer, David, Sr., 83
Austin (Tex.), 33

Bachelder (Kans.), 243
Bachelor Creek, 50, 53
Baker, Arthur I., 73ff.
Baker's Store, 73ff.
Baldwin City (Kans.), 27
Bardsley, _____, 45
Barnes (Kans.), 229
Barton County (Kans.), 183
Bass, Sam, 45–46
Bassett, Charles, 108

Battle of Adobe Walls (Tex.), 82, 89
Battle of Wilson's Creek (Kans.), 136
Baum, Lyman Frank, 171
Baxter, Cyrus, 145
Baxter, John L., 142–145
Baxter, Manford, 145
Baxter Springs (Kans.), 101, 102, 142ff.
Beardsley, _____, 84ff.
Beaver County (Okla.), 42
Beaver Creek (Okla.), 58
Becknell, William, 3–8, 18
Bee (steamboat), 213
Beebe, George M., 203ff.
Beeson, Chalkley M. ("Chalk"), 254
Beloit (Kans.), 178, 207
Benkelman (Nebr.), 31
Bennington (Kans.), 234
Bent, William, 82, 174
Bent's Fort, 15
Berry, Jim, 45, 47
Big Blue River. See Blue River
Big Creek (Kans.), 156
Big Ike, 86
Big John Springs (Kans.), 50, 52
Big Lost Creek (Mo.), 142
Big Springs (Nebr.), 44, 47
Bismarck Grove (Kans.), 251
Blue Mound (Kans.), 142
Blue Rapids (Kans.), 177
Blue River, 28, 115, 167, 177, 178, 207, 208, 214, 226, 243, 246
Bluff Creek (Kans.), 52, 74
Bonham (Tex.), 145
Boone, Albert G., 18
Boone, Daniel, 17
Boone, Daniel Morgan, 211
Born, Henry, 80–89
Born, Ida Dillabaugh (Mrs. Henry), 89
Boston (Mass.), 154, 212
Bourgmont, Etienne Venyard de, 211
Bowersock Mill, 244
Branson, Jacob, 136
Brewster, Gen. W. R., 154ff.
Broadbent, John Fletcher, 232
Brooks, G. D., 120
Brooks, William L. ("Billy"), 109, 110
Brown, George W., 186
Brown Jug (saloon), 23
Brown's Creek (Kans.), 120
Brush Creek (Kans.), 143
Buchanan, James, 203, 205, 219
Buffalo (Kans.), 125. See also Dodge City (Kans.)
Buffalo Creek (Kans.), 120

Buffalo Days (Wheeler), 97
Buffalo Station (Kans.), 45, 84ff.
Bull's Head (saloon), 105
Bundy's Ferry, 27
Burden (Kans.), 40–41
Burlington (Iowa), 146
Burlington (Iowa) Hawkeye, 146
Burlingame (Kans.), 54, 78
Burnett, Abram B., 61–63
Burns, Abe, 244–245
Butler County (Kans.), 180
Butterfield Overland Despatch, 154ff.

Caldwell (Kans.), 104, 110, 225
Calhoun, William M., 154ff.
California, 20, 25, 32, 47, 59, 73
California Express, 39
Calloway County (Mo.), 17, 21
Cameron, Allen, 134
Cameron, Hugh, 133–141
Cameron Bluffs (Kans.), 140
Camp Alert (Kans.), 220
Camp Ben Harrison, 135
Camp Supply (Okla.), 186, 189, 220
Canada, 47
Canadian River, 7, 82
Carrier, Eva, 198
Carson, Kit, 17–18, 82
Carter, Bob, 127–128
Carter, Jim, 127–128
Cascade (Colo.), 153
Case, A. H., 140
Case, Mrs. A. H., 140–141
Cassel, Lew, 115–122
Catlin, George, 10, 209
Cavelier, Robert, 209
Central Branch, Union Pacific, 122, 225–232
Central City (Colo.), 162
Centralia (Kans.), 167
Centralia (Mo.), 79
Chaplain, William A., 134
Chapman Creek, 29, 229ff.
Cheney (Kans.), 253
Cheney Cornet Band, 253
Cherokee County (Kans.), 147, 153
Cherokee Indians, 100, 137
Cherry Creek (Colo.), 214
Chetopa (Kans.), 253
Chetopa Town Band, 253
Cheyenne County (Kans.), 31, 32
Cheyenne Creek, 121
Cheyenne Indians, 82, 120–122, 127–128, 220, 248

Chicago (Ill.), 30, 66, 222, 227, 229
Chicken Creek, 78
Chisholm Trail, 89, 105
Chocktaw Nation, 101
Chouteau, Auguste P., 6
Chouteau, Cyprian, 20, 23
Chouteau, Frederick, 17, 211
Chouteau, Pierre, 20, 23
Chouteau's trading post, 18
Cimarron (Kans.), 39, 40
Cimarron Desert, 6
Cimarron River, 7, 58, 60
Cincinnati (Ohio), 218
Cincinnati Centennial Exposition, 183
Civil War, 23, 32, 52, 74, 80, 94, 100,
    102, 129, 131, 133, 136ff., 154, 180,
    221
Clark, Mrs. Olive A., 181
Clark, William, 209, 211
Clark County (Kans.), 169, 198
Clarksville (Tex.), 8
Clay, Henry, 133, 134
Clay Center (Kans.), 186
Clay County (Kans.), 167, 169
Clay County (Mo.), 20
Cleveland, Grover, 219
Clifton (Kans.), 117, 119, 122
Closing, Henry, 73
Cloud, F. J., 233
Cloud County (Kans.), 117, 120
Clough, E. N. O., 20
Coe, Phil, 106–108, 111
Coffey, _____, 125
Coffeyville (Kans.), 39, 170
Colby (Kans.), 197, 207
Coldwater (Kans.), 249
Col. Gus Linn (steamboat), 214
Collins, Joel, 45, 47
Collins, John, 120–122
Collins, William, 120–122
Colorado, 15, 31, 58, 82, 88–89, 91, 154,
    174, 180, 207, 214, 250
Colorado Fish and Game Commission,
    250
Colorado River, 33
Comanche County, 249
Comanche Indians, 16, 82, 211
Committee for Safety, 96, 98
Commons, _____, 144
Concordia (Kans.), 120
Conrad, F. D., 241
Constable, Grant, 234
Continental Oil Company, 42
Cook, P. G., 187

Coon Creek, 230
Cornish, George B., 241
Corwin, Thomas, 134
Cottonwood Falls (Kans.), 170
Cottonwood River valley, 177, 180
Council Grove (Kans.), 18–23, 50, 73, 75,
    78, 193
Courtland (Kans.), 255
Cow Creek, 65
Cowley County (Kans.), 40–41, 168
Crawford, Samuel J., 228
Cross, Frank, 246
Culberson County (Tex.), 103
Curtis, Charles, 57
Custer, George Armstrong, 80, 130, 220

Dakota Territory, 70, 110, 248, 254
DaLee, A. G., 92
Dalton gang, 39, 88
Darnell, William, 182
Daugherty, James M., 100–103
Davis, Jack, 45, 47
Davis, Jefferson, 204
Davis, Theodore R., 154–162
Deadwood (S.D.), 110
Decatur County (Kans.), 31, 86
Delaware Indians, 9, 80, 136, 173
Delaware River, 208
Delphos (Kans.), 167
Denver (Colo.), 32, 94, 95, 99, 161, 162,
    189, 254, 255
Department of the Missouri, 162
DeSoto (Kans.), 78
Devil's Den, 66–68
DeVore, Brady, 69–70
DeVore, Esther, 69
DeVore, Jacob Elbert ("Ebb"), 69–70
DeVore, James B., 70
DeVore, John, 69
Dewey, Adm. George, 152
Dias, Martias, 14–16
Dickinson County (Kans.), 169, 229, 255
Dillabaugh, Ida, 89
Dobbins, John, 101–102
Dodge, Col. Richard I., 148
Dodge City (Kans.), 6, 34, 39, 82, 86,
    88, 104ff., 110, 130, 131, 188, 197, 198,
    225, 254
Dodge City Cowboy Band, 252, 254–255
Dodge City Peace Commission, 111
Doolin, William M. ("Bill"), 39–42
Doolin, Mrs. William M., 40
Doran, Thomas F., 193–197
Dougherty, Joe, 250

Douglas, Stephen A., 133, 134
Douglas County (Kans.), 9, 136, 173, 249
Downer's Station, 157, 159
Doy, John, 90–93
Dragoon Creek, 50, 53
Dubuque (Iowa), 129
Duffey, William, 108
Dutch Henry, 80–89

*Early History of Wabaunsee County, The* (Thomson), 49
Earp, Wyatt, 110, 111
East Twin Creek, 65
Edwards, J.B., 106
Edwards County (Kans.), 197
Eighteenth Kansas Regiment, 107
Elder, Horton, 143
El Dorado (Kans.), 40
Eldridge House, 27
Elk Creek, 115
Elkhart (Kans.), 58, 250
Elkhorn Tavern, 100
Ellis, H. A., 84
Ellis (Kans.), 43–44, 85, 123ff.
Ellis County (Kans.), 43–48, 84, 96, 125, 129, 197
Ellsworth, Edith, 40
Ellsworth (Kans.), 43, 104, 110, 156, 176, 189, 225
Ellsworth County (Kans.), 198, 211
Elm Creek, 117
Elmont (Kans.), 169
Elwood (Kans.), 91
Emigrant Aid Society, 135
Emporia (Kans.), 73, 75, 76, 177, 194, 255
*Emporia* (Kans.) *News,* 179–180, 249
*Enterprise* (Marysville, Kans.), 231
Ernst, Phil, Sr., 244
Eureka Springs (Ark.), 41
Evans, George, 235
Evans, Snider, Bewell Cattle Company, 33
*Excel* (steamboat), 212
Eychner, V. R., 255

Fall Leaf (Delaware Indian), 80
Farrell, _____, 57
*Far West* (steamboat), 213
Fifth United States Cavalry, 97
Finley, John P., 168
Finney County (Kans.), 198
First Iowa Volunteer Infantry, 146
Five-mile Hollow, 186

Flint Hills, 198
Ford, Bob, 109
Ford County (Kans.), 83, 88, 129, 169, 197, 198
Fort Dodge (Kans.), 129, 130, 186, 187, 220, 222
Fort Elliot (Tex.), 58
Fort Ellsworth (Kans.), 155
Fort Fletcher (Kans.), 156, 157–159, 160
Fort Gibson (Okla.), 143
Fort Harker (Kans.), 156, 176, 220
Fort Hays (Kans.), 125, 129, 130, 186
Fort Larned (Kans.), 65, 220, 222
Fort Leavenworth (Kans.), 15, 27, 49, 55–56, 79, 129, 143, 247, 251
Fort Lyon (Colo.), 58, 82
Fort Riley (Kans.), 29, 55, 168, 185, 198, 212–213, 216, 219, 220, 221, 242
Fort Scott (Kans.), 74, 101, 103, 143, 147, 153
*Fort Scott* (Kans.) *Monitor,* 147, 148
Fort Scott National Cemetery, 153
Fort Smith (Ark.), 88, 100
Fort Union (N.M.), 221
Fort Wallace (Kans.), 220
Fort Wise (Colo.), 221
Fourth Iowa Cavalry, 146
Fourth United States Cavalry, 87
France, 3, 211
Frankfort (Kans.), 167, 177
*Frank Leslie's Magazine,* 33, 148
Franklin (Mo.), 3ff.
Frazier, Catherine, 134
French, _____, 73
French, J. C., 137
Frenzeny, Paul, 194
Fulton, Tom, 52, 54
Fulton County (N.Y.), 134
Furth (Bavaria), 218

Gard, Wayne, 45
Garden City (Kans.), 39
Gardner, Joseph, 91–92
Gardner, Theodore, 91–92
Gardner (Kans.), 219
Garrett, Pat, 89
Germany, 61, 221, 223
Gillett, G. C., 255
Glasco (Kans.), 169
Glen Burn (Kans.), 137–138
Gloversville (N.Y.), 87
Gove County (Kans.), 178
Graeber, G.A. ("Dolly"), 176–177, 215–217
Graham County (Kans.), 197

Grand River, 249
Grant, Ulysses S., 32, 219
Grant County (Kans.), 198
Gratstrom, Edward, 176
Gray County (Kans.), 198
Grayson County (Tex.), 100
Great American Desert, 212
Great Bend (Kans.), 169, 183
Great Salt Lake, 219
Greeley, Horace, 24–32, 148
Greene, Albert R., 214
Greenhalgh, John J., 249
Greenwood County (Kans.), 177
Grey, Alfred, 182
Grice, Gary, 250
Griffin, Leander ("Lee"), 74ff.
Grove County (Kans.), 86
Grover, Sharp, 97–98
Gunshot Frank, 98–99
Guthrie (Okla.), 42
Guymon (Okla.), 58

Hackberry Creek, 86
Haines, _____, 117
Hair, Thomas, 243
Hale, Edward Everett, 210
Hamilton, J. K., 44
Hamilton, James G., 18
Hamilton, T. K., 125–126
Hancock, Gen. W. S., 162
Hancock Indian War, 107
Haney, E. D., 181, 187–188
Hanover (Kans.), 255
Happy Thought mine, 88
Harper, Sam, 57
Harper's Monthly, 135, 155, 162
Harper's Weekly, 154, 162, 194, 220
Harris, _____, 78
Harrison, Benjamin, 255
Harrison, Emily Haines, 175–176
Harrison, Waldo, 175
Hartford (Conn.), 146
Hartford (steamboat), 213
Harvey, George M., 53
Harvey, Joe, 44
Harvey, S. B., 53–54
Harvey County (Kans.), 170
Harveyville (Kans.), 49ff.
Hasbrouk, Lawrence, 154ff.
Hay, George, 91–92
Haynes, Walter, 120–122
Hays, Col. Jack, 14
Hays, Seth M., 17–23
Hays (Kans.), 44, 46, 84, 85, 87, 96, 156, 223

Hays County (Tex.), 33
Hays (Kans.) Sentinel, 86–87
Heffridge, Bill, 45, 47
Heller, Moses, 115–117
Henney, K. J., 255
Henry, Dutch, 80–89
Henry, J. C., 125
Hickock, James Butler ("Wild Bill"), 80, 104ff., 111, 130
Historic Sketches of the Cattle Trade of the West and Southwest (McCoy), 102
History of Kansas, The (Andreas), 135–136
Hobbs, H. B., 51
Hobbs, Wilson, 20
Hodgeman County (Kans.), 129, 169, 198
Hodgson, Allen, 51
Hodgson, Ira, 52–54
Holmes, I. R., 132
House of Representatives, U.S., 203ff.
Hoxie (Kans.), 85
Hoy, George, 110
Hoyt, George, 110
Hudspeth County (Tex.), 103
Hugoton (Kans.), 250
Hulett, _____, 87–88
Huntington, Jeanette P., 150
Huntsville (Ark.), 137
Huntsville (Mo.), 73
Hurd, Jake, 91

Illinois, 60, 142
Independence (Mo.), 15, 75, 221
Indiana, 61
Indian Campaign of 1864, The (Ware), 153
Indianola (Kans.), 28, 55–57
Indian Territory (Okla.), 39, 41, 80, 101, 143, 186
Ingalls, John J., 152
Ingalls (Okla.), 40, 42
Inman, Henry, 168, 220
Iowa, 146
Irving (Kans.), 167
Isthmus of Panama, 32

Jackson, Andrew, 24, 116
Jacob Sass (steamboat), 213
James, Frank, 88
James, Jesse, 88, 109
Janes, John, 78–79
Jayhawkers, 101ff.
Jefferson, Thomas, 211

Jefferson County (Kans.), 171, 173
Jenkins, _____, 243
Jewel City (Kans.), 255
Jewell County (Kans.), 120, 180–181
Johnson County (Ark.), 39
Johnson County (Kans.), 20, 61, 78, 79, 167, 174, 219
Jones, C. B., 88
Jones, "Give-a-dam," 234
Jones, Ottawa, 27
Jones, Russell and Company, 29
Jordan, Dick, 123–128
Jordan, George, 123–128
Jordan, Mary, 123–128
Julesburg (Colo.), 44
Junction City (Kans.), 29, 30, 207, 208, 214, 216, 217, 242, 243
*Junction City* (Kans.) *Union,* 95

Kah-he-ga-wa-ti-an-gah, 61–63
Kansa Indians, 10, 17–18, 20, 22, 208–211, 247
Kansas, spelling of, 208–209
Kansas Band Association, 255
Kansas City (Kans.), 26
Kansas City (Mo.), 17, 102, 135, 153, 173, 174, 178, 207, 208, 210, 212, 214, 219, 226
*Kansas City Star,* x
Kansas Editors and Publishers Association, 148
Kansas Fish and Game Commission, 250
Kansas Hermit (Hugh Cameron), 133–141
Kansas Jayhawkers, 101ff.
Kansas Legislature, 180, 214, 225, 228, 232
Kansas Pacific Railroad, 43, 45, 84, 99, 123, 125, 189, 226ff., 229, 241. *See also* Union Pacific Railway, Eastern Division
Kansas River, 17, 18, 26, 28, 61, 136, 137, 173, 176, 178, 185, 207–216, 233, 242ff., 246, 247
Kansas River valley, 212
Kansas State Agricultural College, 183
Kansas State Historical Society, 23, 49, 53, 55, 137, 232
Kansas Supreme Court, 231
*Kate Swinney* (steamboat), 213
Kaw City (Okla.), 42
Kaw Indians. *See* Kansa Indians
Kaynaird, _____, 101
Kearney (Nebr.), 87
Kearny County (Kans.), 198

Keim, De Benneville R., 96–97
Kentucky, 17, 61, 134
Keys, Ben, 101–103
Killebrew, Pink, 144
King, Melvin A., 111
Kingman (Kans.), 233
Kingston (N.Y.), 154
Kiowa Indians, 82, 220
Kirk, E. B., 187
Kit Carson (Colo.), 99
Koch, Bertha, 224
Kretsinger and Timmons's grocery, 243

La Crosse (Kans.), 253
La Crosse Band, 253
La Grange (Ky.), 137
La Junta (Colo.), 6, 131, 250
Lakin (Kans.), 87, 131–132, 234
Lamar, Mirabeau Buonaparte, 14
Lambdin, Judge, _____, 180
Lane, James H., 136
Lane County (Kans.), 198
Larned (Kans.), 129, 235
La Salle, Robert Cavelier de, 209
Las Animas County (Colo.), 88
Lawrence (Kans.), x, 10, 27, 32, 43, 79, 90ff., 96, 133ff., 169, 173, 177, 180, 205–206, 211, 214, 216, 217, 243, 246, 255
Lawrence Band, 251
*Lawrence* (Kans.) *Journal,* 245
Lawson (Okla.), 42
Leavenworth (Kans.), 26, 27, 30, 32, 57, 91, 119, 180, 219, 222, 247
Leavenworth & Pike's Peak Express, 29
Lecompton (Kans.), 214
Legore, Orlando, 249
Lewis, Meriwether, 209, 211
*Lightfoot* (steamboat), 215
Lincoln, Abraham, 203, 219
Lincoln County (Kans.), 64–65, 198
Lindsay, H. C., 107
Little, W. C., 63
Little Arkansas River, 51
Little Tim, 117–119
Livers, D. Linn, 229
*Lizzie* (steamboat), 213
Lobenstine, William Christian, 221
Lockhart (Tex.), 33
Logan County (Kans.), 51, 99
Log Chain Creek, 50
Log Chain robbery, 54
Lone Star (saloon), 105

*Lone Star Cowboy, A* (Siringo), 89
Long, Archie W., 223
Long, Laura Engel, 223
Long, Stephen H., 209, 211–212
Long Branch (saloon), 108, 254
Long Horn (saloon), 105
Lost Springs (Kans.), 192
Louisiana Purchase, 3
Louisiana Territory, 211
Loving, "Cockeyed Frank," 107–108, 111
Lowell (Kans.), 142
Lyon, Nathaniel, 221
*Lyon Campaign and History of the First Iowa Infantry* (Ware), 153
Lyon County (Kans.), 73–74
Lyons (Kans.), 51

McCall, Jack, 109
McClure, James R., 22
McCoy, Rev. Isaac, 9–13, 61, 209, 212
McCoy, Joseph, 102, 229
McCune (Kans.), 170
McFarland (Kans.), 235
McGee, _____, 64–65
McLouth (Kans.), 171
McPherson (Kans.), 51
Madison Center (Kans.), 249
Malin, James, 148
Mallet, Paul, 3
Mallet, Pierre, 3
Manhattan (Kans.), 27, 29, 30, 115, 173, 181, 208, 214, 243, 247, 255
Manhattan Fishing Company, 243
*Manhattan* (Kans.) *Standard,* 249
Manitowoc (Wis.), 80
Manor (Tex.), 33
Manser, Henry, 41
Marais des Cygnes River, 26, 174, 246
Marion County (Kans.), 192
Marquette, Pere, 209
Marshall County (Kans.), 167, 177, 225ff.
Martin, Jennie Smith, 125–126
Martin, William H., 241
Marysville (Kans.), 115, 226
Massasoit House, 25
Masterson, Bat, 88, 110, 111
Masterson, James, 110
Mastin, Jim, 44
Matson, C. H., 148
Meade, J. R., 249
Medary, Samuel, 203
Medicine Lodge Treaties (1867), 82
Meek, Edith Doolin, 42
Meek, Col. Samuel M., 42

Meeker, Rev. Jotham, 174
Meeker, Nathan, 95–96
Meekin, H. D., 212
Melgares, Gov. Don Facundo, 4–5
*Merrimac* (ship), 154
Merwin, Fred, 158
Mesa Blanca, 58–60
Methodist Mission, 20
Methodist missionaries, 17, 20
Mexican Revolution, 3, 4
Mexican War, 20
Mexico, 8, 14, 15
Mexico City, 67
Meyers, Rudolph, 64
Meyers, Skinney, 64
Meyers, Mrs. W. H., 64
Michigan, 61
Milan (Italy), 221
Miller, E. L., 255
Mineral County (Colo.), 88
Minnesota, 115
Mission Creek, 17
Mission Township (Kans.), 62–63
Mississippi River, 70, 246
Mississippi Valley, 212
Missouri, 3, 47, 50, 51, 60, 78, 101, 232
Missouri Historical Society, 225
*Missouri Intelligencer* (Franklin), 3, 4
Missouri Penitentiary, 91
Missouri River, 4, 5, 91, 92, 119, 161, 173, 176, 178, 207ff., 212, 222, 230, 232, 246
Mitchell, William, 20
Mitchell County (Kans.), 207
M'Laughlin, — — —, 5
Moberly (Mo.), 73
*Monitor* (ship), 154
Moore, Ely, 165–167
Mormon Trail, 219
*Morning Star* (steamboat), 213
Morris County (Kans.), 18
Morse County (Kans.), 170
Morton County (Kans.), 58–60, 169
Morton County Fairgrounds, 250
Moses and Clayton south ranch, 169
Mound City (Kans.), 232
Mount Oread, 10, 11, 12
Muddy Creek (Kans.), 28
Murrary, Gene, x
Museum of Natural History (University of Kansas), 246

*Narrative of John Doy of Lawrence, Kansas, The* (Doy), 93

National Guard, 178
Natoma (Kans.), 66–67
Nease, Bob, 250
Nebraska, 31, 43, 70, 80, 87, 88, 169, 208, 219, 248
Nelson, E. W., 255
Nelson, Fred, 123–128
Nelson, Peter, 229–230
Neosho River, 18, 20–22, 142, 175, 179, 234, 249
Ness County (Kans.), 84–85, 129, 183, 189
Neutral Strip, 101
New Hampshire, 24
*New Lucy* (steamboat), 213
New Mexico, 7, 8, 14, 40, 51, 60
New Orleans (La.), 16, 116
New Spain, 3, 4
New York City, 32, 150, 218, 222
*New York Tribune*, 24, 25, 29, 31
Newton (Kans.), 225
Nicaragua, 47
Nicodemus (Kans.), 197
Niggley, Mike, 230
Nixon, Tom, 45, 47
North Fork of the Smoky Hill River, 94, 97
North Fork of the Solomon River, 85, 86
North Lawrence (Kans.), 177
North Platte (Nebr.), 69
Norton County (Kans.), 31, 169
Nuremburg (Bavaria), 218

O'Dell, O. F., 74ff.
O'Dell's store and saloon, 78
*Official Military History of Kansas Regiments*, 137
Ogden (Kans.), 29, 219–220, 222, 224
OK Corral, 110
Oklahoma, 58, 82, 132, 249
Oklahoma Panhandle, 7
Olathe (Kans.), 26, 78–79, 167
Old Fruit (saloon), 105
O'Loughlin, John, 129–132
Onate, Juan de, 209
142 Mile Creek, 52, 75, 77
110 Mile Creek, 50, 52, 78
Overland Mail Company, 52
Oregon, 51
Oregon Trail, 219
Osage County (Kans.), 50, 168
Osage Hills (Okla.), 40
Osage Indian Mission (Kans.), 179
Osage Indians, 6, 18

Osage River, 9, 61
Osawatomie (Kans.), 24–25, 26, 27
Osawkie (Kans.), 27
Osborne County (Kans.), 66, 67
Oskaloosa (Kans.), 90, 172
Otoe Indians, 118, 120
Ottawa (Kans.), 9, 27, 174
Ottawa County (Kans.), 29, 168, 175
Otter Creek (Kans.), 174
O-X Ranch (Okla.), 58
O-X Trail, 58
Pagosa Springs (Colo.), 89
Palmyra (Mo.), 73
Palo-Duro Trail, 58
Panhandle Eastern Pipeline Company, 250
Papan brothers, 173
Park's Fort (Kans.), 123, 126
Parks, Mrs. _____, 255ff.
Parrott, Marcus, 205–206
Pasadena (Calif.), 69
Pattie, O. J., 248
Pawhuska (Okla.), 40
Pawnee City (Kans.), 29
Pawnee County (Kans.), 174
Pawnee Creek, 129
Pawnee Fork, 174
Pawnee Indians, 11, 12, 16, 31
Pawnee River, 127
Pea Ridge (Ark.), 100
Pecos River, 4
Pennsylvania, 134
Perine, _____, 158
*Perry* (steamboat), 213
Perth (N.Y.), 134
Peters, Abe, 234
Peyton, J. Q. A., 55, 56
Phelps, Mary, 138
Phillips, W. W., 56
Phillips County (Kans.), 31
Phil Sheridan (Kans.). *See* Sheridan
Pike, Joshua A., 91–92
Pike, Zebulon M., 4, 211
Pike's Peak, 214
Pilcher, William, 194–195
Pipe Creek, 29, 30, 116, 117
Pipher, Harry, 243
Pittsburgh (Pa.), 214
Platte City (Mo.), 91
Platte River, 182
Point of Rocks, 58–60
Point of Rocks Ranch (Kans.), 58
Ponca City (Okla.), 42
Pond Creek (Kans.), 162

Popenoe, W. P., 182
Pottawatomie County (Kans.), 169,
    181–182, 249
Pottawatomie Indian reservation, 28
Pottawatomie Indians, 28, 61–63
Potts, George, 245–246
Prairie City (Kans.), 27
Prairie Dog Creek, 31, 86
Pratt, Caleb S., 206

Quantrill, William C., 78–79, 251

Raber, Charles, 176
Randall (Kans.), 255
Raton Pass, 6–7, 15
Rawlins County (Kans.), 87–88, 197, 198
Reader, Samuel J., 56, 136
Red Cloud (Nebr.), 87
Reddington, _____, 43
Red River, 100
Red Vermilion River, 28
Reedy, William, 74ff.
Reid, Albert, 215
Reisinger's Creek, 31
Republican party, 24, 26–27
Republican River, 29, 31, 115, 116–119,
    207, 208, 214, 242ff., 246
Republic of Texas, 8
Rhodes, Eugene Manlove, 40
*Rhymes of Ironquill*, 152
Rice County (Kans.), 6
Richardson, Levi, 85–86, 107–108, 111
Richmond (Mo.), 79
Riley County (Kans.), 169, 219, 223
Rittenhouse Academy, 134
Robinson, Charles, 136, 206
Roberts, Ben, 79
Roberts, John, 79
Roberts, John C., 120–122
Rochester (N.Y.), 150
Rock Bluffs (Tex.), 100
Rock Creek, 28, 52, 73, 74
Rocky Ford Dam, 243, 246
Rocky Mountains, 29, 176, 212, 233, 248
Rogers, W. B., 87
Rooks County (Kans.), 66–68, 197
Ross, John, 137
Roxbury (Mass.), 210
Ruggles, Cornelius W. N., 96
Rugles, _____, 75
Rush County (Kans.), 129
Russell (Kans.), 66, 83
Russell County (Kans.), 198
Russell, Majors and Waddell, 27

Russell Springs (Kans.), 51
Ruthden Station (Kans.), 156, 159
Ruxton, George F., 19–20

St. Benedict's College, 232
St. Joseph (Mo.), 25, 109, 226
St. Joseph and Denver City Railroad, 226
St. Louis (Mo.), 35, 135, 211, 222, 225, 254
St. Louis Fur Company, 247
St. Mary's (Kans.), 57, 217
St. Mary's mission, 28, 55
Salina (Kans.), 174
Saline County (Kans.), 169, 211
Saline River, 65, 83, 175, 186, 207, 243
Salt Creek, 27
San Francisco Mint, 45
San Juan Mountains, 89
San Juan River, 88
San Miguel (N.M.), 7
Santa Fe (N.M.), 3, 4, 5, 7, 8, 14, 15,
    18, 58, 89, 94–95, 131, 162
Santa Fe Trail, 3–8, 18, 20, 23, 26,
    49ff., 58, 59, 60, 74, 75, 77, 87, 192,
    213, 219
Saratoga Springs (N.Y.), 134
Sarcoxie (Indian), 173
Savage, Joseph, 251
Schoenmakers, Father John, 179
Scott County (Kans.), 198
*Scribner's Magazine*, 193
Second Arkansas Cavalry, 137
Second Kansas Cavalry, 137
Sedalia (Mo.), 182
Sedgwick County (Kans.), 69–70, 170,
    197
Seiger, _____, 75
Senate, U.S., 203ff.
Senix, Jacob, 91, 92
Seventh Iowa Cavalry, 146
Seventh United States Cavalry, 80
Shannon, Wilson, 136
Shawnee (Kans.), 26
Shawnee County (Kans.), 17, 61, 182
Shawnee Indians, 9
Shawnee Mission (Kans.), 20, 61, 174
Sheldon, Eli, 46
Sheridan (Kans.), 43, 85, 94–99
Shields, Clara M. Fengel, 192–193
Shunganunga Creek, 63
Sibley, George S., 18
Silver Creek Ford, 40
*Silver Lake* (steamboat), 214
Simmons, Thomas, 91, 92
Siringo, Charles, 89

Sitler, _____, 85
Sixth United States Cavalry, 125
Smith, Doug, 244
Smoky Hill River, 51, 94, 97, 156, 174, 178, 197, 207, 208, 212, 214, 243ff.
Smoky Hill Springs, 160–161
Smoky Hill valley, 176
Soldier Creek, 28, 55
Solomon River, 30–31, 85, 86, 116, 117, 173–174, 178, 181, 207, 214, 234, 243
Soule, Silas, 91, 92
Sour Bill, 98–99
Sousa, John Philip, 255
South Fork of the Solomon River, 207
Spanish–American War, 152
Spanish Fever, 232
Spear, Stephen Jackson, 53
Spearville (Kans.), 40
Springfield (Mo.), 136, 142
Spring Hill (Kans.), 26
Spring River, 142, 143, 144
*Spy* (Worcester, Mass.), 212
Stanton (Kans.), 26
*State Journal* (Topeka, Kans.), 55
Stevens County (Kans.), 58
Stewart, John E., 91, 92
Stonehouse Creek, 211
Stranger Creek, 27
Stuck, J. Cooper, 136
Sullivan, Matt, 110
Sulphur Fork Prairie (Tex.), 8
Summit View Cemetery, 42
Sumner County (Kans.), 109, 110, 178
Sweetwater Creek (Tex.), 111
Sylvan Grove (Kans.), 64, 65

Table Rock Creek, 175
Tabor Opera House (Denver), 255
Tallman, T. B., 120–122
Taos (N.M.), 15
Tavernier, Jules, 194
Taylor, Zachary, 134
Tedlie, John, 41
Texas, 8, 14, 16, 33–35, 80, 82, 132, 145, 162, 182, 254
Texas County (Mo.), 100
Texas longhorns, 34, 105, 143, 180, 193, 225ff.
Texas Panhandle, 7
Texas Rangers, 8, 14
Texas' Santa Fe expedition, 14–16
Thomas, _____, 247
Thomas County (Kans.), 189, 197
Thompson, James, 84–85

Thomson, Matt, 49, 52
Tiernan, _____, 232
Tilghman, William Matthew, 42
Tillotson, Charles, 78
Timber City (Kans.), 249
Topeka (Kans.), 24, 27, 28, 30, 32, 53, 55, 56, 62, 107, 151, 152, 153, 169, 171, 173, 176, 180, 214, 232, 242, 252, 254, 255
Trail (saloon), 105
Travis County (Tex.), 33
Treasury Department, U.S., 134
Trinidad (Colo.), 88
Turtle, Howard, x
Twin Creeks, 65
Tyler, A. M., 243

Union Army, 136ff., 145
Union Pacific, 44, 47, 197
Union Pacific Railway, Eastern Division, 94, 96, 214, 229, 241. *See also* Kansas Pacific
Uniontown (Kans.), 61
University of Kansas, 10, 133ff., 148
U.S. Army Corps of Engineers, 178, 214
U.S. Army Signal Bureau, 168
U.S. Cavalry. *See also names of individual units*
*Useful Worker* (Cameron), 138
U.S. House of Representatives, 203ff.
U.S. Senate, 203ff.
U.S. Treasury Department, 134

Vail, Rev. William F., 174–175
Verdigris River, 177
Vermilion River, 177
Vermont, 24
Vigilante Committee, 96, 98
Virginia, 194

Wabaunsee County (Kans.), 49–54
Wakarusa River, 208
Wakefield (Kans.), 167
Walker, "Big John," 18
Walker, Northrup, and Chick, 22
Wallace, Leslie, 235
Wallace County (Kans.), 169, 197, 198
Walnut Creek, 126
Walruff, C. J., 224
Ware, Eugene Fitch ("Ironquill"), 146–153
War of 1812, 3
Washington, Jacob, 245
Washington, D.C., 134, 135, 168, 205, 255

Washington County (Kans.), 231
Waterville (Kans.), 225–232
Waterville (N.Y.), 225
Watrous (N.M.), 7
Watson and Record's butcher shop, 243
Weakly, J. C., 83
Webb, W. E., 98–99
Webster, Daniel, 133, 134
*Weekly Picayune* (New Orleans), 16
Weichselbaum, Theodore, 218–224
Wells Fargo and Company, 43
West, R. P., 122
Western Hotel, 44
Western Trail, 34
Weston (Mo.), 91
Westport (Mo.), 17, 18, 174
West Twin Creek, 65
West Willow Creek, 88
Wetzel, William, Jr., 53, 54
Wheeler, Col. Homer W., 97–98
Whig party, 24
White Rock (Kans.), 181
White Rock Creek, 118, 119

Whiting, A. B., 185–186
Whitney, Hank, 98
Wichita (Kans.), 69, 88, 104, 183, 225
Wild Cat Creek, 28, 243
Williams, Hezkiah G., 33–35
Williams, Lizzie Johnson, 33–35
Williams, Mike, 106
Willis, S. J., 91, 92
Willow Creek (Kans.), 143
Wilson, John, 40–41
Wilson County (Kans.), 177
Wisconsin, 80, 107
*Wizard of Oz, The* (Baum), 172
Wolf Creek (Kans.), 116
Woodson County (Kans.), 177
Worrell, Henry, 102
Wright, Robert W., 186–187
Wyandotte (Kans.), 26
Wyandotte Indians, 9

Yott, Clarissa Bell Burnett, 63

Zaun, Charles, 85